The Mouse and The Myth

This work is dedicated to my favorite Disneyland partner, my husband, and my own personal Peter Pan, Bruce Robert Koehler. I love you! Thank you for supporting this wish my heart made every step of the way.

Acknowledgements

Many people helped make this book possible. I'd like to thank a few.

Thank you to my parents, David and Carolyn Santos for teaching me that our first and only duty to each other is to enact love.

Thank you to my best friend, fellow Din-no-phile, cheerleader-in-chief, and editor Britta K. Phillips for all the support, love, and vintage Disneyland goodies. We've been at this party for 20 years and in no way is that depressing. I literally couldn't have written it without you.

Thank you to my friend and colleague Bonnie Willers for the support and discussion. I guess we're done solving the world's problems now, or at least I'm taking a break. It's your turn, and I know it'll be amazing.

Thank you to my Disney Studies colleagues Dr. Priscilla Hobbs and Dr. Amy M. Davis for your brilliance and for the sisterhood we've created. May all your Disney dreams come true.

Thank you to my publisher John Libbey for taking on a project from a fledgling author. Your patience with me through this process has been an unexpected blessing.

The Mouse and The Myth

Sacred Art and Secular Ritual at Disneyland

Dori Koehler, PhD

British Library Cataloguing in Publication Data

The Mouse and The Myth: Sacred Art and Secular Ritual at Disneyland

A catalogue entry for this book is available from the British Library

ISBN: 978-0-86196-727-8 (Paperback)

ISBN: 978-0-86196-932-6 (Electronic book)

Cover design: Pat McCallum.

Published by
John Libbey Publishing Ltd, 205 Crescent Road, East Barnet, Herts EN4 8SB,
United Kingdom   e-mail: john.libbey@orange.fr; web site: www.johnlibbey.com

Distributed Worldwide by **Indiana University Press**, Herman B WellsLibrary—350,
1320 E. 10th St., Bloomington, IN 47405, USA. www.iupress.indiana.edu

Printed and bound in the United States of America..

Contents

Chapter 1

Tell Us a Myth, Wendy-Lady!

All Disneyland really is, you see, is a projection outward of the phenomenology of the imagination. And, if they can't go into their own imaginations, they might just as well go into Walt Disney's and he'll help them. And that's what religions have done all the time. – Joseph Campbell[1]

The test of psychology is not, does it work? The test of psychology is: Is it fun? Does it amuse you? Does it delight you? Does it wake you up? Does it talk to your soul? Does it say anything to your soul that makes you see further or feel deeper or are inspired more . . . or that the world around you is more animated or that you are more animated or that there is some beauty, or some love or some tragedy; some real things happening [. . .] . – James Hillman[2]

Introduction

In the academic discourse between myth studies and archetypal theory, many are quick to accept a conventional attitude that contemporary popular culture is antithetical to the development of a psychologically fulfilling relationship with the imagination. These critics seem convinced that this is especially true of American popular culture. And frankly, they're not entirely wrong. The frenetic pace of contemporary life can keep humanity disconnected from each other, a state that leads to both alienation from and negligence of the imagination. Lack of attention to the imagination is psychologically hazardous, because through it – specifically through its relationship to ritual – one cultivates an authentic connection with what Rudolf Otto refers to as the numinous:[3] the

---

1   *Pathways to Bliss*, 17.

2   *Surfing L.A.*

awe-inspiring transcendence humanity has traditionally understood to be the touch of God(s). We yearn for what comparative mythologist Joseph Campbell insists is the most basic of existential needs: the experience of something real, a magical encounter between mundane events and the mysteries that exist beyond our empirical senses.

Whether we interpret these numinous moments to be the soul's voice, the mind, or synapses in the brain, we cannot ignore humanity's yearning for them. This need is traditionally expressed, both individually and collectively, through the languages of mythology, theology, and psychology. Although at first glance these disciplines may seem unrelated, they address the same desire – the development of a hermeneutic of the divine. They form a philosophical pyramid that develops and categorizes rituals steeped in thought, intuition, and action. Greek words – Logos (word or the structures of reason), mythos (story, discourse, or plot), theos (numinosity or God), and psyche (breath or soul) – essentially speak about the same things. These are languages we use to discuss big questions, such as: What does it mean to be human? How do we express our emotions? What do we do with our knowledge that some things are unexplainable? Is there truth in what seems to be miraculous? Does truth exist beyond empirical data? How do we relate to that truth?

Participation with myth and ritual is an outlet for this drive to make sense of our embodied condition. Participants of cherished mythic traditions do so by finding language to describe these transcendent moments. We tell stories to explain complicated emotions. We also engage in meaningful rituals, which then become hermeneutical metaphors. Mythology is essentially the soul's metaphorical language processed through story. Likewise, ritual is the physical performance of the soul's metaphors. Campbell writes:

> The life of a mythology springs from and depends on the metaphoric vigor of its symbols. These deliver more than just an intellectual concept, for such is their inner character that they provide a sense of actual participation in a realization of transcendence. The symbol, energized by metaphor, conveys not just an idea of the infinite but some realization of the infinite.[4]

He understands this relationship between symbol and transcendence to be the first, and perhaps the most vital, function of mythology. Following contemporaries C.G. Jung and Mircea Eliade, he proposes that symbols have the ability to bridge the gap between the numinous and the mundane. These symbols are the building blocks rituals use to shape culture. Despite any biases that argue against the imaginative efficacy of popular culture, the fact still remains that the Disneyland Resort offers such an experience to the devout patron, utilizing images, symbols, and the poetics of narrative to transcend the world outside the

3   *The Idea of the Holy*, 5.

4   *Thou Art That: Transforming Religious Metaphor*, 6.

park, beyond what Disney calls *The Berm*,[5] while continuing to shape and craft the mythology of the organization.

As I analyze Disneyland's place in mythic ritual, I remain convinced that the excursion to Disneyland in Anaheim can, and does, function as psychologically transformative ritual, demonstrating that it becomes so through the way it crafts a unique interaction between traditional aspects of ritual: the soul's journey to the imagination, the pilgrimage to a temple or shrine, an enchantment with image and spectacle, and an ever-evolving renewal practice. Furthermore, I see Southern California itself as iconic, and that Walt, his contemporaries, and subsequent artists utilize such factors as climate, movie magic, and Disney's own trusted brand as purveyor of myth to make the park such a place. Disney's kind of theme park could only have come about through the alchemical cauldron of Hollywood's mid-20th century film/fantasy industry.

This kind of protected container for immersion into fantasy is a vital aspect of psychological health, interpreted more fully through the lens of myth and ritual studies. The analytical psychology of C.G. Jung and James Hillman as well as Joseph Campbell's extensive study of mythology are useful guides to understand these concepts more profoundly. In particular, Jung's analysis of symbols and signs as the language of the soul, his definition of archetypes as the psychological energies that make up our complexes, and his belief in the malleable nature of archetypes offers a framework for orienting the following analysis. In probing these assertions through a Jungian lens, I postulate that secular ritual can function like sacred ritual, and that the presence of playful wonder and awe is vital to an encounter with the transcendent. As a Disney patron who personally experiences altered states of consciousness at Disneyland, and as one who witnesses it in others at the park during each new visit, I hold firmly and unapologetically to an insider's point of view. I do not, however, suggest that a trip to Anaheim's mouse temple affects all patrons in the same manner. I simply propose that the relationship between Disneyland and the patron is more profound than it may appear. It can be a fundamental and fulfilling encounter, which Disneyland does by re-visioning traditional standards of myth and ritual through the poetic language of Disney's American myth. One last note: It's also important to state that this book focuses self-consciously and specifically on The Disneyland Resort, as it is the original Disney theme park, and frankly, the only park that bears the physical touch of the original cult leader, Walt Disney. Although an analysis of Walt Disney World in Florida and the global Disney

---

5   This book uses the term "berm" in both a literal and metaphorical sense. Disney's constructed berm refers to the digging of a ditch in order to create a shelf, or wall, of soil. The term comes from Dutch and refers to the military practice of the digging of trenches for protection and camouflage. A berm was built around Disneyland. It was originally constructed for the sake of holding the illusion of transportation into another kingdom. In the early years of the park, the berm blocked out the vision of cars, telephone poles and the sounds of nearby busy streets, such as Katella Avenue and Harbor Boulevard. It still serves this purpose, but it also serves as a metaphor for thresholding at the Magic Kingdom. The berm is Disneyland's border crossing.

theme parks would make for a fascinating study, doing so would be a herculean task, likely larger than one book and definitely beyond the purview of this project.

Why Disney Studies? Why not?

Scholars in the field of Jungian myth analysis spend quite a bit of time discussing what is often called a conscious process of mythmaking, or the mythopoetics of contemporary popular culture. They follow Campbell's lead. He often argued that popular storytelling is low art, that as such it is contrived which makes it devoid of any mythic, psycho-spiritual depth, which is deeply ironic if one considers that this work spawns the creation of *Star Wars*, a series Campbell personally loved and contributed to, and another franchise now owned by Disney. These arguments against Disney storytelling as true myth generally note its ties to capitalism, insisting that a focus on profit is innately anti-mythic. Detractors argue that real myth springs spontaneously from a culture's communal soul, which in essence makes intentionally crafted art not art at all. The presence of capitalism in sacred locations often creates a cognitive dissonance for those who would idealize what they believe a temple should be.

This notion that the existence of consumption at Disneyland eradicates any true presence of the sacred is not only an untrue, shallow reading; it's also a self-defeating argument. When it comes to *collective* culture, it is impossible to separate stories and practices from the economic structures in which they are couched. There are plenty of examples to be found among the temples of ancient peoples, medieval and Renaissance holy sites, Hindu shrines, and in the Christian televangelists of today, such as the *700 Club* and the well-known *Hour of Power*, previously filmed at the Crystal Cathedral in Garden Grove, California, located only a few miles from Disneyland.[6] While clearly not unproblematic, they are nonetheless meaningful to their devoted faithful. Economics are always a factor in the creation of temple culture.

As a self-proclaimed apologist for Disney, I often find myself arguing against this academic mainstream. However transformative patrons at the Disneyland Resort may believe their experiences to be, many thinkers still question Disney's mythic value. These discussions fall victim to a kind of elitist anti-populism, which is strange and unfair as the critiques leveled against Disney's stories – romantic drivel, racist themes, cultural stereotypes, sexist and misogynistic imagery – are rarely argued against Disney's source material with such vehemence. The fact is that all stories hold within them the capacity to be judged

6   In an ironic twist, the Crystal Cathedral was sold to the Roman Catholic Diocese of Orange County, California. The OC's newspaper, The OC Register posted an article on April 23, 2016 that details the past plans for the Cathedral, concerns from patrons, and the latest attempts to rein in costs. The fate of the Cathedral is of great importance to people living in Orange County, because it is a popular tourist destination whose image is indelibly linked to both its home in Garden Grove and neighboring home to Disneyland, Anaheim. http://www.ocregister.com/articles/diocese-713286-million-cathedral.html

positively or negatively according to the cultural standards of the moment. Douglas Brode addresses this irony when he suggests that Disney's attempt at bridging the divide between high and low art might be at the center of the intellectualist attacks on Disney.

He argues that financial success can work against an artist's attempt to be accepted by art world elites.[7] He goes on to write that Walt Disney was less concerned with how his art would be accepted by the elite, as he was that it would be well loved by the public. All forms of art fascinated Walt, but art meant little to him, if he could not share it with his audience in a way that they could understand and that resonated with them on an emotional level. Academic critics of Disney often orient from a Marxist perspective, accusing Disney's kind of populism of at best being hollow shades of myth and fairy tale and at worst being the *whiskers* behind a capitalist machine enslaving both workers and patrons alike. Richard Schickel, Henry Giroux, and Jack Zipes[8] are just a few notable thinkers that have taken a critical swing at Disney for having a negative, or at least problematic, impact on American culture. These critiques of Disney became more passionately pointed as the inflation of the 1980s gave way to the nihilistic anti-capitalist orientation of the 1990s and the first two decades of the 21st century. As the anti-Disney movement in the academy grew, a fusion occurred between Marxist and third wave feminist critiques, bringing with it a whole new level of disdain for Disney, as well as the complete rejection of the Disney princess and what is often referred to as *princess culture*. Although I can't say that these critiques are entirely wrong or unfair – they're not – I can and do argue that they are often myopic. I favor a Yes/And approach that seeks to broaden perspective, as it is only when we continue to encounter larger truths that we begin to encounter healing, both culturally and psychologically.

That Disney critiques have now become the rule in the academy rather than an exception is true, but it is also the case that there is nothing new about this dismissive attitude toward Disney. As early as the 1940s, the American academy was already silencing thinkers who dared to suggest Disney as both a valid topic for study and a place that makes truly significant art. In 1942, art historian Robert D. Feild published a book titled *The Art of Walt Disney*. In it, he details the work he personally studied at the studio from 1939 to 1940. According Steven Watts, "Feild believed that Disney's films had pioneered a new type of creative expression, undermining the outworn assumption that 'music, painting, sculpture, and architecture…alone are art'."[9] Feild's work is both compelling and comprehensive. He spends hours interviewing artists and even Walt himself. Despite the rigor of his study, many of his colleagues disagreed with his choice of topic,

---

7   *Multiculturalism and the Mouse: Race and Sex in Disney Entertainment*, 257–258.

8   Henry Giroux *The Mouse that Roared: Disney and the End of Innocence*, Richard Schickel *The Disney Version: The Life, Times, Art, and Commerce of Walt Disney* and Jack Zipes *Fairy Tale as Myth/Myth as Fairy Tale* and *Fairy Tales and the Art of Subversion*.

9   *The Magic Kingdom: Walt Disney and the American Way of Life*, 101–103.

vehemently arguing against his findings. Harvard chose to release him from his position before the publication of his book, a decision that made for a scandal within the department that was never satisfactorily addressed.

Clearly this kind of bias against the positive efficacy of Disney's work has deep roots in the American academy. Although not specifically about Disney, a similar type of argument against popular culture occasionally surfaces in depth psychology as well. In his essay, "A Myth is as Good as a Smile", David Miller critiques such re-working of contemporary myth, suggesting that a person finding soulfulness in the stories of capitalist societies are in danger of projecting " [. . .] fake soul and fake world" on them.[10] From this perspective, a central reason to study mythology is to make sense of the soullessness of our time; to tell us what we are not and to help us see through the absurdity of contemporary life. Truly though, why participate in anything if it is simply an exercise in seeing through the emptiness of our own existence? Of what enduring use is a mythology really if it does nothing other than show us our own emptiness?

Before answering that question, I'd like to pose a related one. Why become an apologist for Disney if the topic can get you fired, if not completely ousted, from the academic community? *Answer*: Disney offers something of value that is deeply lacking in our current psychological milieu –an emphasis on the importance of play and on the transformative nature of love. Miller also writes, "People are hungering for an understanding that mythology and its study can make possible . . . the humor, imagination, and love myth promotes".[11] While there is a fair amount of truth in all critiques of contemporary American popular culture, asserting that they are fake simply because contemporary storytelling reflects the capitalist societies from which they originate is poor logic. Myth is continually remade, reworked, and revised. Stories shape the world, as we know it today just as vitally as they did in ancient times and places. There is nothing more deeply engrained in our culture today than the popular pursuits of media. And furthermore, what is Greek theater, Shakespeare, the offerings of any great novelist but the popular culture of their era? Simply put, while it's imperative that we study Disney because a thorough understanding of popular culture is indispensable to intellectual vitality, it's vital that we participate with Disney because their myths promote play and love through an encounter with joy; a perspective that is indispensible to psychological wholeness.

If, as Jungian theory suggests, archetypes are universal and eternal,[12] they live behind any and all cultural clothing. Studying, digesting, and integrating the dynamics that intertwine myth and ritual are more than just academic pursuits, bound to be buried in a library. From this perspective, it is experience that

10 *Depth Psychology: Meditations in the Field*, 190.

11 *Depth Psychology: Meditations in the Field*, 185–186.

12 Jung, C. G. The *Structure and Dynamics of the Psyche (1916/58)* CW 8 and *Archetypes and The Collective Unconscious* CW 9.

constitutes the authenticity of a life lived. Truly understanding the myths and rituals of a culture means holding the value of story and ritual in balance no matter where they reside. Disneyland is the conscious creation of this kind of lived experience, a conscious manufacturing of what should constitute story. Although it's possible to suggest that contrived story is antithetical to mythmaking,[13] we must not ignore that when those who study story talk about *mythmaking*, they also tend to follow it with the word process. This indicates recognition of something at least crafted, if not also contrived.

Satisfying true mythic hunger means engaging with the material in front of us, and delving into both the darkness and the light of that material. For the sake of crafting a discipline, students of mythology have begun by delving into rich and complex material, traditions that are millennia old, soaking up their wisdom and considering the possible blessings offered by these traditions. As hauntingly provocative as these traditions are though, a thirst remains for research that considers the links between ancient wisdom and the myths and rituals of the current moment, and not only with what religious studies scholar Wendy Doniger refers to as *Other Peoples' Myths*.[14] In fact, and I believe Doniger's work point to this as well, projecting Western analysis on other peoples' myths while also patently rejecting facets of our own as unworthy of study and dispossessed of value can be a dangerous exercise in cultural appropriation. That being said, I'll leave it at this – popular storytelling distills a facet of cultural soul into a particular mythic moment, and if for nothing else, that makes it worth our time.

A Land of Golden Dreams?

As a child of Californian parents with strong, proud ties to our Azorean Portuguese and Friesian Dutch immigrant backgrounds, I grew up immersed in a micro culture that engaged California as *Wonderland,* a mysterious place filled with unknowns, but also a physical manifestation of the imagination with all the joys, pitfalls, dangers, and absurdities inherent to both real life and fantasy. To my child's eyes, home seemed at once labyrinthine and kaleidoscopic. My grandparents had a passionate love for California, both physical place and, although they were largely unaware of it I'm sure, metaphor. Although I grew up listening to stories of the *old country* and the pilgrimage west in the early decades of the 20th century, I was also taught that the land was the source of our livelihood. For them, California is the physical embodiment of the dreams our family immigrated to America to fulfill. They passed this love onto me, and although they were completely unconscious of it, they were nonetheless vital in

---

13   In the context of archetypal psychology, mythmaking has generally been understood as the artistic expression that arises spontaneously from what Jungians call psyche/soul.

14   Doniger's book is a seminal piece in comparative religion and myth study. She draws connections between story and the way cultures use story to understand themselves in a deeper way.

the construction of my belief that California has a unique archetypal place in the American mythic imagination.

The community in which I was raised held a firm belief that their state was a beacon of creativity and bounty. To us, California is a kind of ritual playground forged out of an image of paradise, a place where everything, through hard work, ingenuity and devotion, seems possible. For me, this begins with the land itself. California is a large state – the third largest by land mass and the largest by population. I've often joked that if you want to know what America looks like, visit California. With its myriad types of landscape and infinite microclimates – forbidding deserts, warm, sandy beaches and windswept rocky ones, awe-inspiring mountains, rolling hills, and lastly its vast amount of fertile agricultural ground – California is a global microcosm. This kind of natural environment lends itself to a *if you can dream it, you can do it* attitude, clearly typified in the myths of Southern California.

My mother was raised in Artesia, California, a community that lies at the intersection between Los Angeles, San Bernadino, and Orange counties. She was fifteen years old when the theme park opened in 1955. As they were professional colleagues in the agricultural industry, my grandparents were personally acquainted with the owners of Knott's Berry Farm, another theme park used as a touchstone for Walt Disney. I grew up visiting Knott's, and stories of those early days permeated my childhood. This relationship with Knott's, its mythic reverberations with Disney, and the presence of these theme parks shaped the Southern California that my mother's family knew, and my father's resonance with the *Mickey Mouse Club* and Fess Parker as *Davy Crockett* continues even to the present day. Until his death in 2010, Fess Parker was something of a local celebrity in my hometown of Santa Barbara. He was always controversial, whether he was building a new hotel or championing the rights of the Chumash, but he was also never too busy to talk to anyone about life in general or his experience of working with Disney in particular.

My husband worked with Fess on his landscape for some years. We held our wedding reception at his hotel near the beach in Santa Barbara. Over the years that I've been researching this book, I've come across many people who either knew Walt personally, or have worked with Disney in some way. These kinds of connections with Disney are the rule, rather than the exception in California, particularly in Southern California. Disney personally affects everyone in some way or another. Everyone knows people who work for Disney, has personal feelings about Disney and in some fashion, has had their lives shaped by Disney. I was just shy of three years old when I first visited Disneyland, even though the farming community where I lived with my parents was approximately 250 miles away in Central California. Although my memories of this trip are vague, I do remember sitting on my father's shoulders and touching Pooh Bear's paws. I visited Disneyland several times during my childhood, and even then I understood the park as a place that provides a psychological container for the magic of playful imagination. A container or psychologically safe environment, much like a therapy couch, is a vital aspect of myth and ritual.

Although this may seem naïve and idealistic in the face of history, one cannot forget the innovation and creativity that has traditionally bubbled over from the mythic cauldron of 20th-century California, whether it is Sid Grauman's *Chinese Theater*, Howard Hughes's *Spruce Goose*, Steve Jobs's *Apple*, or Walt Disney's *Disneyland*. If, as William Doty advocates, "Myth is understood as referring to the fundamental religious or philosophical beliefs of a culture, expressed through ritual behavior or through the graphic or literary arts, and forming a constitutive part of society's worldview",[15] then iconic centers for the creation and distribution of a culture's stories and traditions are bound to develop in places where these stories are born. Myths are, as folklore theorist Alan Dundes indicates, stories that tell us how things came to be.[16] These big stories relate to the sacred locations to which the stories belong. In Disney's case, these stories begin in, and in a sense always belong to, *mythic* California.

In some ways, California will always be more imaginary than real. From the earliest period of Spanish and Portuguese exploration, the name *California* carried the mythic projection of Europeans. The name harkens to the imagination. It evokes Spanish and Arabic exoticism, the reversal of western cultural norms, which considering the state's reputation as a place that nurtures all kinds of subculture may be closer to the truth than one would immediately suspect. California's name is widely believed to originate from stories written around the year 1500 by a Spanish novelist named Garci Ordonez de Montalvo. These stories tell of a magical island located somewhere west of Spain and ruled by a formidable queen – either Arabic or African, depending on whom you ask – named Califa.[17] The island of these stories is a paradise – beautiful, dripping with gold and the mythical milk and honey. The inhabitants of Califa's island are alluring, statuesque, powerful, warrior women who prefer the company of each other, only inviting their men to the island once a year for the purpose of reproduction. According to Californian legend, Spanish explorers mistakenly believed Baja to be an island when they encountered it in the sixteenth century. Their imaginations were stirred by the possibilities presented by the rugged and enthralling sights they encountered. One can imagine that the fertile lands and colorful landscapes must have convinced the sailors that they had landed on Califa's island.

These transcendent, mythic encounters set a precedent for an imaginative interpretation of California that still exists today. Despite tragic and certainly complicated socio-cultural histories that result from this disconnection between

---

15 William Doty, *Mythography*, 13.

16 *Sacred Narrative: Readings in the Theory of Myth*, 1–4.

17 Sometimes called Calafia or Califia.

fantasy and reality, myth continues to thrive. Even in the 21st century, this fantasy of Califa is called to mind in the imagination of Californians. An agricultural company from California's San Joaquin valley, an agricultural valley often called the *breadbasket of the world*, takes its name from this mythic queen. On the website for *Califa Farms* they write, "Great things come from California: the movies, gold, Lemon Limeade that tastes like endless summer".[18] A quick Google search for *California Tourism Commercials* provides all the evidence one needs to prove that Queen Califa's mythic impact still exists today in many Californian endeavors. The imagery associated with her is everywhere both in the way Californians understand themselves and in the way they project their products beyond state borders.

Another Spanish legend that guides the mythic history of California is the story of the *lost city of El Dorado*,[19] which pops up shortly after the first conquistadors arrived in Central and South Americas. El Dorado is widely understood to be a fictional place, manifested in the wealth of the forests and jungles of the Americas. In contrast the Califa's island – a utopian paradise pregnant with intoxicating feminine power, the city of El Dorado constellates the ambition of a masculine explorer, a conquistador. A king rules this lost city, not a queen. And the city represents ridiculous amounts of wealth, in contrast to a heavenly locale where no one needs to strive. These stories speak to the driving forces of psychological need that live behind American colonialism and the ensuing myth of Manifest Destiny.[20] They fulfill the fantasy of *lottery ticket* wealth acquisition – the idea that if you peek through the trees you will find every material thing you desire. Although the Spanish legends of El Dorado are not set in the state of California itself, Spanish presence in early California fused with the gold rush energy of the 49ers, a group of fortune hunters that descended on Northern California during the mid-19th century when gold was discovered in foothills of the Sierra Nevada mountains. When this happened, the lore became part of Californian identity. Throughout a large part of the 19th century and into the 20th the idea of coming *out to California* became synonymous with acquiring wealth and opportunity.

Utopia, beauty, freedom of body, engagement with imagination, and the chance of wealth acquisition, these are America's earliest myths of California, and as its child, Disneyland is born of this lineage. As an environment that is more imaginary than real, Disneyland is the physical manifestation of a surrealist romantic enticement. This mythic energy is so present in the atmosphere of

18 http://www.califiafarms.com/products/citrus-juice/lemon-limeade

19 http://science.nationalgeographic.com/science/archaeology/el-dorado/

20 Manifest Destiny is a belief that was broadly accepted by Americans during the 19th century. It held US settlers were preordained to conquer and expand across North America. Historians agree that it had three basic themes: the special virtues of American people and America, a special mission to redeem and remake the west into a mythic agrarian image, and that this destiny is unshakeable. Problematic though it may be in terms of postcolonial theory, this myth certainly influenced Walt Disney's upbringing.

Southern California that it becomes fused with the place itself. Both Los Angeles and Orange Counties have frequently been populated by restaurants shaped like large brown hats, show venues that place the patron in the middle of a medieval joust, Hollywood back lots, studios, and all manner of themed parks and spaces. The region's culture is rooted in the process of crafting story, of making Surrealism real. In its surrealism, Disneyland is a quintessential example of Southern Californian mythology.

Though these images of California continue to be present today, they were at the height of their power in the early part of the 20th century when a group of extremely creative storytellers came west for new opportunities, or perhaps simply for one grand opportunity: to develop, tell, and sell stories in burgeoning fields of new media. These stories piece together a journey narrative that conveys American identity through the lens of Los Angeles, a city that has been cast in a global role. It 's a single region able to depict everything from the plains of Kansas and the bright lights of Time Square to the battlefields of Europe and the temples of Asia. Those involved in the early development of the city of Hollywood accepted this role, but as storytellers always do, they told the stories their way. And, to this day, the west coast maintains a certain heft as a realm of enchantment. Visitors continue to flock to studio backlots or tours of classic Hollywood sites and attempt to stake out celebrities, as evidenced by the gossip show *TMZ*, the candlelight vigils that occur whenever a beloved celebrity is lost, or the throngs of fans that will wait for hours for a glimpse of luminaries in their award season attire.

The voyeuristic nature of Hollywood's entertainment media has been vital to the development of mass culture. Although the mythmaking inherent in film-making is no longer confined to the studios as in the past, a psychological association continues to link Hollywood to storytelling and mass culture. Perhaps the most complex and artistically liberating medium within film has been animation, from early hand-drawn cartoons to contemporary CGI used to enhance live action features. Walt became fascinated with animation early in his life, and after his first attempt, Laugh-O-Gram Studios, failed, He hopped on a train to Los Angeles. The move made sense. His uncle and his brother Roy lived there. He arrived star struck and soon recognized that Southern California, with its moderate climate, open spaces, and unstructured social conventions offered the best atmosphere for an artist working within this new art form. He found California to be conducive to the development of his vision, and out of this new two-dimensional medium of animation came three-dimensional Disneyland, a place that becomes an *axis mundi*,[21] a psychological respite for the imagination of much of the world.

If, as the Greek term *mythos* suggests myth is the speech or narrative that tells the story of *us* for those to whom the stories belong, then Disney's myths face

---

21 *Axis Mundi* or Center of the World.

west toward Hollywood, the genesis of an American pan-mythos that helped to fashion mass culture. Although the myths that emerge from every corner of this nation reveal vital aspects of what it means to be American, it's Hollywood,[22] as the original home of film and television, perhaps particularly from the 1930s through the 1960s, that became entrusted with the role of mirroring our stories back to us and projecting them out to the world. Where else would these stories come from than California, *The Golden State*,[23] America's mythical sun drenched land where stars shine during the day and walk among us? The gold of Queen Califa's island and the bounty of El Dorado come to life in the imagination when the myths of California present it as a magical place *where dreams come true*.

Nostalgia and Transcendence at Disneyland

The capacity to love is the heartbeat of Disney's myth that advocates for a balance between our own individuality and our relationships with others. At the center of this myth lies the individual's story. A trip to Disneyland is an interaction between the individual character's stories and the ways in which each story contributes to the collective story; a fact that exists even in the Company's conservationist message that *Every Tree Has Character*. Individuality, however central to Disney's mythology, does not mean simple selfishness and conceit. Relationships and a community of patrons in relationship to each other have always been central to Disney myth, placing the individual's story within the context of familial bonds. One of the best examples of the importance Disney places on relationships is the memory book that is the windows on Main Street, U.S.A. Each window notes an important position in the Disney cosmos: *tune-makers* (The Sherman Brothers), *proprietors* (Elias Disney), and *purveyors of fine coonskin caps* (Fess Parker) to name just a few. Each one of these windows corresponds to a real person who has had a vital impact in shaping the Disney brand. They are called out by name, etched in glass, and given a role in the park that fits in connection to the role they played in real life. They become a part of the place itself.

When Disneyland's 50th anniversary was in full swing in 2005, Disney launched a call for family photos to be installed in different locations around the park. Their request was simple: send in a photo of yourself or your family enjoying the park and your photo would be added to a loosely impressionistic, Monet-like photo in which each individual photo became one small part of a large photo

---

22 Some might actually argue that this is no longer the case, since the old days of studio films are no more. Indeed, many production companies are moving their work to places where filming is more financially feasible, such as Austin, Texas and to European locations such as Ireland and The Czech Republic. However, the stars always return home to Hollywood as a kind of axis mundi for such events as The Academy Awards. This suggests that, as a place, Los Angeles still maintains its power as an Olympian image, the place where the stars live.

23 It is often thought that California is called The Golden State because of El Dorado and the gold rush, but is actually called that because of the golden desert hills of California's farm land that glow with golden grass and yellow gold California poppies.

that eventually came together to form the image of a character. This project proved to be incredibly popular, and it is a perfect example of the way Disneyland works to create an atmosphere of American-style *E pluribus unum*.[24] The individual's story is key at Disneyland, and the individual's story creates the story of the collective.

That patrons are devoted to Disneyland even in the face of all the destructive flaws of its corporate model, suggests to me that there is reciprocity between the park and the visitor, and that this reciprocity is re-created on every visit through the process of interactive storytelling. No two trips are the same. The visitor to the resort enters the storytelling process, and through a relationship with the environment and characters, becomes a living part of the story. The early Imagineers understood intrinsically that unlike other amusement parks, a theme park experience allows the visitor feel involved in the mythopoetic process of story-crafting. It both personalizes the park for the individual visitor and crafts a mythology to blanket the group of participants.

Fiercely meticulous sales and marketing departments may be responsible for much of Disneyland's success, but the true life's blood of the park endures in the mythic imagination of the people who continue to live the story. Creativity through continuous change is a driving mantra of the Disneyland Imagineers, though they also respect continuity and tradition. American myth and nostalgia are two topics that are completely intertwined, as are Disney and nostalgia. Everyone who has commented on Walt, from Steven Watts to Neal Gabler, discusses Walt's love of, use of, and obsession with nostalgia. Too often though, in my opinion, those who comment on nostalgia malign it. It is often thought of as uncritical sentiment, as story polished just to make the audience feel happy. Those who appreciate nostalgia are often accused of being deluded and/or simple minded. Richard Schickel once called Walt out for his sentimentality about the past saying that if he had any politics at all, it was the politics of nostalgia. In the 2015 documentary on Walt for PBS' *American Experience* series, he said that he thought Walt wanted to *be* the image he put forward to the world. According to Schickel, Walt wanted to be the healthy person, physically and psychologically, that he projected to the world. But, according to the PBS documentary version of him, he just wasn't that person.

Walt's artistic response to the complexities of an often-painful human existence was to create the reality he wanted to see through an encounter with nostalgia. Although many have suggested that this *Disney version* is dangerously myopic, it is also the greatest gift Disney has to offer. The Disney lens provides a cathartic space for healing the pain of social, spiritual, and cultural alienation. The etymological root of the word itself offers an indication of why it's indispensible to Disney mythmaking. Nostalgia is a combination of two Greek words, nostos (home) and algia (pain). The pain of being separated from home, of having lost

---

24 "Out of many, one.

home, of being torn away from home, or having home taken away. Few experiences are more evocative of the American experience than that. Tom Hanks' *Saving Mr. Banks* version of Walt addresses this desire for reconnection with home and a healing of the lost inner child. In a touching scene that takes place in P.L. Travers' home, he tells the story of the abuse he suffered during the difficult days of his childhood and then he asks Travers why, if one had the ability to change their story, would they not choose to do so. To him, that's what storytellers do. They fix the broken parts of myth. As I see it, that's where the healing potentiality of nostalgia lives. At the end of the nostalgic drive is a desire to be released from the pain of having broken stories, to be returned to a time and place where both the stories and the people they reflect are whole.

Californian myths and a culture of nostalgia coalesce at Disneyland. The mythic projection becomes a mythic reality as the patron is bathed in the sun drenched arms of a land of plenty – of wish fulfillment, of wonder, ruled by princesses and charming princes, where Jedi knights keep villains in check, and every desire of leisure time is catered to in a glorious land of comfort and delight. There is darkness there, certainly, as Senator Bernie Sanders recently questioned when he called out Bob Iger on the compensation the corporation offers its employees. Some have even gone so far as to refer to living in Anaheim as *living in the shadow of the mouse*. As an external manifestation of the imagination steeped in the myths of California, however, this all makes sense. This tension is central to Californian myth.

In the series finale of AMC's critically acclaimed show *Mad Men*, American anti-hero Don Draper drops out of his life and heads west to California. After a short jaunt to Los Angeles, he heads up north to a retreat space, obviously Esalen Institute in the Big Sur area of Monterey County.[25] While in this gloriously sacred space overlooking the Pacific Ocean, Don has a breakdown. Later, the series ends with him sitting in a lotus position meditating with a smile on his face. The scene then fades out to the iconic 1971 Coca-Cola commercial that features a generation of young people, the very generation that was raised on Disneyland's early years, on the hilltop singing *I'd Like to Teach The World to Sing*.[26] This scene is intentionally ambiguous. An implication of this, which is also true about Disneyland, is that for American culture, interaction with the bliss of Califa's realm is irrevocably fused with the search for the eternal city of gold. These are the mythic realities of California. In Disneyland, we find a nostalgic encounter with this idea – a belief that this will return us to wholeness from the pain of loss, both specific and unspecific. Inside this kind of mythic reality, Disneyland is remarkably effective.

This psychological respite is positioned as a comforting encounter with Disney's uniquely Californian perspective on global myth. It brings Disney's stories alive

25 http://www.esalen.org

26 https://www.youtube.com/watch?v=ib-Qiyklq-Q

in a way that allows the patrons to give themselves over to transcendence. And it does this for the sake of creating feelings of warmth that are central to satisfy the patron's need for nostalgia. I have enjoyed countless trips to Disneyland, many of them as an annual passholder, and I am consistently amazed at the delicate balance Disney holds between a reverence for the past and a devotion to Walt's principles of progressivism. In March 2009, on an unbelievably beautiful day in Anaheim, I had an experience that made the mythic impact of Disneyland particularly clear to me. Up to that point, in all the years I spent visiting Walt's original hub for physicalized storytelling, I had not noted much about patterns of behavior among the patrons. It had always been clear to me that there was intentionality behind the things that Disney was doing, and I enjoyed other *Disn-o-philes* as though they were friends, instead of simply strangers I would most assuredly never meet again. This day though was a bit different.

As my husband and I strolled across the Hub, a town square-like locale which centers and acts as a bridge between the different lands of Disneyland, I noticed a gathering of guests standing in front of Sleeping Beauty's Castle, a situation that is not uncommon at Disneyland, especially where characters are gathered or attractions are located. We decided to stop and listen to the Disneyland Marching Band. Mickey Mouse, Minnie, and Goofy joined them as they danced to the tune the band played. It was all so typical – that is, until something happened that completely changed the way I understand both Disneyland itself and the Disneyland patron.

The band finished their set, and as Mickey Mouse (the band leader) brought the music down low, Walt's voice came over the loud speaker, reciting the opening day speech. "To all who come to this happy place, welcome. Disneyland is your land. Here, age relives fond memories of the past [. . .] and here, youth may savor the challenge and promise of the future. Disneyland is dedicated to the ideals, the dreams and the hard facts that have created America [. . .] with the hope that it will be a source of joy and inspiration to the world."[27] A reverential hush came over the crowd of people, the likes of which I had previously only seen in settings dedicated to worship. We listened to Walt's words, this prophet, priest, and king of his own land of enchantment, dreams and magic,[28] and as we did I felt a palpable energy being generated between the audience and myself. Eventually the speech concluded and sound was brought down. I was deeply moved as a poignant silence came over the park. It is extremely rare for pure silence to fall over any part of the park, and when it does it is usually in anticipation of something. On this occasion though, the silence felt more like a completion of sacred liturgy. It seemed to me that we were hearing a divine voice

27 http://www.disneydreamer.com/DLOpen.htm

28 Occasionally, there were those who would suggest that Walt Disney should run for mayor of Los Angeles. His response was simply that there was no reason for him to become a mayor when he was already king of his own land. http://d23.disney.go.com/archives/collecting-dreams/ *Disney News,* Winter 1993.

speaking. The group was both transfixed and transformed. The moment of silence ended, and as the crowd went on to their next moment of fright and fun, I came away with an experience that cemented Disneyland's importance to me as the center of pilgrimage.

I'm not sure whether the crowd present that day was conscious of the transformation that occurred at that moment. Perhaps it was something I noticed because of my sensitivity to archetypes and deep mythic patterns. Either way, as I enjoyed another sunny day in the park, it became clear to me that simply being in this place had affected a change in consciousness, not only on myself, but also on many others around me. As I stood in line for the Pirates of the Caribbean attraction, I noted the crowd itself. Around me stood people of all ages, races, national origins, religious creeds, political affiliations, and sexual orientations. It became clear that the crowd willingly suspended the issues humans generally find divisive. Somehow and for some reason, patrons of Disneyland choose to leave these distinctions of nationalism, politics, and subversive morality outside the main gate. Patrons talk to strangers. I have even had parents ask me to watch their children while they run to the restroom. A sense of safety reigns supreme, as Disneyland patrons seem convinced that they are unified by their adherence to Disney's ideology. And with respect to exceptions that do occur, people generally seem happy. This kind of willing suspension of disbelief, the ability and eagerness to submit to the realm of fantasy is central to all ritual, and it is integral to the transcendence necessary in order to make an effective ritual.

For many of these patrons, Disney's mythology is a living system similar to that of Gene Rodenberry's *Star Trek* universe, J. K. Rowling's *Harry Potter* series or George Lucas's *Star Wars* epic. These franchises are splendid cosmologies birthed of gifted storytellers, which come alive as epic myths through interplay between the imagination of the storyteller and the imagination of the receiver. Myth and storytelling are interwoven in this way making it almost impossible to define one without the other. Not all stories are mythic, but certainly all myth is conveyed through some kind of image or narrative structure. Ritual, however, provides the mysterious link between images, which often precede a mythos itself and the physical world. The magic of Disneyland lies within this mysterious link. These storytellers play with distinctions of good and evil, carrying the same utopian desire in their franchises that make Disney's offerings so popular. They speak to humanity's desire for peace, freedom, and the sacrifice necessary to reach for these ideals. Through Walt's myths, the names of such legends as Mickey Mouse, Fess Parker (Davy Crockett), master Pixar filmmaker John Lasseter, and Walt Disney himself become icons and contemporary bards of an unfolding ritual tradition. They, like other myth-makers of the modern and postmodern era, sense the need for myth and ritual and, through the theme park experience, seek to integrate mythic images, past and present, with folk and fairy tales from around the world. The massive outpouring of devotion available at the parks, as well as identification with all things Disney, suggests to me that the vein of collective, archetypal psyche has been tapped.

The D23, an online contemporary fan club and hub for Disn-o-philes, exemplifies the way in which people patrons engage with Disney storytelling as the basis for mythic community. In September 2009, I attended the first D23 Expo. This organization, developed by the Disney archivists at the studio in Burbank, seeks to incorporate the love of Disney nostalgia, with contemporary ways of sharing information. Their Internet site, for example, is full of trivia and comic gems, as well as the latest information on theme park renovations, film releases, and events. When they launched in 2009, the massive reaction to the project surprised even the creators of D23, which, incidentally, stands for Disney 1923 – the year Walt came to California – and the Expo is now a biannual event. Subsequent Expos have taken place in 2011, 2013, and 2015. The next Expo commences on the weekend of July 14–16, 2017.

Over 40,000 people converged on the Anaheim Convention Center in 2009, purely for their love of Disney. It was an experience that, in its jovial energy, felt more like a family reunion than a conference. This group demonstrated a devoted, quasi-religious fervor for the Disney mythos, much like what one sees at Disneyland, leaving energy in the air that was truly magical. The unprecedented popularity of the theme park is evidence of both the magic of the place itself and the skillfulness of those who pull the strings behind the scenes. Journalist for the website MousePlanet.com and Disney enthusiast David Koenig describes what Disneyland does in sheer numbers. He writes that "More than twelve million guests each year come to sample Southern California's purest slice of paradise, and for the most part, they believe the fantasy".[29] This magic, like any other transformational endeavor, is calculated and worked out in a presubscribed ritual that is scientific in its consistency, a consistency that works on a global scale. The Disney phenomenon is not simply an esoteric Southern Californian attempt to artistically render myth within a cultural expression of American art and ritual. It is a global phenomenon that couches these expressions through the stories that create Californian identity.

Disney's theme park, with its mythic images and interactive rituals, can and does fulfill certain psychological and spiritual needs for myth. Although it does not heal or reassemble in total the fractured nature of American myth, it does offer an option for a momentary suspension of it. During each trip to Disneyland, as I watch oceans of Disney worshippers, led by the memory of their leader Walt and his priests the *Imagineers*[30] partaking in interactive attractions, I become more convinced that the Disney mythos is alive and at least extended to all corners of humanity. In an era when global myths seem to center around despair, American

29   *Mouse Tales: A Behind-the-Ears Look at Disneyland*, 18.

30   This is a term Walt Disney coined by combining the words imagination and engineers.

politics make us all cringe, and Hollywood continues to churn out one disaster film after another, Disneyland offers a safe haven for the imagination.

It becomes a container for it, and although it cannot unify culture at large, it can offer a playground for humanity to have a unified experience of imagination while navigating the difference between child-ish-ness and child-like-ness. This intersection between play and meaning is the place where Disney's archetypal bounty lives. In the context of this, a trip to Disneyland can be likened to a temple pilgrimage. Although it is often suggested that it is a temple to consumerism and capitalist economics – a strong and important point to recognize – I would suggest that an environment built entirely on consumerism would eventually consume itself. Disneyland continues to stand because it is a temple to the imaginative power of myth, the creative action of ritual, and the transformative bonds of love, familial and otherwise. ✳

Chapter 2

The Pilgrimage to Psyche-Land

Western culture is too comfortable with itself to change overnight [. . .]. It is more realistic to think about the spiritual needs of family and self as a starting point for social transformation than to begin thinking we can change Hollywood . . . To make Self each person's own best spiritual project is to avoid the crush of the gigantic modern Machine. Ritual enables us to live a life that is much closer to what our souls aspire to [. . .]. – Malidoma Patrice Somé [31]

In the Beginning…

*O*nce Upon A Time, there was a man named Walt Disney. From childhood, he was compelled to be an artist, a storyteller, which to his imagination was the same as being a wizard. These dreams grew to maturity with him. When he was ready, he assembled some of the world's most gifted artists to build a whimsical kingdom. He wanted his land to be a place where people can feel safe to play and enjoy one another. The idea came to him while spending family time with his daughters at a carnival in the Griffith Park area of Los Angeles. Walt understood the importance of family bonding. By all accounts, he was a loving and attentive father, and he always made sure that he kept his weekend days free to spend with his daughters, Diane and Sharon. He knew, as he was incredibly busy building his own ventures, that *quality time* is an elusive thing for most contemporary families. He also knew that spending this kind of time is vital to the construction of healthy relationships.

Walt relished this weekly time with his daughters. He'd sit on a park bench eating his bag of peanuts or popcorn as the children rode the carousel or visited other

---

31   *Ritual: Power, Healing and Community*, 79.

attractions. In those early days of his studio expansion – the mid 1930s through the early WWII years – Walt and his daughters visited several different carnivals and zoos, all with a similar result. The girls played and dad waited patiently, eating his snacks, and dreaming about a park of his own. As he sat on one of those legendary park benches, the "original" one of which is now located in the space between the Mad Hatter and the Opera House at Disneyland's Main Street, U.S.A., a particular thought constantly invaded his fertile imagination. Why, he mused, was there no place where parents and children could partake and play together? This question was the catalyst he needed to build a park of his own.

Over the next couple of decades, Walt spent much of his time trying to decide exactly what a Disney park would look like. Where would he build it? Would it be in Burbank next to the studio, or would he find property elsewhere? What kinds of attractions did he want it to have? He knew it had to be a place where families could come together and play together. It had to represent the way he understood his work's offerings to the world. But when he looked around at other amusement parks, he was unimpressed. His wife, Lillian, reminded him that amusement parks were often kind of seedy, not really the kind of places people wanted to spend a lot of time. So, he began to collect ideas, thoughts about what he believed he could do better.

A few guiding ideas came back to whenever he thought about his park. Its stories had to led by a guiding ethos of sentimentality of connection, or as he was fond of saying, it had to have *heart*. It had to be clean and safe, and it had to embody what he thought childhood in America should be. His plan was to take the park patron along on a guided tour of the way he understood Disney's mythic contributions. Although he would not have used the language of myth in the way scholars that follow in the footsteps of Campbell have come to understand it, he was certainly aware of his brand's mythic impact. Watts writes that by the early 1960s:

> Walt clearly understood that "Disney" now symbolized an amalgamation of qualities and that he personally had evolved into a many-sided image: a revered national moralist, an example of American achievement, a trusted guardian of the nation's children, and a representative of average citizen, and their vales, tastes and desires.[32]

Indeed, Walt knew exactly what it meant for stories to have the Disney touch. He took this responsibility seriously. Because he felt so strongly about the significance of his brand's contributions to American identity, he never spoke of the creation of Disneyland as purely a money making endeavor. More often he referred to it as a kind of passion project. He believed the park to be his three dimensional interpretation of America's ideals, which he considered Disney to be "uniquely equipped to dramatize...send them forth as a source of courage and inspiration to all the world".[33] In this sense, Walt is an American prophet.

---

32 *The Magic Kingdom: Walt Disney and the American Way of Life*, 405.

He sensed the need for sacred play – a need he intuited because he lamented the neglect of childlike imagination in the world around him. In response to this neglect, he created a space that resonated deeply with Cold War America and continues to resonate today.

Walt died in 1966. Grief ripped through his corporate family, and as a result Disneyland went into a period of deep mourning. By the early 1980s, some expressed concern about the future of the brand Walt worked so hard to build. Then came Michael Eisner and the Reagan era. With Walt's long time friend in the White House, America reignited its consumerist drive. Disneyland was reborn during the hyper-consumptive era of the 1980s, fusing a new Fantasyland with changing images of Tomorrowland. It has gained momentum since then, becoming the temple to America's fantasy escape that it is today. Currently, Disneyland has grown from its original Disney property to include *Star Wars*, *Indiana Jones*, and Marvel. It has expanded its definition about who and what belongs in the park, but it continues to present itself as a place that offers playtime between children and adults, a release from the pressures of contemporary life, and a place of magic where all dreams come true. Despite the steadily rising cost of tickets and local hotels, the crowds at Disneyland are larger than ever. It seems that Walt's desire to create a three dimensional nostalgic locale as shield against the traumas of life has succeeded beyond anything he could have ever imagined.

How Did We Get Here?

Between 1954 and 1966, with the last cries of the Second World War and the Korean Conflict fading to silence, the first whispers of the Vietnam conflict being heard, and the dawning of the Age of Aquarius on the horizon, academics began to delve deeply into a new awareness, into what they called consciousness-raising fields of study: second-wave feminism, deconstructionism, ecopsychology, post colonialism, and the racial reverberations of the Civil Rights Movement. America in the 1950s and early 1960s had much in common with the Victorian age of Walt Disney's personal mythic history, both eras of homogeny and thinly veiled contempt against anything that might be viewed as culturally subversive. In many ways, it was a time of extremely polarized political viewpoints, much like our current moment. Somehow, amidst a nervous status quo of the Cold War's atomic age and the cultural homogenization of the red scare and McCarthyism, a burgeoning American interest in Eastern religions and the depth psychoanalytical traditions of Freud and Jung brought the language of consciousness to the lips of many social critics.

Although this era has often been remembered for a paranoid need for control, Walt, often thought of as Hollywood's ultimate conservative studio head, utilized his position as cultural bard to smooth out the edges and find some kind

---

33 *The Quotable Walt Disney*, 55.

of middle ground. He helped a generation of America's youth find their own way of telling story and, through his unique brand of family entertainment, brought together the conservative and liberal facets of society. Brode addresses this issue in his book on Disney culture and sixties subversivism. He writes:

> America, in Disney's broad view, is not liberal or conservative, progressive or traditional, Democrat or Republican. The genius of the system resided in a symbiotic relationship of each complementary opposition – an ever-shifting balance between rugged individualism and commitment to community.[34]

The Disney studio as led by Walt Disney fashioned a sense of community through the creation of a market for youth. These stories attempted to transcend the issues that divide in order to create a specific brand of storytelling, which, though not an altruistic effort, is nevertheless a noble pursuit. That being said, Walt has also been the subject of much controversy. Many of his animators, most notably the legendary union organizer Art Babbitt and *Snow White and the Seven Dwarfs* veteran Bill Tytla left the studio during a devastating and extremely ugly labor dispute in 1941. Walt's choice to testify in front of the House Un-American Activities Committee (HUAC) during the dark years of the Hollywood black list era did not help his image among Hollywood creatives. He has been called a fascist, a control-freak, and a megalomaniac, opinions that if not fully vetted are certainly up for debate given historical facts about him, his business policies, his politics, and his choices. His passion for education and entertainment, however, was always clear. He loved telling stories, and it was this passion, combined with a unique championing of the American family that helped pave the way for a new generation of 1960s social activists.

With an entire generation of youth poised, thanks in large part to Disney's influence; to take ownership of the power of their own mythic voice(s), one might assume that these changes would be entirely positive. However, Jung's theories show, the aspects of soul not brought into consciousness (shadow) are bound to find a way into consciousness (ego) often through subversive culture and behavior. This generation raised on Disney's myths, though more culturally conscious than the generation before, was ultimately just as unable to obtain balance as any other, and, much like the cosmos of Lucas' Jedi, psychological wholeness proved just as elusive amidst the civil unrest of the Vietnam era and the hyper consumerist times since then as it proven to be during the 1950s *Ozzie and Harriet*[35] era, a time that depicts the family as a homogenized, un-self-reflexive happy home.

The socio-political movements of mid 20th century culture were an attempt to test the limits of freedom. Earlier experiments, such as the transcendentalist

---

34 *From Walt to Woodstock: How Disney Created the Counterculture,* 37.

35 *The Adventures of Ozzie and Harriet* was a situation comedy that aired on American television from 1952 to 1966. This show, which aired on ABC, the same network that garnered a deal with Walt Disney for his *Disneyland* show, presents an iconic sense of what is considered typical of the era. It stars real-life parents, Ozzie and Harriet Nelson and their children.

communes of the mid-19th century and the carnival, role-reversal atmosphere of the flapper parties of the 1920s sounded similar intimations of freedom and subversive thinking. Amidst the angst of the 1960s at the end of Walt's life, social norms began to be overturned. A proclivity for questions without answers began to dominate many of humanity's myths. With the prevailing mantra amongst youth of *Question Authority*, many Americans began to believe that perhaps the only truth is that there is no truth or, conversely, that *everything* is truth.

In the previous chapter, I explored the complications that arise when a scholar in the fields of myth and depth psychology chooses to analyze Disney. As previously mentioned, it's also is important to note that these complications go beyond the fields of myth and depth psychology to include a broader distaste for Disney in the context of subcultural movements. During the transformative years of the mid-late 20th century, an intractable attitude toward the demonization of American culture in general as one built on the soullessness of capitalism gained ideological momentum, as well as a belief that engaging with spirituality and being transformed by it requires wholesale rejection of everything popularly *American*. Many of those who were aware of the driving myths of this culture began to suggest that a genuine connection to humanity was somehow to be found in the powerful stories of the ancients with near exclusivity.

Campbell's work, particularly his book *The Hero With a Thousand Faces* first published in 1949, champions the impact of mythology. By the mid-1960s, a generation of young adults who were raised on Disney's folklore and fairytale were eager to find new ways to engage with ancient stories. This appreciation for myth may be understood as one of the most positive steps that was taken during the 20th century toward psychological healing, what Jungians call individuation or the integration between self (wholeness) and shadow (that which is unconscious) into consciousness. Again though, as Jung intuited, that which is unconscious is just that. It reflects that which we either do not know, or have forgotten, and such is the case with the movement toward mythic appreciation.

In the midst of an earnest desire to both reclaim wisdom from the past and promote tolerance, a culture of self-loathing has developed in the American academy. In this attempt to acknowledge the traumas of the past, we forget that humanity has the option to live in joy. Disneyland reminds us that there are seasons for every human experience, and those seasons include play and delight. These jubilant activities must be acknowledged for what they are: moments of child-like bliss. If not, our society may fall prey to a cycle of self-loathing, trauma, terror, and mourning which in turn gives rise to polarized, dogmatic thinking. In the last sixty-plus years, humanity has felt the pain that comes with psychological growth, as we continue to endure a constant reshaping of our identity. We keep searching for deeper points of social connection, but this self-reflexivity has not come without a price. In some sense, we struggle to re-engage our ability to believe in anything, including our own spirituality and, most importantly, ourselves.

Abject terror seems to be the defining emotion of the first decades of the 21st century. Images of apocalypse, a world in flames, of transformation and revelation, captivate this era's mythmaking. News outlets offer us little in terms of psychologically balanced believers. Television manipulates us to fear every possible nightmare – the terror plot, the gory murder, the natural disaster, the corrupt angry politician, and the broken economy. Video games and virtual reality media are gripped by stories of dark armies covering the globe. The film industry continues to crank out disaster films, such as *2012*,[36] depicting the destruction of the planet and, all the while, science reminds us that there is some truth to it all, and that life on our planet is barely hanging onto its natural, delicate balance.

Even at Disneyland, we sense that a shift is on the horizon. Dark images are central to Disneyland's dark rides, balancing out the simplicity and innocence. In fact, the fairy tale motifs of death and danger are present even in the most seemingly innocuous attractions at Disneyland. This dark material finds a devoted following at Disneyland, inspiring the blockbuster franchise of films based on the popular Pirates of the Caribbean attraction. One time Disney animator Tim Burton has produced work has also been particularly effective in this vein. The lead characters from his 1992 classic, *The Nightmare Before Christmas*, Jack and Sally, have found a niche at Disneyland. *Jack is my Boyfriend* t-shirts and Sally plush dolls, as well as all kinds of merchandise from the film, are everywhere. Each year, beginning in early September, the Haunted Mansion attraction is transformed into an encounter with Tim Burton's tweaked image of what happens when *Halloween does Christmas*. As the years pass and the franchise's popularity continues to increase, Halloween does Disneyland all year long.

We anticipate apocalypse. But apocalypse suggests revelation, and that revelation is not yet clear. Humanity is more stressed out, depressed, medicated and disconnected than ever, which begs the question: where is our sense of play? We live with an overwhelming awareness that these are the last days of something significant, but the nature of that something is hidden. These feelings of foreboding are compounded by the confusion of suffering from a spiritual identity crisis. The desire for peace and tolerance remind us that pantheism ISN'T atheism, the uncertainty of which makes for an American culture situated in the context of a global culture for whom spirituality is completely out of balance. The darkest parts of the imagination have a monopolistic control on our minds; much of lightness, frivolity, and play have disappeared from daily life. Humanity has become so gripped by the darkness that the term *wholesome*,

---

36 Roland Emmerich, 2009.

which suggests a process of coming into fullness or completeness of being, loses meaning as anything other than kitsch.

One might suggest that contemporary culture is inherently post-mythic and post-ritual, at least in the traditional sense. It might be argued that imagination and the ability to cultivate a ritualized relationship to the imagination are irreconcilable with contemporary culture in a time when the religious complex seems to be, as television comedian turned filmmaker Bill Maher calls it, *Religulous*.[37] Some might even suggest that much of humanity has reached the pinnacle of what sociologist Max Weber referred to as the disenchantment of the West, and that magical wonder simply has no part in this environment. In good postmillennial[38] form, perhaps the answer to all these observations is yes, no, and maybe. A yearning for magical ritual often becomes the proverbial *Dumbo* in the room as the simple act of immersion into sacred consciousness continues to be surrounded by the divisive energy of fundamentalism and xenophobia. The religious impulse can be a dangerous thing to navigate when it literally means life or death. Although contemporary religious young people continue to flock to liturgical traditions of all kinds, secular rites have begun to claim a vital hold on the soul of humanity. This kind of environment calls for the creation of new containers for the sacred that unite humanity across all of its diversity.

As parents and mentors, the baby boomer generation began this process as they focused on the development of their own identity and living in a conscious manner. The blessings of their journey toward enlightenment continue to echo into the contemporary moment. In many ways though, this generation also succeeded in self-destructing, both psychologically and spiritually, often taking its children and grandchildren with it. If you ask the general public about their participation in ritual, they might spout some rhetoric about the tragedy of its loss, but precious few will actually be able to speak about the way they participate in it, or even suggest a way to reclaim it. William Doty speaks to this *anti-ritualistic* attitude. He believes there has developed in society, and specifically to what he refers to as "ritoclasm", the simultaneous fear and dismissal of traditional modes of ritual.

---

37 2008.

38 The term postmodernism, which has its genesis in the mid 20th century, refers to an era that, in truth, no longer applies to contemporary culture. Nineteenth and early 20th century Modernism sought to deconstruct what appeared to be broken systems hailed by Nietzsche as the affects of the death of God, as well as acknowledging the mythic wasteland of culture. Postmodernism, post-Holocaust-ism, and post-deconstructionism are philosophical attempts to speak to the brokenness of the modernist movement by acknowledging not just brokenness, but oblivion itself. It is hallmarked by an apocalyptic sensibility. What I call postmillennialism refers to contemporary myth commentary's refusal of the idea that there is nothing left of the broken containers. It is a new romanticism, which, though it is an heir to deconstructionism, attempts to reconstruct. My sense of postmillennialism is in line with the Hebrew concept of Tikkun Olam, which is the idea that although our actions do shatter the world, it is our responsibility to find the pieces and put them back together. This is the task of the postmillennial commentator on contemporary ritual processes.

> It is difficult to advocate a healthy respect for rituals, when one first must deal with a ritoclastic mind-set which denies that rituals ever can be considered positively, when rituals are considered to represent primarily a negative deadweight from the past, or when the self-reflexivity of our postmodern culture intrudes its suspicions of any activities that are held to represent transcendental values.[39]

The true state of contemporary culture's ritual practice is even more distressing than a metaphorical smashing of the rituals of the status quo. Many rituals are simply left unattended. Categorized as meaningless, rituals were often systematically deconstructed before they were destroyed, leaving not even a hint of what a ritual might look like for the next generation to re-invigorate or re-fashion it. As the sacred traditions of the past were dismantled, the pieces were not, as is standard operating procedure at Disneyland, stored away for future use. And though many have neglected the rituals themselves, humanity has not lost its need for ritual. They are as present as ever, waiting to be re-discovered and re-named – a process, which requires re-learning what it means to fashion them and appreciate the ones that we engage in at present.

One of many in the academic and artistic communities who address the dismantling of culture's mythic imagination, Campbell advocates for a new myth, a myth that speaks to all of humanity. *Star Trek* creator Gene Roddenberry was another, suggesting a new humanism, one that focuses on what humanity shares in common rather than on its differences. They insist that there must be a way to unify humanity through its diversity in a free and peaceful way. Their modernist neo-romanticism also predicates the development of an American neo-utopianism. Walt is, arguably, the most influential of all these neo-romantic utopians. A shrewd, intuitive businessman with the affectionate heart of a folk hero, he began to popularize this brewing tension between romanticism and modernism by creating his own interpretation of it for American consumers. The reach of his mythic legs is long as it straddled across Main Street, U.S.A.,[40] with one foot planted firmly in the nostalgia of Frontierland and one foot floating freely in the ether of Tomorrowland both anchored by the realm of Fantasyland. Consciously and unconsciously, Disneyland embodies the ephemeral, ambiguous nature of postmodern, and now postmillennial, ritual. It balances the tensions between ambitious drive, fastidious social control, and freedom of imagination.

Everything Walt Disney Imagineering[41] designs is created for the purpose of manipulating the senses in such a fashion as to present the tensions of American life in a fun and psychologically safe, playful way, with (of course) an emphasis on the characteristics that make America a positive idea. When the notion struck Walt that there ought to be a place where children and parents could play

---

39 *Mythography,* 390.

40 This term may be understood to gain at least part of its impact due to Disney's development of the icon. It has come to be a cultural buzzword for small, grass roots values in business.

41 Originally known as Walter Elias Disney (WED).

together, it was because he sensed a psychic void left when modernism began to point at humanity's hollow ritual shells, many of which had already begun to unravel at the edges. In designing Disneyland, he responds to this void. He knew, perhaps because he was able to tap into the unconscious psychology of culture, that the world is becoming increasingly *smaller after all*. And with mounting paranoia growing from the rapidity of social changes already waking around the edges any truly meaningful sacred space would need to reflect both the growing trends toward pantheism and social equality.

All living creatures need the downtime of playtime, but humanity remains unable to balance needs with behaviors. Many contemporary outlets for play offer self-destructive tendencies, as Marion Woodman suggests in a documentary on her life when she talks about the presence of addictive behavior. Woodman argues that fear drives our lives. She says that we act out in addiction because we live in a culture that doesn't understand metaphor, and because we don't have an appropriate channel for the metaphors that our souls actually long to express.[42] And, she's absolutely correct. The gratification Disneyland offers has the potential to follow this propensity toward addiction, but while it is true that consumption is out of control, it is also true that for all its destructive aspects, Disney's mythic message continually focuses on some of the most integral parts of what it means to be human: love, the importance of one's unique voice, and the bonds of family and community. Far from being a perfect pilgrimage, an encounter with Disney's myths can be interpreted as a choice to engage in the fractured fairytale that is American mythic tradition; through a container that, if wielded in a positive manner, might just have the opportunity to enact healing through stories that those mired in consumer culture might actually understand.

American culture often links both sacred and secular ritual to places that are ideologically sacred rather than physically sacred. In other words, our sacred locales develop out of ideology rather than the sacred nature of the land being the impetus for meaning. Places such as Graceland, Washington DC, Mount Rushmore, and Disneyland often offer profoundly moving experiences as artificially created places to go, a physical manifestation of the shift in consciousness, not necessarily by encountering the natural world itself. Crafting such places has traditionally been the realm of religion. In a secularized context, however, this can be problematic, as America recognizes no official state religion. Disney scholar Karal Ann Marling writes "In a pluralistic society, where experiences of church, school, and ethnicity were not universally shared, Disney motifs constituted a common culture, a kind of civil religion of happy endings, worry-free consumption, technological optimism, and nostalgia for the good old days".[43] This begs the question: If Americans are indeed without a unifying religion, how is ritual made without religion?

---

42 *Marion Woodman: Dancing in the Flames*, 2010. https://www.youtube.com/watch?v=z3h4n-_NEgU

The archetypal theories of depth psychology speak about this and in so far as they offer alternative spirituality, they are a helpful way to understand not only how the soul finds meaning in this kind of deconstructed environment, but also how myth and ritual can transcend a specific religious context. These theories lend themselves to an exploration of Disneyland as an environment of archetypal vitality; an atmosphere for ritual an examination of which begins with a definition of some of archetypal theory's most commonly understood terms and methods. When Jung writes of archetypes, he means to refer to the psychological energies or complexes that arise from what he calls the personal and the collective unconscious. These energies are the seat of our emotions and our actions. They are the catalyst for an epistemology of the divine. He theorizes that archetypes themselves are ineffable or indefinable, because they encompass all the possibilities that live within the archetype. In other words, the archetypal *mother* is indefinable because within it exists every possible facet of what mother is or ever could be. It is the pure energy itself, and there is no way to grasp it all.

By contrast, archetypal images are the symbols and images that humanity makes in response to the ephemeral presence of archetypal energy. Much like the emotions in Disney/Pixar's recent film *Inside Out*,[44] they are the expression of artists and myth-makers of a given culture in response to the presence of archetypes. Although resonance between the archetypal images of differing cultures does often exist, archetypal images speak to the story of a specific people. Indeed, they are often so esoteric as to speak to the story of an individual person. When the resonance of specific kinds of archetypal images exists on a larger scale to a group of people, stories and choreographed events are developed to form ritual behavior, which can be defined as bodily interaction with both archetypes and archetypal images.

The essential purpose of ritual is to create transformative experiences of what a person or group of persons knows to be sacred. Doty suggests that "Ritual may be an important means of organization of the self, and it provides a means of relating the personal and the transpersonal, a making-personal of that which transcends individual human experience; it is one of the ways to integrate the expressly biological and the expressly cultural [. . .]".[45] Understood in this sense, rituals are the meaning-markers for humanity. Campbell insists that myth is vital for the development and maintenance of a culture and society. However focused on the narrative myth as he may be, it's clear that he understood the role of ritual-making in the process of myth-making. Further illuminating Campbell's theories about the intersection of myth and ritual, Doty writes, "[. . .] ritual does not merely represent ideas. It does not just illustrate mythological abstractions, but is an immediate acting out that bridges and unifies the somatic

---

43   "Disneyland 1955: Just Take the Santa Ana Freeway to the American Dream", 201.

44   *Inside Out*, 2015.

45   *Mythography*, 312.

and ideational, the bodily and the mythic."[46] Of central importance to myth-making is the ability to integrate sacred stories with rituals that are transformative. In order to begin to understand how to do this, one must define hermeneutic parameters for the word mythology itself, a word that can literally be interpreted as story language or discourse language.

As I understand it, myths are not the stories themselves; they are like streaks of lightening across a night sky. They are detectable only to the sensory organs of the soul. Myth is the psychic energy itself. It is the touch of the archetypal. Depth psychologist Thomas Moore suggests that the realm of myth is the realm of pure imagination.[47] It is not that myth is in and of itself imperceptible. However, without a vehicle, myth is impenetrable, impossible to grasp and cannot be processed by human senses. Myth's vehicle is logos: the Greek word for language, also understood as a building block of communication and the guiding orientation of reason.

Myths are the elements themselves, the impressions, the colors, the ephemeral moments of inspiration, leaving behind only the memory of their presence. Logos, by contrast, is practicality. It weaves together colors in order to craft a tapestry. Logos is the process of fashioning a narrative structure out of the impressions of myth. Together, mythos and logos speak the language of the soul. Out of these elements, humanity fashions ritual. The work of western myth and ritual scholars of the late 19th and early 20th centuries has focused on a chicken vs. egg argument. They debate definitions of each and questions of genesis. Myth and ritual theorists sometimes attempt to prove the supremacy of myth or ritual one over the other, but no complete theory has emerged. I believe this is because the two are symbiotic, inextricable and mutually begotten. In reality, it is impossible to separate the two for long enough to truly consider the question. As soon as mythic images emerge in both consciousness and language, they are robed in ritual and vice versa.

The word "ritual" derives from the Latin base *ritus* and receives its lineage from the Indo-European root *rime*, an ancient word of shared Icelandic, Germanic, Irish, Welsh and Latin origin, which means, "number or reckoning".[48] Rituals, therefore, are meant to keep the rhythm of life. They are conduits for transformation, and they allow for the integration of numinous ecstasies in our daily lives. Without ritual, the soul has no audible voice in the physical world. Ritual is somatic interaction with humanity's deeply ingrained archetypal patterns. It's the work of the flesh that connects the mundane to the numinous and engages the body with story. But its parameters have traditionally been too narrowly drawn and too controlled. Fragmentation and self-reflexivity are features of the contemporary ethos. It makes sense that the stories we tell and the rituals we

---

46   Ibid., 312.

47   *Rituals of the Imagination*, 20.

48   *Oxford English Dictionary* online.

live reflect this. If it is true, as so many have suggested, that Americans have lost the ability to make meaningful rituals, then this situation reflects a lack of connection to the imagination. A disconnect between the body, mind, soul, and spirit may reflect the lack of connection between the transcendent experience and the poetic imagination which, until the Enlightenment, was the place where ritual and religion intersected in the western world.

How and when disconnect occurred is of interest here, as it relates directly to the creation of Disneyland as a ritual. The root of the breakdown of communication between the mythic and ritualistic aspects western psyche (at least, as some may experience it today) can be understood as the result of the heightened rationalism of the Enlightenment era, an era when skepticism reigned.[49] America was born, ideologically, spiritually, and philosophically out of this era. Many early colonial Americans favored a vehement – and in their eyes a fundamentalist – rejection of religious icon, ritual, and spectacle. From its earliest inception, American culture attempts to separate religion from ritual. It attempts to literalize the narrative, stripping Christian myth to rationalistic fact.

The ethos of this era moves further into the realm of perceived religious experience with Nietzsche's proclamation of the death of God.[50] This proclamation intuits a paradigm shift in the psychological life of European culture, which eventually becomes the reality for American culture. The death of God suggests the death of a certain style of consciousness. It hails death, in Nietzsche's understanding, to the human ability to be transformed by a metaphysical mindset. What Nietzsche seems to begin to sense is the loss of the ability to see the world around us as an animated playground for the archetypal, the disappearance of gods and monsters and the triumph of human rationalism against what was deemed to be simple illusion or an imaginary Marxist *opiate for the masses*, which can now only be acceptable as a mode for entertaining children. The theme park was born out of this environment. A trip to Disneyland is a pilgrimage that revives magic through a combination of the craft of miniaturization, the psychological liminality of emotion, and the mastery of storytelling.

However impossible it is to measure empirically, the presence of passion, emotion, and pathos reifies the existence of soul. This leads to the rise of psychology: a scientific, rationalistic way to measure the movements of the soul. This style of consciousness attempts to fold the work of religion into the methods of scientific empiricism, but the problem with this method is that the mythic worldview science constellates is responsible for the disconnection between science and soul. I'm not attempting to demonize either science itself or the scientific method, just to argue that culture must allow for the presence

49 One might suggest, actually, that the roots of this go all the way back to the ancient Greek cynics and skeptics. Hellenistic philosophy also favored rationalism, and likewise often found it difficult to engage with mysticism.

50 *Thus Spake Zarathustra*.

of magic, opening the psychological channel for the enchanting possibilities that are nothing short of vital for the sake of a fulfilling ritual life.

In traditional societies, be they tribal or otherwise, ritual's purpose is to create a sense of belonging to a community. It opens a channel between the spiritual and physical realms. This brings to mind Campbell and Otto's theories of the awesome function of mythology and its relationship to the holy. David Lyon[51] suggests, like Jung, that the impulse to religious practice points to something symbolic, and that this symbolic way of experiencing the world offers an interpretation of the soul imperceptible through any other means. Mythic rituals offer meaning and belonging. The simple necessity of ritual has been a something that western cultures have often placed in the darkest part of psychological shadow over the past two hundred years.[52] This creates a cognitive dissonance because the soul is drawn to images and begs for transformation. The tendency to ritualize as a natural function of the soul shows itself both consciously and unconsciously. Lyon writes "Religious symbols and stories are like so much else in contemporary culture, cut free-floating fluid. They do not disappear. Rather, they reappear as cultural resources."[53] Disney's rituals are quintessentially American, reflecting a tenant that there are truths which can unify humanity, and that those truths relate directly to individual freedom. In the case of American ideology, these truths are humanist truths, not theological truths, which makes Disneyland a humanist ritual.

A recent article from *Tablet Magazine* illustrates the power of Disneyland as secular ritual in an extremely powerful way. Writer Menachem Butler talks about a visit Elie Wiesel, the late and much beloved author, political activist, and Holocaust survivor made to Disneyland just over a decade after his liberation from Buchenwald camp. As Wiesel worked to find life again after experiencing what can only be called the apex of the most brutally systematic genocide ever perpetrated on the world's stage, he had an encounter with Walt's utopian park that was both magical, awe-filled, and transcendent. Butler notes "in early 1957, Wiesel was slowly recovering from his injuries after being hit by a car in Manhattan's Times Square. In an effort to raise his spirits, Wiesel's editor from *Yediot Aharonot* Dov Yudkovsky and wife Leah came to America for a visit."[54] Wiesel, who had idealized his childhood years before the war fell in love with Disneyland, calling it "a Garden of Eden for children here in this life".[55] He felt transfixed and transformed by his time there, detailing the theming and the presence of cast members. This Disneyland visit proved deeply cathartic for

---

51 *Jesus in Disneyland: Religion in Post Modern Times*

52 It would be naïve to suggest that the reasons for this are uncomplicated. A certain amount of psychological distance from rituals of belonging was necessary for people crafting a nation based on ideological connection rather than ethnic or religious homogeny.

53 Lyon, 134.

54 http://www.tabletmag.com/jewish-arts-and-culture/books/206125/elie-wiesel-visits-disneyland

55 Ibid.

Wiesel. It is beautiful to consider how Disneyland can heal the wounds of even the most traumatized among us simply by recalling the joyous connections we make easily as children.

Wiesel's interpretation of Disneyland makes the utopian power of humanist ritual clear in the most bittersweet, heart lifting way. The power of ritual comes from its ability to emotionally move the person experiencing it. When it works, it is awe-inspiring, numinous, sacred, and transformative. All these adjectives can be applied to Disneyland, which offers a bridge between the needs of soul and the insufficiency of culture to meet those needs. This is increasingly necessary in a time when the guiding mythic ethos is often abject objectivity. By offering an alternative to skepticism and fundamentalism, Disneyland becomes an alternative ritual; one that is actually predicated on the needs of the individual soul in relationship with the community rather than in conflict with it. In doing it through the eyes of children, it encourages participation.

A Campbellian Hermeneutic of Disneyland

Like Walt Disney, Joseph Campbell is a paradoxical figure. Perhaps the greatest paradox in his work is that as Campbell spent years searching for a transcendent experience of myth, he was then compelled to classify it. He created four classifications of mythology, which he believed to be an infallible way of answering whether or not a group of stories classified a mythology. All of his functions of mythology relate to ritual, and all four can illuminate an understanding of Disneyland as ritual. In fact, one might simply replace his word myth with ritual since, as I've previously suggested, the two are impossible to separate.

According to these parameters, the first of these functions of mythology is to arouse a sense of awe in the mind and the heart of the participant. Mythology is, most importantly, an apparatus that exists to endow perspective on humanity. Great as human hubris often is, myths remind us that there are overwhelming, often titanic, powers that can consume us. Myths stir apprehension in the core of our souls as they overpower us with emotion. Words such as *wonder, magic,* and *dreams*[56] are central to the Disney sense of participation with story, as Disneyland creates an environment of transformed reality. Walt once quipped that anything was possible at Disneyland. The Disney patron returns to the state of consciousness generally reserved for children: simple, animated, and imaginative. It does so through suspension of disbelief and immersion into dream images. This altered state allows the patron to participate, unquestioningly, in Disney mythology as a whole. It offer a state of complete identification with the numinous – a complete and utter experience of both consuming and being consumed.

Secondly, Campbell suggests that myths function to order the cosmos. They

---

56   These are the names of the ships in the fleet of the Disney Cruise Line.

seek to make sense of the physical world, allowing the tremendous presence of the numinous to bring structure to the mundane. This function of mythology overlaps with Mircea Eliade's concept of *eternal return*,[57] a concept that understands mythic ritual as that which returns the world to its primal, holistic state. In the mythic ritual of eternal return, archetypal reenactments of myths create the world anew. This is certainly true every day at Disneyland. The Disneyland experience is made new every morning at the "rope drop" ceremony where an omniscient voice heralds the beginning of a new day renewing the story of Disney's land through the vehicle of sentiment and nostalgia. Although the shape of the park has changed since the addition of Toontown, and indeed will change again with the addition of *Star Wars* Land, the early designs of Disneyland resemble a heart,[58] a symbol of the seat of emotion in American symbolism, and certainly was Walt Disney's favorite word-image whenever he spoke of the power of a story. Disneyland's heart serves as a container for a specific version of the story that *is* the archetypal image of Disney's America. It orients the Disney devotee's sense of themselves and their relationship to the American ethos, as it utilizes psychologically safe stories to allow humanity to reconnect with child-like awareness of who and what Disneyland means to the patron. The patron enters through Main Street, U.S.A., passing a train station, Walt's favorite symbol of progress, and after a trip down Main Street, U.S.A., understood to be a nostalgic snapshot of quintessential America, the Disneyland patron is flanked on one side by the Frontier and the exotic world on one side, the promise of positive progress on the other, with Fantasyland, the center of imagination, straight ahead standing in between the two.

The third function of myth according to Campbell is to delineate a social order and set up standards of morality. Myths create codes of integrity. They create distinctions between different modes of behavior, creating orthodox and subversive standards for a culture. Driver notes that this is also a function of ritual. He suggests that ritual is necessary "…not only to 'fix social life' in the first place but also to restore order when it has been lost".[59] This utopian aspect of Disney mythology is what has been most disparaged by Disney critics as an environment that is so fastidiously controlled in its execution. Historically, those in charge of Disneyland have exacted social controls over patrons and cast members that extend to such things as hairstyles, clothing, behavior, personality, and attitude. Koenig chronicles the cast member experience of this as not just a job. For many, being a cast member is a lifestyle. Cast members often build their entire lives around their work at Disneyland. Some even marry other cast members, and when they leave their tenure at Disney they often go so far as to write books

---

57 *The Myth of the Eternal Return: Cosmos and History*, 17.

58 The Walt Disney Company is well known for their refusal to give permission to use their images in published works. For this reason, I am including the web link where this image can be found instead. http://spyhunter007.com/disneyland_monsanto_house.htm.

59 *The Magic of Ritual: Our Need for Liberating Rites That Transform our Lives and Our Communities*, 136.

about the experience, create Facebook groups, and continue their relationship with the company through consulting and other means.[60]

It's impossible to overstate the pedagogical significance of this behavior. For many, the Disney lifestyle is a way of being in the world. Cast members are indoctrinated into the Disney tradition from the beginning of their training. After receiving their training, they are released into the Disney community, like lay ministers to lead the patrons through their own process of identification with the tradition. The lifestyle extends from cast members to patrons as well. Disney cosplayers,[61] collectors and, annual passholders structure their lives around the stories and behaviors of Disney's myths. The exhortation to *Stay Disney* is common in social media groups where people talk about how they relate to each other and what it means to be a community. Staying Disney refers to a way of viewing the world that is optimistic, full of childhood wonder, loving, and playful. This ethos orients the way patrons interact with each other, creating a web of connection that unifies them through community affection for one another and for Disney's characters.

Lastly, mythology functions to tell the stories and to contain the rituals that carry people through various stages and crises of life. It is certainly beyond argument that Disney's mythology can be understood to fulfill these functions for a global community of patrons all couched, of course, safely in terms of the preferred lens of Disney's mythos. Disneyland is often used as a therapeutic model, a wedding chapel, a memorial center for grieving, and even a place to craft personal mythology and family customs.[62] It encourages the growth of individual story, which extend out to family, nation, and globe.

Events such as Grad Night and Gay Days Anaheim have fulfilled this function. Grad Night is an event that happens every year throughout the months of May and June. It is a rite of passage for many Californian high school students. The students drive in on buses in dressed in formal attire for an overnight romp in Disneyland. The park is closed to patrons other than the graduates. The intimacy of the experience gives the students a sense of ownership of the park, a feeling that helps develop the students' sense of burgeoning adulthood. I participated in grad night as a high school graduate in 1995. We left school as soon as we

---

60 Dave Koenig, *Mouse Tales,* 64.

61 Cosplay, the abbreviated term for costume play refers to the practice of adults engaging in character interaction. They dress up in costume, do makeup, and pretend to be characters at events like ComicCon and the D23 Expo. Cosplay is also the subject of community building online platforms like Facebook pages, Pinterest boards, and Tumblr sites.

62 In 2010 and 2011, the Disney Parks have created two series of commercials, which focus on exactly this function of storytelling and ritual making. The first one is the *What Will You Celebrate?* series. It focused around lyrics of a Corbin Bleu song called *Celebrate You*: "It's the time of your life/You don't want to miss out on right here and now/There's so many reasons why/You don't want to stop/It's your chance live it up/In everything you do/Celebrate you!" The *Celebrate* series presents a sequence of iconic, nostalgic Disney images combined with emotionally swelling music. The second is the *Let the Memories Begin* series. This series allows the Disney patron to participate in the spectacle process by uploading their own videos and pictures to the website for possible inclusion in the commercial series.

were finished with classes and drove in a packed bus nonstop to Disneyland. At sunset, we entered the park and we received parameters of behavior as well as the timeline for the event.

We were to arrive back at the bus at 5am, no exceptions. Although we were chaperoned, it was expected that we would behave as adults crossing the final threshold of our childhood educational experience. Having the event at night with no one else around except graduates added to a feeling that this was a rite of passage, a liminal experience something that was in the process of taking us from one state of being to another. Afterward, we returned to the bus happy and exhausted. Many of us slept all the way home, as we arrived back to our homes in time to greet a new day. We arrived home on what is called *Senior Ditch Day*, which meant we were allowed to go home, rest, and digest this rite of passage before returning to campus for commencement ceremonies.

Gay Days Anaheim is another event that is ritualistic in its nature as it has been one that helps create identity and community for LGBTQ patrons. Held on the first weekend of October every year, Gay Days Anaheim is Disneyland's answer to the Pride movement. Disney has long since been supportive of LGBTQ events, and this one though unsanctioned is nevertheless supported. Participants at Gay Days Anaheim pre-order shirts that denote their participation in the event. It is a powerful statement of solidarity to be there on that weekend in October and see so many people come out in support of each other through their love of all things Disney.

It is a community expression of civil rights, and it is also a pilgrimage that has been reproduced by many different groups of Disney fans since – Bat Day for people who love the Disney villains, Dapper Day and Pin-Up Day for people who love to dress in the by-gone style of the 1940s and 1950s, and many others that while unsanctioned by Disney are clearly approved of by them.[63] Disney fans understand the park they love to be their personal playground. This mindset creates a backdrop for the most important moments in their lives. People are married there, proposed to in front of the castle; they bring their children there to be ushered into the life of the imagination. In short, they live the most integral parts of their lives there.

This function of Campbell's definition of myth is also about ceremony. Mythic ritual exists to create ceremonial identity for people. Over Independence Day weekend 2016, *Orange County Register* posted an article on social media proving that Disneyland creates ceremony for those who sense the lack of it in contemporary society. The story is about an Anaheim area man who had recently written to Disneyland thanking them for selling *Welcome Home* tickets to veterans in the years following the Vietnam Conflict. He points out that veterans of Vietnam are often denied benefits offered to many other war veterans because Vietnam was never officially declared a war. He laments the lack of ceremony, noting

---

63   http://www.laweekly.com/arts/a-guide-to-disneylands-unofficial-dress-up-days-5402663

how his purple heart was "pinned to his pillow" and how even when he exited the military his exit certification was simply sent to him in the mail, not treated with any kind of ceremony or care. With heartfelt, tearful gratitude, he thanks Disneyland for being his "sanity check" and offering a place where veterans are able to go and seek safe re-integration into society.

He talks about how he spent several weekends over the course of a couple of months sitting on benches, watching people, and feeling relaxed. Although he admitted that it was a bit late to tell the staff at Disneyland how he felt since most of the cast members who worked there were probably gone, he still felt strongly enough about it to contact the Disneyland staff. In answer to his letter, he was invited to witness the flag retreat ceremony that Disneyland does every day around dusk. The staff at the park surprised him by announcing his presence and his 50th anniversary of serving honorably in the military, folding and handing him the retired flag, which then prompted several Disneyland patrons to stop, thank him for his service, and share with him their own stories about family and military service. It is clear from the interview the reporter did with him after the ceremony that this is just what he needed. Disneyland not only offered healing to this veteran, it also gave him the closure that his government had chosen not to give him, a ritual moment that might well have finally brought an end to his life as a soldier.

The Soul's Hidden Mickey

In contexts where ritual is functional, the inner, an imaginal aspect of the journey to sacred location is understood implicitly and without the necessity for external examination. In other words, when we live connected to myth and ritual, the soul animates and the divine is everywhere. The trip to Disneyland creates its own kind of mythic consciousness. It offers a new interpretation of pilgrimage for people so often alienated from authentic experiences of the soul that it becomes necessary to make a pilgrimage to the soul in preparation for an authentic experience of it. Mircea Eliade talks about this shift from the mundane to the sacred in our lives – the idea that the sacred can occupy the same space as the most commonplace parts. From this perspective, the shift between sacred and profane aspects of life exists entirely within the supplicant's state of con-sciousness. Understanding humanity's need to take a pilgrimage inward as part of the sacred trip outward adds depth to the concept of the pilgrimage itself, nuance that is essential to the poetics of ritual. From this perspective, the word pilgrimage takes on a new depth of meaning in a deconstructed postmillennial environment where deconstruction often breeds disconnection.

An authentic encounter with pilgrimage, although one of the most central aspects of ritual poetics, is conspicuously absent in contemporary American culture. Because soul and body mirror each other, it is a vital part of the American experience to make the journey to the imagination become part of the journey to the sacred physical place. A pilgrimage requires a conscious soul centered shift, and this shift is its own form of spiritual practice. A key aspect of this shift is the necessity for humanity to separate psychologically from everyday profane existence in order to connect with something sacred. Eliade suggests that these spaces need not be located in distant lands, nor can they be divorced from culture.[64] While a pilgrimage location is indeed an actual physical place, making a pilgrimage is a style of consciousness. As such, it requires psychological development and participation in ritual to make it happen. Sacred sites can hide in plain sight, as is the case with Disneyland.

In this environment, the concept of taking a pilgrimage becomes a metaphor for ritual. The power of metaphor lives in its ability to open the mind to the workings of the imagination by allowing images to speak in paradox.[65] The theories of both C.G. Jung and James Hillman are at the center of an exploration of this type of pilgrimage since analytical psychology's entire existence is based on story's ability to connect to and heal the soul. If we engage with these deep encounters of the soul, they permeate every part of our lives, and as such require no ontological explanation. Such engagement with life is not often the case in the contemporary western world. It is largely because many believe myth and ritual to be meaningless that a conscious analysis of pilgrimage as metaphor is even necessary at all. The psychological pilgrimage in general, and the Disneyland pilgrimage in particular; can thus be interpreted as a metaphor for the inward journey toward psychological vitality. Hillman calls this *soul making*. He suggests that we come to understand what soul is, what the divine is, and what healing is through engaging with the depths of feeling that arises from engagement with the creative process.

This begins when the imagination has room to play. The journey inward itself is a pilgrimage that must occasionally be rejuvenated before turning it outward to experience it in a larger world. In the context of Disney culture, one can interpret mythic renewal through depth psychology's archetypal method of the examination of dreams and amplification of images. To understand the trip to Disneyland as a physical pilgrimage is one aspect of the experience. To interpret the pilgrimage to Disneyland as a way to connect to the imaginal realm of the soul, however, offers layers of meaning and methods of practice with which one's developing consciousness can engage.

The atmosphere that is created by Disney property triggers these psychological shifts before the patron even enters the park. Shuttles, buses, trams, and walking trails all require action. This action provides a process that situates the soul in the context of a sacred experience. For many Disneyland patrons, the pilgrimage begins when they make the decision to take the trip. They research attractions, accommodation and experiences on the Internet and begin to dream about the

---

64   *The Sacred and the Profane: The Nature of Religion*, 20.

65   George Lakoff and Mark Johnson, *Metaphors We Live By*, 3.

trip. They may join groups on Facebook and cull other Disney fans for answers to questions they may have. They may watch Disney movies for months in advance. Some may even go through a process of preparation that is similar each time they take a trip to the park. The might pack the car the same way, drive the same route, and stop at the same restaurants or gas stations, or take the same train every time. Then, when they exit the freeway, get off the train, or get off the shuttle from the airport, they enter the Disney property with its familiar street names and carefully crafted landscaping. One cannot help but be aware as soon as one crosses onto Disney property. Moving across the outer Disney properties into the entrance pavilion, security, and ticket booths to the main gate and eventually across into the park is an effective psychological shift I call *thresholding*.

The Hidden Mickey is a captivating metaphor for of the Disneyland patron's psychological journey inward. Hidden Mickeys consist of hiding the head of Mickey Mouse, in plain sight, but doing so in such a way that it will not necessarily be obvious to the patron As the Imagineers work on the park, they often seek to weave inside jokes into the attractions, many of which bear their names. On Pirates of the Caribbean, for example, the boat follows through a channel where a pirate ship attacks the walls of the city with a canon. Holes, which have been blasted into the wall, form a Mickey Mouse head when viewed from a certain angle.[66] Hidden Mickeys are created through mosaics in tile, painted on walls, or even on menus at some of the restaurants. Sometimes these Mickeys are subtly obvious, such as the one in the preshow of Star Tours prior to renovation of the attraction in 2011. This preshow, a safety video similar to ones generally shown at the beginning of a flight, shows Wicket, the lead Ewok from Lucas' *Star Wars, Episode VI: The Return of the Jedi*, boarding the flight with a stuffed Mickey Mouse plush doll under his arm.

Patrons bring the park and its images to life, while allowing the imagination to wander, wonder and become enchanted. This is the way myth and ritual has always created meaning for the people who engage with them. Park patrons slowly become aware of the powerful presence of these images, and through the process of finding them, experience deeper initiation into Disney's traditions. Hidden Mickeys are an example of the way in which the experience of Disneyland engages with ritual poetics, such as the making sacred of a place and the quest for the sacred. Mickey's image becomes grail-like. The quest for him ferries the patron deeper into the imagination, which often develops a stronger amount of psycho-spiritual dedication to the place.

Lost Parents? Children Inquire Within
Another aspect of depth psychological pilgrimage that Disneyland addresses is

---

66 Arlen Miller has published an excellent book on the subject of the Hidden Mickey. More information is posted on www.hiddenmickeys.org.

the move toward a psychologically balanced family relationship. Despite an attempt on behalf of many contemporary myth-makers to display the family unit as the imperfect yet loving structures they often are,[67] the pathological truth is that many families are so disconnected from each other they cannot recognize their disconnection. Nor do they possess the tools necessary to remedy the situation, even if they do recognize it. Extreme behaviors, such as cutting and tattooing, are an attempt to speak to this relational deadening, simply by attempting to create a ritual that will allow the individuals engaging in these practices to feel. Fierce acts of violence rooted in ideological fundamentalism, from the recent shootings in San Bernardino, at a Planned Parenthood in Colorado, at UCLA, and the tragic massacre at the Pulse nightclub in Orlando, Florida, as well as a spike in teen suicide that occurred a few years ago spurred on by internet bullying, are indicative of the lack of empathy, emotional intelligence, psychological health, and compassion. These unspeakably tragic circumstances are further proof of our national, indeed global, crisis of disconnection from soul, empathy, compassion, joy, and the ritual body. They speak in physicalized terms of the pathos inherent in the human experience. Sadly, even at Disneyland it is common to spot families in crisis: parents shouting at children, siblings ignoring each other, and a basic negligence of relationship is common even in Disneyland's self-proclaimed *Happiest Place on Earth*.

All of this disconnection spells psychological pain for the cultural child complex – the part of our soul that remains childlike and needs to be soothed and nurtured as such. Adults struggle to make meaning for the next generation without having received the training necessary to become a generation of wise ones in the first place. Without, in many cases, receiving any obvious functioning rites of passage of their own, the group of adults known as Gen X, Gen Y, and the Millenials struggle with its roles as parents, as lovers and as partners. The root of this disconnection correlates to the dismantling of psychological traditions in the family unit, or, as Hillman calls it, pathologizing or falling apart.[68] In fact, this painful cultural complex often comes from an undoing of communal, family ritual. Whether from disinterest, a genuine lack of knowledge of what to do, a lack of sense of self, or an imbalance in their work life, many parents are simply absent, both physically and/or psychologically. In this context, today's parents, often find ritual too befuddling to tackle. Despite, and perhaps in some ways because of, the wealth of resources available to contemporary parents – books, internet chat forums, special meet-up groups catering to the supposed needs of parents and children for bonding/playing – the parents of young children seem increasingly less capable of taking on the mantle of authority figure than ever before.

---

67 ABC's *Modern Family* and recent films like *Our Family Wedding* (Rick Famuyiwa 2010) and *Dan in Real Life* (Peter Hedges 2007) are an example of this.

68 *Re-Visioning Psychology*, 64.

Because psychological sensitivity begins in a child's family unit, the vital importance of family is central to the rituals of Disneyland. The park is designed for
the use and enjoyment of the family as a whole. As the family unit is the genesis
of all ritual, and in contemporary culture it is this unit that has been responsible
for the systematic stripping away of much of tradition, it makes sense that an
effective pilgrimage in this environment would be one that would touch the
heart of the child complex, attempting to bring balance between the psychic
energies of the child and the parent. Victor Turner suggests that pilgrimage is
externalized mysticism, the interior, mystical life made public. This kind of
mystical experience made physical holds in balance the experience of the child
in the context of a family. If the family unit is unable to provide a safe
environment for its members, Disneyland becomes an object of guidance for it.
Speaking of the 2011 film *Gnomeo and Juliet*,[69] for which she voiced Juliet, actress
Emily Blunt speaks to the exact issue guiding the Disneyland ethos. She argues
that:

> If I had kids, I would not want them to see more violence in the movies. When I
> was a child, you'd go to see a difficult movie, discuss it with your parents and the
> experience would pass. Kids today don't have a chance to breathe. It's always around
> them, so why not give them a break at the movies? It's their only chance at
> innocence.[70]

Disneyland offers relational bonding without the risk inherent in the dynamics
of the family's interpersonal dealings. These dynamics can be called the cultural
family complex. These structures are often broken, just as our cultural rituals that
attend to them often are as well. They also require a soothing balm. Disneyland
builds a laughing place, a space of ease and innocence, and it does this by moving
the patron's emotions like chess pieces on a board. Karal Marling[71] argues that
every part of the park, from the size and color of the buildings to the costumes
and the programs they create are all intended to soothe the mood of the patrons.
Assurance against all the ills of the world is the first priority of the image-makers
at Disneyland. They prefer that thrills never become too scary, images never
become too disturbing and the experience never becomes too challenging.

Many detractors of Disneyland critique this orientation. How can a place offer
anything of substance, of authenticity if the environment is unchallenging? I
posit that the answer to this question can be found in to grounding themes of

69 It is interesting to note that in an incredibly Disneyfied move, this film is self-consciously happy in contrast
    to the original Shakespearean tragedy. Patrick Stewart, veteran Shakespearean player, offers his voice for
    the role of William Shakespeare's statue. During the most sensitive moment in the narrative, he jokes with
    Gnomeo about how their story sounds familiar and that Juliet will be dead by the time he returns. When
    the lovers are reunited, Gnomeo looks at Juliet and comments about how much better their version of the
    story is.

70 The film, *Gnomeo and Juliet*, is a computer-animated version of the iconic Shakespearean classic, *Romeo and
    Juliet*, told through the point of view of garden gnomes. Not surprisingly, the studio that released the
    product, Touchstone Pictures, is a Disney subsidiary. This article was published in the *Orange County Register*
    on Friday, February 11, 2011.

71 *Designing the Disney Parks: The Architecture of Reassurance*, 79.

Disneyland: play and love in the family complex. This interwoven relationship between the two at Disneyland is empowering. Disneyland's environment levels the psychological "playing field" between parents and children, extending a certain amount of safe power to children. They can engage in an environment geared directly to them, as at attractions like Autopia, where children are allowed to drive; and "no license is required."[72] Likewise, parents are encouraged to get in touch with their child-like selves, wearing silly hats, skipping, laughing, singing, and believing, as they all leave behind pressures of jobs, bills, and the complexities of parenting, and for men in particular, this permission to play helps release oppressive confines of American masculinity. Thus, the often-impenetrable moat between child and adult finds a drawbridge.

Since love, in all its various forms, is the defining myth of Disney, a soulful pilgrimage to Disneyland is one that seeks to celebrate and connect with love. All of Disney's stories, yes each and every one, speaks to the transformative nature of love. All of Disney's characters are changed, magically, psychologically, ontologically, through an authentic encounter with love. Disneyland offers this transformation through the genre of what has traditionally been known in myth as otherworld or underworld and fairytale. It creates an otherworld within our physical world to attend to the most alienated but integral aspect of us: the simple affection of the family unit. In addressing our longing for childhood through the context of innocence, it balances what Hillman calls the cultural, archetypal Puer/Senex dialectic, literally the eternal child and the old wise man. Not surprisingly, Hillman wrote and spoke a lot about this dialectic in his later years, juxtaposing these two archetypes. He suggests that this dialectic is out of balance in contemporary life, and that balance of it is perhaps the greatest psychological challenge facing the collective soul today.

The balance between these two archetypes is effectively achieved at Disneyland through stories of Walt, the mythic man who embodies the balance between youth and age. In pondering this, I am reminded of Disneyland's 10th Anniversary Special, when a 65-year-old, Walt dressed in a smart suit saunters around the park wearing Peter Pan's hat decorated with a plume slashed across the side as he quips that "anything's possible at Disneyland". This image of him transcends time and becomes an icon of the Disney tradition holding in balance what he calls "fond memories of the past" and the "promises and the challenges of the future". It's Disney's ethos in image form: happiness, joy, love, and play. Through this image, as the leader of this tradition, Walt guides his cultural family complex to make a pilgrimage to the underworld, the symbolic landscape of the Disney ancestors, a symbolic attitude that is vital to the experience, as it revitalizes itself on a daily basis, through the public's acceptance of Uncle Walt's mythic impressions as a boy, man, visionary, and bard.

---

72 Direct quote from the attraction.

The Animated Shaman

Human imagination has immense power to animate, to bring life to story, and Walt was a master of accessing the collective imagination. Initiated *Disn-o-philes* often imagine him as a kind of contemporary American cult leader. Some refer to him as Uncle Walt, a highly appropriate title as family business was at the heart of everything that Walt and Roy Disney did. The Disney name conveys a fusion of myth and ritual to patrons. As with many other aspects of ritual poetics, the creation of an effective pilgrimage requires intervention of some kind of guide, a priestly figure like Virgil in Dante's *Divine Comedy*. It requires weaving a comprehensive hermeneutical thread and the education that develops the internal guidance necessary to find and follow the thread. It is impossible to overestimate the importance of this kind of guide in facilitating such a journey.

Artists, poets, bards, seers, priests, shamans, seekers, philosophers, medicine men, mystics, or magicians,[73] whichever a group chooses to call them, these vital healers stimulate the psychic abilities of a people group united by a mythology to turn inward and make the mystical journey to the soul. The experience of these intuitively sensitive individuals follows a pattern. They are often called shaman, known as the "the prototypical otherworld traveler".[74] Their stories follow a similar pattern, similar to Campbell's hero's journey. They hear a call, follow the call, incur a deadly wound of some kind, survive the wound, make the journey to the otherworld, have their experience, and return with alchemical knowledge that allows them to speak and enact healing to their people. All of these things are notable in Walt's life. As a child, he felt a call and followed it. He survived illness, war, psychological devastation in the form of childhood abuse, bankruptcy, the loss of a child, and studio unrest. And he journeyed to the imagination, returned, and led others there as well.

A shaman must also be charismatic and hermetic in their ability to be hero-storyteller that returns with deep and magical wisdom and guide, a guardian who is able to provide an opening between the mundane and the magical worlds. In the case of American culture and, indeed, for much of the world, Walt embodies this role. Although very much a part of the physical world, he maintains mythic status. As an embodiment of the shape shifting, mercurial trickster archetype, he is America's great priest of comedy. Steven Larsen notes that this kind of figure is wise when he "legitimizes and externalizes the inner laughter".[75] The shaman is a tour guide to the soul, and as a symbolic mediator between the traveler and the metaphysical realm; part of their responsibility to their community is to provide a safe passage for the soul's transformation to occur.

By the time of his appearance on the Disneyland television show in 1954, Walt

---

73 With respect to variations and distinctions, this exploration will stick, consciously, to Eliade's term of shaman, suggesting that the shaman is the psychological facilitator for a people's inward journey.

74 Carol Zaleski, *Otherworld Journeys*, 13.

75 Steve Larsen, *The Mythic Imagination,* 270.

had already cemented his place in the context of American popular culture as a trusted mentor and purveyor of mythology. Mickey Mouse bolstered America through the worst times of the Great Depression and Cold War Era. The technical achievements of *Snow White And The Seven Dwarfs* blew the audience's minds. *Dumbo* soothed the anxious soul. *Davy Crockett* captivated a generation of children. To America, all these stories come from the mind of Uncle Walt, a man so deeply identified with his stories that he could simply appear to a television audience and magically, with a snap of the fingers, transport them anywhere. His audience found him trustworthy, a clean-shaven image that appealed to the majority of Americans with televisions. He reminded them of their neighbor next door or their favorite uncle, rather than a wealthy head of one of the most well respected studios in Hollywood. With his unassuming Mid-western attitude, and willingness to be a "ham actor",[76] he immediately set viewers at ease.

At the genesis of the Disneyland television show, he was already a trusted guide, exactly the kindly voice many Americans would happily follow, like the children in the fairy tale followed the Pied Piper. This trusted guide continues to be the imaginal magician behind Disneyland. Although his presence seems to disappear from the park in what is called the "Eisner era",[77] his spirit like that of many a great cult leader, is still present at Disneyland. It's often indescribable, but always indelible. Disney historian Christopher Finch wrote that, "He was a visionary – but a visionary who had the common touch that enabled him to take the mass audience along with him into uncharted territory".[78] His touch was the alchemical work of the truly archetypal storyteller, and people simply loved him for it.

In the context of folk culture, he had an uncanny ability to understand, both intrinsically and by careful study, what kind of images and experiences would resonate with his patrons. In the last six years, since the end of the Eisner era, the image of Walt has reappeared once again with enormous amounts of energy behind it. In large part, that has been the work of his daughter, Diane Disney and one of her sons, Walt's namesake, Walter Elias Disney Miller. His image has reappeared in the form of books, images, and quotes on t-shirts and collectables, particularly those available directly to D23 members. Their mission is clear: to make it well known that Disneyland is Walt's Magic Kingdom, and that his vision continues to govern the kingdom.

---

76 *Walt Disney: The Man Behind the Myth*, 2001.

77 Between 1984 and the 2005, a period during which Michael Eisner was chief executive officer of The Walt Disney Company and which also saw unparalleled growth in the company. Eisner also oversaw the opening of several other parks worldwide, as well as the great Disney animated film renaissance which began with the release of *Who Framed Roger Rabbit?* in 1988.

78 Christopher Finch, *The Art of Walt Disney: From Mickey Mouse to Magic Kingdom*, 10.

Welcome to Pixie Hollow

In order for ritual pilgrimage to be effective, the person participating in it must experience transcendence. This kind of transcendence from the mundane is often marked by a journey to some kind of fairyland, an enchanting land of magical characters. It is a powerful part of the mythology of many different cultures. In Ireland, for example, a tradition and culture that was part of Walt's personal heritage and thus a huge part of his own mythic orientation, a breathtaking fairy queen promises eternal love and beauty when she seduces one of their most beloved heroes, Oisin. He disappears into the shadowy realm of Tir Na Nog, the land of youth, for 900 years. While living with the fairies in this surreal and ethereal parallel reality, human time stands still for Oisin. In this story, the land of the fairy is a land *in illo tempore*.[79] It exists somehow simultaneously out of time and before time. After living in bliss for almost a millennium, Oisin feels the need to return to his human home. He returns, believing that it has only been a day. Before he leaves, his fairy queen cautions him not to allow his feet to touch the earth, but he is pulled off his horse by another rider, and as his feet touch the ground, he is transformed into the nine hundred year old human being he has become. The moment his feet touch the ground, the magic ends. The opening to the otherworld closes to him.

The Odyssey itself is a series of journeys into ecstatic experiences. Poets, like Homer, are gifted in the ability to stir the emotion necessary to create a container for ritual transportation enacted this mythic system for the ancient Greeks. Contemporary mythic systems continue to play this out. C. S. Lewis's epic series *The Chronicles of Narnia*, J. K. Rowling's *Harry Potter* series, Lewis Carroll's *Alice in Wonderland* and J. M. Barrie's *Peter Pan* are just a few examples of modern-age myths that feature the journey to the otherworld, the fairyland, the land of enchantment and imagination. This tradition of a magic land, the home for the imagination where ritual transportation occurs is the tradition with which Disneyland aligns. Transportation to a magical (Wonder) land seems particularly poignant in a culture as alienated from the imagination as ours. Likewise, Odysseus, while on the long journey home to Ithaca, also comes across such an enchanted lair, full of magic and existing out of time. He encounters the sorceress Circe who, after transforming his men into pigs and seducing Odysseus with her charms, lulls him into oblivion with her for five years, the length of which seems to Odysseus to be merely a few days. As his clarity returns, Odysseus desires to return home, and Circe's desire for him compels her to return his men to their previous state as human beings, after which she kisses Odysseus goodbye and sends his party on their merry and - except for Odysseus - doomed way.

A vital aspect of the otherworld journey story is a descent to the underworld, the realm of the ancestors or the land of the dead, represented in the Christian

---

79 The phrase meaning "in that time" is meant to be evocative of a time outside of time.

tradition by the story of Christ's harrowing descent into Hell and in the Greco-Roman traditions by the afterlife plunge to the underworld in both Homer's *Odyssey*[80] and Virgil's *Aeneid*. This motif reoccurs in mythologies all over the world and in ritual practices of all kinds, and it is particularly important to the stories of both the modern and postmodern eras. It symbolizes the importance of meditation, of listening closely to the voices of the past. It represents hereditary knowledge, or Jung's concept of the collective unconscious. Hereditary knowledge is the kind of knowledge that is often untapped. It represents the soul's descent into shadow, the dark aspects of soul that are unknown to the conscious ego, and in the mythic traditions to which Americans are heirs, the journey to the underworld is signaled by one of two types of narrative twists: death, and the descent to either Hell or an underworld of some sort.

From a semiotic perspective, there are several reappearing symbols at Disneyland that herald of this kind of descent in story. In his book, *The Myth of the Descent to the Underworld in Post-Modern Literature*,[81] myth and literature scholar Evan Lansing Smith calls these symbols "necrotypes".[82] Although Smith's work is specific to the literature of the postmodern era, it also applies to the stories of Disney, as they are products of postmodernism and the current postmillennial moment. He coined this phrase to refer to archetypal patterns that relate directly to the journey to the underworld.

As Walt himself was a modernist in many ways, it makes sense that he would be interested in this motif. Necrotypes can be understood as images that carry allegorical significance, because when used in a story, they often have a singular, correlative meaning. Examples of necrotypes can be found all over the Disneyland Resort in the form of bees, mirrors, birds, eyes, mountains, trains, and rivers. Smith suggests that these images appear as a central hallmark of postmodernism ". . . [in] an elaborate, ludic, and self-reflexive manner",[83] all of which describes the nuances of Disneyland's worldview. The realm of dreams, watery reflections, and fantasy are central to Disney's journey. These images are mythically potent in both ancient and modern myths. They draw the patron deeper into the myth.

The journey to the underworld begins with what I've previously called thresholding – the conscious creation of a physical reminder of the psychological changes required by entrance into the sacred space. Again, at the Disneyland Resort, this begins as early as the exit off of Interstate Five. The streets surrounding the resort are lined with perfectly manicured lilies and palm trees. All the

---

80   Walt Disney Pictures' *Hercules*, which was released in 1997, featured Hades, the Greek lord of the underworld, as the villain of the piece. Character actor James Woods voiced him.

81   Smith, 2.

82   Ibid., 3.

83   Ibid., 3.

foliage surrounding the resort is impeccably pruned in a similar manner, making it clear that the land belongs to the resort. The sidewalks and iron railings are also homogenized in such a way as to make it clear that they are on Disney property. And this theming continues as the patron continues deeper and deeper toward the park, until the illusion becomes complete. This trip to the other-world/underworld is similar to the way that James Hillman talks his theories of experiencing archetypal energies. He suggests that in order to begin to generate a healthy relationship to the soul, it is necessary to take a trip "through the looking glass" into the realm of archetypal images.

To him, because archetypes arise from the soul, they carry psychic energy and have a life of their own.[84] To engage with archetypal images, therefore, is to visit them in their own worlds. To encourage a mythical sensibility is to reconnect with our childlike ability love and interact with our imaginary friends. To Hillman, cultivating this kind of soul making is at the heart of a polytheistic world view – a way of understanding the world that allows for deeply affecting, powerful archetypal images to transport us, permeate us, and change every aspect of our beings. He suggests that our culture is out of balance largely because it has become so monotheistic, and that our monotheistic way of viewing the world robs us of imagination as it ultimately destroys our ability to connect with myth and ritual. He writes about the contemporary alienation to images, suggesting that polytheistic approaches to religious impulses are the healthier mode of expression because the soul finds its fullest expression through a variety of kaleidoscopic images.

Hillman calls this personifying, allowing the unconscious to speak for itself. This is the primary modality of poetic or religious practice, and tending the psyche must start with personifying, a longing that Walt Disney acknowledged in creating Disneyland. The Disneyland maxim that *every role is a starring role at Disneyland* suggests the dignity of this material. Personalization requires owner-ship of these images, and not necessarily in a dogmatic fashion, but in a way that cares for the imagination, as Hillman reminds us "Imagination itself must be cared for as it may well be the source of our ailing".[85] Caring for the imagination requires being willing to feel the imagination.

Hillman writes that the unconscious soul will produce thoughts, experiences and images through dreams, active imagination, and other quiet moments of the soul. Before the soul can make a pilgrimage, it is necessary for the pilgrim to reconnect with the aspects of soul that yearn for pilgrimage. In *Re-Visioning Psychology,* he develops a cohesive psychological theory that presents a method for this kind of development of one's soul. He suggests that the journey to otherworld of imagination requires the recognition of the home of the imagi-nation as a real thing separate and distinct from other mundane aspects of life.

84   James Hillman, *Re-Visioning Psychology*, 17.

85   James Hillman, *Healing Fiction*, 73.

This perspective brings to mind Dumbledore's famous quote to Harry Potter: "Of course it is happening inside your head, Harry, but why on earth should that mean it's not real?"[86] This kind of thinking stands in opposition to an ego-consciousness that would insist that thoughts, feelings, images, emotions, and other psychic materials are fabrications of the individual's mind and nothing else. These theories, which develop out of Jung's concepts of the collective psyche and the collective unconscious, hold tension between multiplicities in relationship to the psyche. It's an epistemological approach that opens consciousness to the numinous breakthrough of magic and a palpable encounter with the otherworld of the imagination.

In its active sense, ritual is magic. Magic engages with ritual as it makes art out of the rhythms of life, and it is this understanding of Magic, which is, of course, one of Disney's defining terms. Magical moments, magical memories – Disneyland is filled with them. Whether they refer to the thrills of the Matterhorn or the simple joy of taking a picture with loved ones, Disneyland patrons recognize that the park is filled with these magical moments. Any kind of magic requires participatory submission by the patron to the enchantment of a magician. This is a kind of conscious willingness to enter into the unconscious realm, even if it does mean engaging with Walt's psyche and the psyche of the Imagineers who have worked with Disney, creating the theme park experience since 1955.

A Fairyland Filled With Dreams

The spiral journey down into the underworld is often connected to practice of understanding dreams. This spawned a practice in psychological circles known as *Lucid Dreaming*, which suggests that one may be in the dream world and yet may be able to control the dreams. One might argue that places and spaces such as Disneyland are similar, as they offer a safe environment for the fulfillment of dreams. It is, as the park's marketing executives have often suggested through their advertisements for Disney's theme parks, *a place where dreams come true*. Although it is clearly not a container for those who suffer from acute psychotic illness, it does offer a contained model for the wish fulfillment of certain segments of society in a dream-like atmosphere. Stephen LaBerge suggests that, "When we awaken, laughing with delight from a wonderful dream, it is not surprising to find that our waking mood has been brightened with feelings of joy".[87] Dreams are one of the purest connection points between ego consciousness and the unconscious.

Disney dreams, however, are not identified with material from the Jungian world of the uncontrollable unconscious. Disney dreams are wish fulfillments. They represent the passions of the patrons as shown by the Disney's classic film,

86 *Harry Potter and The Deathly Hallows*, 723.

87 Stephen LaBerge, *Lucid Dreaming: A Concise Guide to Awakening in your Dreams and in Your Life*, 10.

Pinocchio, in what is arguably the most immediately identifiable of all Disney songs, past and present, *When You Wish Upon a Star*. For most Americans, and in fact for a large majority of the world, just a few notes of this song conveys an immediate affiliation with Disney's parks and television show. This song, written by Leigh Harline and Ned Washington, was developed for inclusion in the 1940 classic about the puppet whose dream was to become a real boy. It is the theme song for Disney, and particularly with the lyric, "when you wish upon a star / your dreams come true", it encapsulates the dreamy environment of Disneyland. This environment allows for the concept of living and controlling one's dreams while simultaneously doing so in an environment where one can immerse fully without fear of the nightmare. For example, when the Disney parks offer promotions such as the *year of a million dreams*, it suggests that whatever it is the patron dreams, or wishes, as Disney's mythology conflates the two, is possible, in such a way that will be edifying and enjoyable for the masses.

In that sense, Disneyland's pilgrimage can also be understood as an exercise in what Jungians call active imagination. Traditionally, active imagination has been practiced as a quiet, meditative encounter with the archetypal through contact with the unconscious. This kind of practice is often difficult to engage and may require the presence of an analyst. Jung asserted that his concepts would not be useful for the common folk. He insisted that if it were possible for a person to remain safely tucked within a tradition, then it would be better for them to remain there. Disneyland offers such an environment. In engaging with Disneyland, patrons are encouraged to connect with the characters they find most resonant. Disney characters follow a certain set of rules, according to Disney's typologies: Mickey and friends, princesses, villains, animal sidekicks, et cetera.

If, as I've suggested, many in the contemporary world are heirs to a culture of the alienation of imagination, one could argue that it is necessary for individuals to climb into the psychic realities of others in order to be able to experience it at all. Film/animation historian and Disney expert Amy Davis proposes "What does seem to be agreed upon by psychiatrists and psychologists studying the impact of media upon children, however, is that visual media have an influence on children (and on adults, for that matter) because film appeals to the sense of fantasy, even when the images being portrayed are 'realistic' (such as with documentaries)".[88] This is the reason why Disneyland works. It provides an environment that allows patrons to enter into the images of the films, and the characters that the patron encounters through the interaction between the parks and the films becomes psychologically potent for the patron as it offers a physical entrance point for psyche at the theme parks.

---

[88] *Good Girls and Wicked Witches*, 30.

A Pilgrimage to Heart

In 2007, Walt Disney Pictures released a film called *Meet the Robinsons*. It is very loosely based on the book *A Day with Wilbur Robinson*.[89] The film tells the story of a young inventor named Lewis and his journey to find his family, self-identity, and the place where he belongs, physically and psychologically. Lewis is an orphan, and his passion for invention, though it is encouraged by the caring guidance of the woman who runs the orphanage,[90] nevertheless makes Lewis feel like an outcast. His roommate, a snarky sidekick type, quite understandably harbors frustration toward Lewis because he works on his inventions all night, keeping him from the precious sleep necessary to win his baseball games. Needless to say, he does not welcome Lewis's inventions. Furthermore, Lewis suffers from a string of invention mishaps and failures, which further avert his chances of being adopted.

On the day of Lewis's greatest failure as an inventor, he meets a boy named Wilbur Robinson. Wilbur tells Lewis that he is from the future and offers to take Lewis back in time to see his birth mother if he will go back to the past to fix his memory extractor, an invention that has just blown up in his face at the science fair. Lewis refuses to go fix it, and Wilbur takes him into the future to prove who he is. While in the future, Lewis discovers that he himself is the inventor who has made the future such a utopian environment, and that Wilbur is actually his son. Wilbur's journey to the past to get his father to fix his invention was spurred on by the entrance of a sinister man in a bowler hat, who, as it turns out, is Lewis' orphanage roommate. He has lived for many years with a growing hatred toward Lewis because, as he sees it, Lewis is responsible for the negative direction his own life has taken. Lewis journeys to the future, and eventually also to the past to see his birthmother, and both are catalysts for the development of his own identity.

It is clear that the director of this film identifies deeply with the emotions of its young protagonist and with the journey that the Disney mythos offers the imagination. In the film's commentary, director Stephen J. Anderson says as much. He notes that he grew up as an orphan, and that Walt Disney and the products of Disney were instrumental in the formation of his own sense of identity. This film is the perfect example of the kind of journey Disneyland may elicit in the psyche of the family visiting the park. The references to the park are clear and numerous, and the film ends with one of Walt Disney's most famous quotes: "We keep moving forward, opening new doors and doing new things, because we are curious and curiosity keeps leading us down new paths".[91] Indeed, this quote has been referenced throughout the film, as *Keep Moving Forward* is the Robinson family's motto, and this point is discussed at some

89   Written and illustrated by William Joyce.

90   Voiced by Angela Bassett.

91   *The Quotable Walt Disney,* 85.

length in the extras on the DVD release of *Meet the Robinsons*. Disneyland's cultural ethos is rooted in a desire to create a childlike wonder for all the patrons of the environment, and a critical aspect of that is joy and security. In the song from the movie *Little Wonders*, by American songwriter Rob Thomas, we have these lines:

> Let it go, let it roll right off your shoulder. Don't you know the hardest part is over? Let it in, let your clarity define you. In the end, we will only just remember how it feels . . . . Let it slide, let your troubles fall behind you. Let is shine until you feel it all around you. And I don't mind if it's me you need to turn to. We'll get by, *it's the heart that really matters in the end* . . . . All of my regret will wash away somehow. But I cannot forget the way I feel right now. In these small hours.[92]

The heart, Disney's stories continue to insist, is truly the thing that matters in the end, and without a journey of play, connecting to the heart is impossible. This story, much like the pilgrimage to Disneyland itself can be, is a journey of recognition and reconnection.

Disney's concept of heart centers on interpersonal connections made in their controlled environment. Immersion into their version of ritual process requires laughter. Disneyland allows time to fall away as play creates an interactive atmosphere. The ability to play and to laugh is an essential aspect to psychological well being because it reflects a dynamic between symbols and the soul. Play represents the lack of stagnation in the process of mythic ritual. It's also enactment. There is a reason that the medium of theater is called *play*. Campbell once wrote that "Mythologies present games to play: how to make believe you're doing thus and so. Ultimately, through the game, you experience that positive thing which is the experience of being-in-being, living meaningfully."[93] To enact play is to create a world. Playing, whether on the stage, in a sandbox at a park or skipping down Main Street, U.S.A. at Disneyland, is transcendent. It opens a channel to awe, releasing one from the profane nature of physical life.

Acting is creation, and creating a world through enactment makes play – what is often called – a *liminoid* experience. These kinds of experiences are similar to what Victor Turner called liminal ritual moments in that they place the person having the experience in a psychological state where they are separated from the rest of their social group. Johan Huzinga explores this idea:

> The concept of *ludic liminality* points to leisure and play as places for exploratory search for the metaphors that advance human creativity, and it points to ritual as play (because rituals are constructed the same ways play activities are: delimited arenas for the activities, marked and regulated schedules, rules and statuses applicable only in the ritual/game, and so forth).[94]

Ludic liminality allows for the connection of sacred space with levity. It allows for the inversion of social norms, which would otherwise interfere with the

---

92 Italics mine.

93 *Pathways to Bliss*, 6.

94 *Homo Ludens*, quoted in Doty, 401.

experience of the sacred. However, Disneyland's version of lucid liminality does so by allowing the entrance of humor and silliness to what could otherwise be a serious endeavor. I will consider ideas related to liminality and spectacle in chapter five, examining the concept of the carnival and the liminal nature of spectacle. With respect to the journey itself, however, Disneyland is an environment that gives psychic permission to the patron to *go there*. The patron affects a psychological change simply by crossing the threshold into the park.

Through entertainment, Disneyland purports to be a space allocated to the physical manifestation of the freedom to live one's dream,[95] whatever that may be, as long as one's dream is as innocently kitschy and silly as the dream of the next person. Disneyland is a temple to the love of amusement – a temple to a style of consciousness that is sorely needed in a society burdened by apocalyptic consciousness. Freedom, imagination, equality, and fun are enshrined at Disneyland through the use of seemingly innocuous thrills, which Walt and the Imagineers crafted intentionally for that reason. All of these depth psychological concepts lead the devoted park patron, like Theseus through the labyrinth, on a pilgrimage to the soul. While scholars, psychologists and cultural critics in myth and depth psychology spend time and energy attempting to create new ways to encourage the process of developing consciousness, Disneyland does this effortlessly by simply giving the imagination permission to play. It weaves together the different threads of the depth psychological pilgrimage, focusing directly on fantasy. It offers ways to prepare the middle ground of the imagination for adults and children, turning outward into the physical manifestations of ritual. It may seem simple, but this avenue to the imagination has been neglected for far too long. Like other journeys to mythic ritual, Disneyland offers another lens with which to view these methods, and an understanding of this place as such leads to a natural progression of questions as to how Disneyland evolved into the sacred space it has currently become.

---

95 Dream, in this case, refers to the closely guarded passions of one's heart.

Chapter 3

The Evolution of Disney's Temple to Entertainment

Herbie, I just want it to look like nothing else in the world. And it should be surrounded by a train. – Walt Disney[96]

Walt Disney had built the Versailles of the twentieth century – but it was a Versailles designed for the pleasure of the people rather than the amusement of the nobility. – Christopher Finch[97]

California's Animated Axis Mundi

I've previously discussed how the fusion of mythic and ritualistic approaches to the imagination offers an opportunity for psychological healing. I've further suggested that these approaches moved into the shadow part of our consciousness, meaning they are engaged now largely through unconscious action. Developing awareness of the ways the journey to mythic imagination is neglected by culture offers an opportunity to develop new possibilities to understand ancient, archetypal facets of what it means to be human. This includes exploring new types of ritual, the pilgrimage to temple being a central piece of it. As one moves into the practice of pilgrimage, the soul begins to turn inward toward a reflective journey before the pilgrimage outward can have any truly transformative significance. Once this style of consciousness develops, it

---

96 *Walt Disney Imagineering: A Behind the Dreams Look at Making the Magic Real.* The Imagineers, 17.

97 *The Art of Walt Disney: From Mickey Mouse to the Theme Parks*, 398.

becomes possible to notice the ways contemporary secular culture participates in refashioning traditional psychological and spiritual patterns. Hillman refers to this as *seeing through* to the mythic imagination behind culture.[98] From this perspective, a pilgrimage may be just what humanity needs to apply a soothing balm to the mythic imagination. Ian Reader writes that

> Underpinning all of these strands is the notion of rebirth and return: rebirth to a new life after pilgrimage, rebirth of the shattered community, rebirth and reaffirmation of the recreated community and communal identity. Pilgrimage then, involves restoring the complete and painful ruptures of the past, healing the wounds of bereavement, loss and disruption and making the participant(s) whole.[99]

Like Campbell's hero's journey, the process of going on pilgrimage includes the recognition of a need or call, the journey, the experience of the temple, and a return back to society with the gifts garnered on the journey. The zenith of this kind of sacred journey is the actual experience of the temple itself. In fact, if one understands the hero's journey to be similar to Jung's concept of individuation – to have an encounter with sublime mythic energies and to experience psychological growth through that encounter – then one might suggest that the pilgrimage to temple is the ultimate hero's journey.

The word "temple" is defined as "An edifice or place regarded primarily as the dwelling-place or 'house' of a deity or deities; hence, an edifice devoted to divine worship".[100] This term is applied liberally across cultural boundaries and eras. It has become an archetype itself, as it is reinterpreted through image *ad infinitum*. As dwelling houses for the gods, temples inspire veneration and reverence. As an archetypal symbol of what Mircea Eliade calls the *axis mundi* or the *navel of the world*, the temple conveys a responsibility for crafting an identity for the people to whom it belongs. Eliade's metaphor for temple as *navel of the world* fits the archetype perfectly. The navel is the genesis of the physical connection to our mothers; it conveys the beginning of our consciousness and the rooted nourishment of our developing relationship to it. The things that create identity – family structures, art, work, relationships, and cultural standards just a name a few are vital to offerings of temple culture. An interpretation of temple as *navel of the world* places those participating with temple culture at the genesis of everything that makes us who we are as beings. In the sense that the temple is the beginning of and the grounding to cultural and personal identity, understanding it as the metaphorical navel of the world is central to interpreting its cultural significance, a choice that the creators of Disneyland made from day one when Walt exhorted that "Disneyland is dedicated to the ideals, the dreams, and the hard facts that have created America, with the hope that it will be a source of joy and inspiration to all the world".[101] An outing to Disney's park in Anaheim

---

98 *Re-Visioning Psychology*, 118.

99 *Pilgrimage in Popular Culture*, 222.

100 *Oxford English Dictionary* online.

is one of a growing list of secular activities that have become connected to the concept of pilgrimage.

The presence of Disneyland is central to Californian culture. In fact, locals sometimes treat it like a community center. According to stockholder reports, travelers from across the globe also feel the call of Anaheim's original theme park, though foreign patrons account for a relatively small amount of park patronage. Disneyland is a cultural icon, a human made image that embodies the sacred for the sake of reflection, as well as a mythical home to which many may journey to reconnect with something of ideological value. Although current commercials generally refer to Walt Disney World rather than Disneyland as they once did, they still ask that old question: "You've just won the Super-bowl/Miss America/Olympic Gold! What are you going to do next?"

This question gets at the root of a truth that American culture often obscures, the need for sacred space. This need for sacred connection is deep in the soul of humanity. As numinous sacred space is, it can also be fun. Sacred space can provide an opportunity to entertain the patrons that help edify it. In contemporary America, we often use tourism and entertainment to fulfill the traditional structures of pilgrimage. Timothy Dallen notes, "To undertake a pilgrimage carries with it an implicit assumption of a physical journey, hence the often cited maxim by Turner and Turner (1978: 20) found in most discussions of pilgrimage: 'a tourist is half a pilgrim, if a pilgrim is half a tourist'."[102] Tourism itself is a form of pilgrimage, and the rituals of temple culture are effective, in part, because of their use of entertainment. The fact that these rituals amuse the patrons who engage with them allows the practice to touch the soul of those for whom they are found edifying. Indeed, the entertainment industry itself is complicit with the poetics of the sacred, offering a heightened style of consciousness necessary for the experience.

Simply moving into the territory of temple itself causes this kind of shift in consciousness. A temple is an archetypal environment, a sacred mountain that is simultaneously a mystical axis mundi and a very real place. According to Eliade, "Man constructs according to an archetype. Not only do his city or his temple have celestial models; the same is true of the entire region that he inhabits, with the rivers that water it, the fields that gave him his food, etc. . . . "[103] Disneyland plays with our global obsession with celebrity culture by inserting the idea that the guest is the center of the park's cosmos. The park patron becomes part of the show as it makes them a central player with Mickey and the gang. Disney pumps scents into the air, plays with architectural perspective, and manipulates mood through the use of color, song, and behavior to shift con-

---

101 http://www.disneydreamer.com/DLOpen.htm

102 *Tourism, Religion and Spiritual Journeys*, 39.

103 *The Myth of the Eternal Return: Cosmos and History*, 10.

sciousness and make the patron a part of the show, instead of merely a witness of it.

Masterful manipulation is present in the form of the sensory spectacle. This kind of manipulation has led many to understand Disneyland fans as uneducated fools who are unaware of the curtain being drawn before their eyes, but this is simply not the case. This kind of illusory sleight of hand has been utilized at temples throughout the history of humanity. Even the ancient oracle at Delphi relied on magical wonders created by the priests, whose job it was to kneel behind stones and provide a voice for the oracle. This is not foolishness, but a functioning ritual, through which the soul experiences an altered state of consciousness. It is the magic of entertainment, a magic that has been an aspect of temple throughout the millennia. Full mythic immersion requires suspension of disbelief. Through the acceptance of crafted magic, devotees truly experience the transformative nature of the temple.

In his seminal work *The Decline of the West*,[104] Oswald Spengler cultivates a theory that understanding a direct correlation between the ancient worlds of Hellenized Greece and Rome elucidates what he believes to be the decline of Western Civilization – a theory he develops through experiences he had in the depths of World War I. While, clearly, this work is the philosophical stance of a modernist, the idea of a connection between the social and cultural constructs of contemporary America and those of ancient Rome has captivated the imagination of many a myth commentator.

Campbell and Jung in particular were fascinated by what they considered to be the influence of ancient Roman imagery on American symbolism. This return to Romanesque culture is common to culture. Neo-classicist influence is all over early American architecture and currency. Walt Disney, however, was a modernist. His work is a product of the same zeitgeist as Spengler. This means that he responds to the lineage of Rome, but he also sees the devolution of it in his contemporary world. This connection between the mythic constructs of America and Rome is evident if one considers the comparisons between Disneyland and the Pantheon through the mythic consciousness pantheism cultivates.

In the center of Rome's *eternal city*, stands a symbol of Roman commitment to its own utopian myth – the Pantheon, a home to all the gods. In ancient times, it was a sacred space for both the mythic and religious imaginations to engage across cultural lines. Whatever the socio-political reasons behind the building of this temple, the psychological impact is still the same. It reassures the visitor that no matter what their religion, culture, or creed, their god is welcome in Rome. William L. MacDonald calls it "The temple of the world".[105] Its impact on world architecture is undeniable, and although dedications to all gods were

---

104 *Der Untergang des* Abenlandes, 1918.

105 *The Pantheon: Design, Meaning and Progeny*, 11.

not uncommon, particularly in the Hellenized world, the broad influence of the Roman Empire turns this particular temple into a mythic icon, an image that symbolizes Rome's humanistic ideology that, in the contemporary imagination, belongs equally to all citizens. The temple dates to the pre-Christian era of the Emperor Hadrian, and although its worship was abandoned shortly following the rise of Christian power, it remains as a standing image to the prevailing impact of the convergence of mythic and religious consciousness in both ancient and contemporary Rome.

As a space that springs from Walt's Hollywood-style imagination, Disneyland responds to the presence of the religious impulse in a similar capacity. A temple is, most importantly, a house of worship, and clearly Disneyland is such a place devoted to a uniquely secular form of worship. It offers the veneration of different kinds of gods: the self-conscious worship of ideals. Disneyland's participation in the traditions of temple cult practices – the veneration of icons and the physical immersion of spectacle, exemplify its status as a temple. It is filled with the trappings of a traditional temple experience: a place that offers a house for the sacred images connected to the gods and an atmosphere for ritualizing the stories sacred to a people. While the playful reverence with which Disney patrons treat the park is evidence of the park's status as a sacred temple, Disneyland resists the use of overt references to spirituality and dogmatic distinctions.

Many have considered Disney's ethos to be exclusively Christian, and while the broad aspects of Christian morality are at play at Disneyland, as this tradition is the most influential tradition in the context of the Disney artists and Imagineers that created the park), it is not at all true that Christianity rules the Disney ethos. Brode suggests this when he quotes Bob Thomas's biography, *Walt Disney: An American Original*, "'Walt considered himself religious, yet he never went to church. The heavy dose of religiosity in his childhood discouraged him; he especially disliked sanctimonious preachers. But he admired and respected every religion, and his belief in God never wavered. His theology was individual.'"[106]

The mores of the Christian ethos are present at Disneyland, but doctrinal fundamentalism is not. Scholars have often questioned the meaning behind the glaring lack of churches on Main Street, U.S.A., an issue taken up by Diane Disney-Miller when she relays an anecdote about an interchange between her father and a minister. When asked about the lack of churches on Main Street, U.S.S., he simply replied that he had no desire to privilege one tradition over another.[107] Instead, Disneyland cultivates what Watts calls, "The Disney Doctrine": "a notion that the nuclear family, with its attendant rituals of marriage, parenthood, emotional and spiritual instruction, and consumption, was the centerpiece of the American way of life".[108] Even on opening day, when Walt

106 Thomas, qtd. in Brode, *From Walt To Woodstock: How Disney Created Counterculture,* 106.

107 *Walt Disney: The Man Behind the Myth* 2001.

religious leaders to dedicate the park, he brought in military chaplains, a catholic priest, a protestant minister[109] and a rabbi, to represent the faiths dominant in American society at the time. Though this is still a reflection of a particularly Christian/Jewish American bias present in 1950s Southern Californian culture, the fact still remains that Disneyland is an intentional reflection of the midcentury American sensibility that the dogmatism of religion is a private matter, and therefore best left outside of the arena of mass culture.

This utopian message of Disneyland is at the center of what to my mind is the most compelling tension of the place. Disneyland is the product of a society made of varied and multilayered spiritualties. American ideology is rooted in the drive toward liberation of the soul, yet, in that liberation there is a contradiction. Is it possible to practice all religions and none simultaneously? America is built on the idea that it's possible. By recalling ancient societies that emphasized freedom of religious practice, such as the Hellenized world, Disney has created a similar kind of environment where patrons find unification in ideology rather than in religious doctrine. Brode writes, "In his films, Disney – while all but ignoring organized religion – emphasizes the spiritual side of life".[110] In this environment, any cultural artifice that becomes as iconic a place for community building, such as Disneyland, hinges on shared ideology as a means of creating culture. In the case of Disneyland, "The Disney Doctrine" is the unifying religion of the temple. It's the source of Disney's myths and the cosmic god(s) responsible for Disneyland's creation. It finds its expression through Disney's foray into the mediums of stage performance, film, and television.

A Thrilling Ride on the Top of the World
Disneyland serves a physical, temporal purpose that speaks to the practical function of temple cult as much as it serves a purpose as an icon. Simply put, the park *is* temple culture. It employs all the trapping of such an endeavor: the sensory participation, the suspension of disbelief, the vitality of the image, the luminosity of the landscape, the imminence of the invisible, and the presence of merchandizing. To truly experience it as such requires an appreciation of the concept of temple as the center of the world, the *axis mundi*. Myth-makers utilize various archetypal images to express what is essentially the same concept, a symbolic center for the most cherished stories and rituals of a people. The center of the world can be many different things. It can be a tree, a crossroads in the desert, or a holy mountain. It can be a natural locale imbued with sacred energy, or it can be crafted specifically to evoke such a thing.

Eliade suggests that a celestial, archetypal image exists upon which all temples

108 *The Magic Kingdom: Walt Disney and the American Way of Life*, 326.

109 The minister was Walt Disney's nephew Reverend Glen D. Puder.

110 *From Walt To Woodstock: How Disney Created Counterculture*, 106.

are based. He indicates that all temples represent the summit of the archetypal *Sacred Mountain*. It is on this summit that the mythic *axis mundi*[111]is built. Disneyland reinterprets the celestial image of the mythic mountain. It utilizes what Walt called *weenies*, great architectural landmarks that draw the eye and direct the flow of traffic, vital to the design of the park. Although some of these weenies are intended to look like buildings, and in reality all of them are backlot buildings,[112] many of the weenies are Disney's interpretations of the mythic mountain. These mountains provide the physical manifestation of the psychological or symbolic space they seeks to create. This symbolic center is the genesis of all mythic creation, as well as the point of convergence for the cosmic regions: heaven, hell and earth.

From the perspective of archetypal psychology, Disney's mountains can be understood to offer an opportunity for the development of consciousness. They flank the park, surrounding the patron with points of entry, ritualistically, into shrines, immersing the visitor in the archetypal experience of each land. Although technically there are three mountains at Disneyland, in reality there are four. That is to say, three of the mountains in Disneyland reflect geological structures similar to those found in nature: Matterhorn, Splash Mountain, and Big Thunder Mountain. Space Mountain appears to be a mountain or sculpture from another realm. Each one of these offers a nonverbal cue regarding the story into which the patron is about to immerse, and the attractions are housed inside these mountains. All four of these attractions are thrill-ride experiences or roller coasters, a detail that suggests, perhaps subconsciously, that the numinous experience of the holy mountain of traditional temple is intended to be an ecstatic one.

These mountains represent different pieces of Disneyland's cosmology: Matterhorn, a romanticized image of the home of the European fairy tales of Disney's mythic canon; Splash Mountain, a kitschy image of the American South; and Big Thunder Mountain Railroad, a caricatured version of the westward expansion and America's doctrine of Manifest Destiny.[113] In its role as the mountain that isn't a mountain, however, Space Mountain presents the patron with something less tangible, and therefore less susceptible to distillation into romanticism and caricature. Space Mountain reflects Disneyland's myths of a utopian tomorrow and the excitement of technology. It's the only one of Disneyland's "holy mountains" that offers an attraction that transcends Earth. The vehicle for it is a rocket that catapults the patron deep into space through a circular motion. The dark vacuum of space renders the track of this attraction invisible. To me, this attraction most effectively recreates the experience of the mythic mountain, as it offers the rider a view of an atmosphere few humans

---

111 *The Myth of the Eternal Return: Cosmos and History,* 7.

112 Particularly Sleeping Beauty's Castle, Haunted Mansion, and It's a Small World.

113 For more about this, read *Walt's Utopia: Disneyland and American Mythmaking* by Priscilla Hobbs.

have actually seen. For this reason, Space Mountain is the height of Disneyland's liminal experience and places Tomorrowland next to Fantasyland as the home of pure fantasy. Through the mystery of the thing that has not yet, but may soon, come to pass, it offers a unique kind of transformative experience. The combination of these myth themes and the physically thrilling structure of the attraction itself encapsulate the ethos of both Tomorrowland and the archetypal image of the *holy mountain*.

Mythic Timelessness at Disneyland

In an essay written with Steven D. Hodscher, Yi-Fu Tuan writes, "To be there is to have arrived: no need therefore to worry about being elsewhere. The timelessness of 'center' ritually evoked in the cosmic city, as at least hinted at in Disneyland . . . 'perpetual spring' itself conveys a sense of timelessness: it certainly conforms with accepted images of Eden or paradise."[114] Tuan suggests that the climate in Anaheim makes it the perfect place for the creation of Disneyland. According to the Anaheim and Orange County Convention Bureau and climate change notwithstanding,[115] the annual average temperature in the city of Anaheim ranges between 75 and 85 degrees Fahrenheit. As a general rule, the temperature in Anaheim is stable. Although there can be days in both summer and autumn when the mercury can rise to over a blistering 100 degrees Fahrenheit, that kind of heat rarely last for more than a few days at a time.

Its proximity to both the ocean and the arid Southern Californian desert generally keeps the temperature at an acceptable level at night. This also keeps humidity in balance. Consequently, most types of flowers bloom in Anaheim all year. Seasons are virtually imperceptible there. Disneyland's landscaping personnel work tirelessly to continue the illusion of the turning of the seasons in Anaheim. They plant thousands of annuals that bloom and are spent within weeks every quarter to move the season forward. During most of the year, the honeyed smell of sweet alyssum scents the air. Petunias and peonies line the paths. At Christmas time, red and white cyclamen line Main Street, U.S.A. During the traditional Halloween Time[116] celebration, the iconic flowery Mickey head in the garden at the front gate, the front boundary of the berm, is replaced with miniature pumpkins that create the shape of Mickey's head. And yet, the air is still scented with the same smells of churros and popcorn, sweat and sunscreen.

Even amid the change in the foliage, the climate creates a reassuring backdrop

114 "Disneyland: Its Place in World Culture", 195.

115 www.anaheimoc.org/Articles/Archive/Webpage10455.asp.

116 Halloween, as one might expect, is as important a time at Disneyland as Christmas. Main Street, U.S.A. celebrates a traditional Midwestern harvest festival complete with windows lined with glowing pumpkins, Frontierland boasts an homage to the Mexican celebration of *Dia de los Muertos*, and an evening event allows children and adults to attend a private party where they can dress in costume go trick or treating.

for the creation of a surrealistic, magical temple that exists to reverse the patron's experience of the world outside. Marling notes:

> The act of entry was a rite of passage telling the stranger to shake off the customs of that other place – the formless sprawl of Los Angeles out beyond the parking lot, the town two or three stops back along the railroad tracks. Here, on this spot, the day started afresh, with a new set of rules. And the first of the admonitions built into the fabric of Disneyland was this: Arise and walk! Walk, all together now, straight down Main Street from the train.[117]

> Entertainment is clearly vital to the experience of temple. Patrons are held in rapt attention to the magical exhibitions of the temple priests, and since the earliest days of silent film, the cultural environment of Los Angeles has been responsible for developing temples to entertainment and mass culture. Disneyland is a product of that environment.

Animating Disney's Temple to Entertainment

To entertain is to engage. Without an emphasis on this kind of engaging spectacle, it is impossible to create the kind of communal experience necessary to create a functional temple. Walt's sense of the impact of entertainment in creating an environment for storytelling was profound. He understood that entertainment is not simply an escape. It is a necessity. Entertainment media functions as a way of allowing for the presence of role-reversal, something Turner recognizes as central to the creation of ritual when he develops his concepts of *liminality* and *communitas*.[118] In this environment of *communitas*, which he defines as an organic creation of transformative community ritual, the culture of temple forms the boundaries around the place.

Turner indicates that there is a nuanced but vital difference between the concept of the *liminal*, the betwixt and between space in ritual, and what he calls the *liminoid*. At the heart of the difference between these two terms is the distinguishing feature of entertainment: volition. *Liminoid* experiences are those experiences that, however psychologically effective they may be, are not compulsory rituals. They are part of a distinctive group of rituals that rise to meet the particular needs of the individual. Because they are not mandated by society, their emphasis on choice offers patrons the unique ability to feel as though the ritual belongs to them in a deeply personal way. This kind of ritual seems especially enticing to Americans, who often wear democratic philosophy on their sleeves like the cause-consecrated ribbons celebrities pin to their clothing during award season. They reflect a full-scale acceptance of the philosophical concept of free will.

As a *liminoid* ritual, Disneyland would not exist without these Southern Californian entertainment media. Film shares this history with the stage but is effective in nuanced ways of its own. Likewise, television, as an outcropping of both

---

117 *Designing Disneyland: The Architecture of Reassurance*, 86.

118 *The Ritual Process: Structure and Anti-Structure*, 95.

theater and film, brings together the characteristics of stage and screen, delivering to the consumer from within the comfort of their own home. Its power develops out of a deep understanding of the potential of amusement to craft ritual through an exploration of, and a manipulation of, a community's own sense of identity, mythic sensibilities and hunger for fun. The poetic containers of sacred space exist for the sake of the development of mythical points of congruence in the world. They are eternally reworked through the archetypal images of the culture doing the poetic work.

In the context of contemporary American culture, industries of entertainment are directly responsible for the re-visioning of the archetypal image of the temple. Storytellers bear the joys and the burdens of creating culture, both consciously or unconsciously. As both entertainer and illusionist, storytellers carry the responsibility for creating environments of social reversal. Disneyland's storytellers willed it into existence through an arc of archetypal human experience that traces itself directly from stage to silver screen, to small screen and beyond to the theme park.

Any truly functioning temple relies on the ability of its storytellers to convince and transport devotees through poetic work. Glamour magic, a common type of spell in the practice of magic traditions, is it's own type of poetic work. It is the practice of shape-shifting, manipulating the senses, and holding another in power. Witches, shamans, bards, actors, and animators all share this kind of transformative art. As discussed in previous chapters, the experience and craft of magic are the stock in trade of myth-and ritual-makers. Performance art is magic. All mythic ritual is by nature magic. In the contemporary world, Disney is the most successful purveyor of this kind of magic.

Any experience that surpasses the mundane nature of daily life is magical. It produces truth through illusion, which Hillman suggests is the true purpose of fiction when he writes "Authenticity is *in* the illusion?".[119] The quest for finding transcendent truth in the illusion is what makes for an effective ritual performance. Crafting the illusion of performance is never incidental. It requires the skill and precision of a master. Within the context of temple culture, Disney creates glamour in its parks by conjuring the spectacle of performance. A rich understanding of Disneyland as a temple requires the consideration of the development of these mythopoetic media, as well as the impact they have had on each other in the context of Disneyland's cultural environment.

The Imitation of Life

Imagine: The air sizzles with an energy that is made of more than the bodies involved in the staging. Costumes are donned, as actors touch up their make up, prepare, and practice their lines backstage. Behind the scenes, people dressed all in black work wires and lifts, prepare to move stage parts, and prepare special

[119] *Healing Fiction*, 39.

effects. The business backstage takes place with lights up and loud voices. Actors shout to each other, offering quips and criticisms, as the others who work the show use walkie-talkies to contact each other regarding technical issues. Directors each have their own style. Some pray, some chastise, some go just as deeply into character as the actors themselves. The options for activities backstage are endless, and as loud and rowdy as the backstage cast may be, there is a sense that a community of persons is about to create something together.

The house, the place where the audience sits, is usually a stark contrast to the kind of activity going on behind the stage. Patrons find their seats. An orchestra or a pre-recorded track plays as it comes closer to time to raise the curtain. Patrons read their programs or engage in polite conversation with persons next to them. They are largely aware that *dramatis personae* are about to arrive on the stage before them for the sake of conveying a story. What they are often unaware of is their own participation in the creation of the drama. The patrons who sit patiently in their seats, waiting on pins and needles for the curtain to rise, place themselves in a state of psychological sensitivity as they prepare to cross the threshold to a world that is completely foreign. The curtain finally rises, and like Alice peering through the looking glass, the audience looks on as an entire cosmos is created. The cosmic creation that occurs in this experience is also a relationship; a connection between the troupe itself and the audience in contact with them. This relationship manifests through a threshold: the stage.

This is a portrait of contemporary stagecraft. For thousands of years, dramatists have been an essential touchstone for cultural myth. They have marked the passage of time by enacting the stories of particular festivals and held the primary responsibility for creating the psychological states necessary for participation in rites of passage. Storytelling is a vital aspect of the development of psychological wholeness, even if it is as informal as a conversation around a home-cooked meal. Nevertheless, most societies recognize that separate ritual spaces for dramatic storytelling are as necessary as the storytelling itself, and stage performance is one of the most powerful forms of storytelling. Much like the stage itself, the impact of art lies in an intricate combination of strategic concealing and revealing. In his work on the absolute psychological necessity of aesthetics, Hans Georg Gadamer writes: "If we really have had a genuine experience of art, then the world has become both brighter and less burdensome?".[120]

This is equally true of the stage. It utilizes its natural qualities to produce an illusion, that when effective, is almost unbreakable. And, in doing so, it offers a catharsis intended to lighten the patron's psychological load. There is no better description of the significance of Disneyland. Sam Smiley notes that "Artists don't want to end the world; they wish to create it".[121] For the purpose of this analysis, it would be just as valid to argue that through the practice of recreating

120 *The Relevance of the Beautiful*, 26.

121 *Playwriting: The Structure of Action*, 4.

it, they wish to ritualize it. There is an alchemical aspect to the creation of a story through stage, screen, or paint and moving image. Ritualizing these mediums is an ancient ritual practice. Through its use of the tools of entertainment, engaging with pilgrimage can create a heart-lifting encounter with temple.

The theatrical stage creates a synthesis of drama, storytelling, and art through its use of multimedia platforms for entertainment. [122] Both ancient and contemporary societies utilize drama, weaving ritual into mundane life through humanity's daily experience. Traditionally stage drama participates in this. By its very nature as a vehicle for story, it opens the soul to the divine through an authentic connection with emotion. Drama's stirring of emotion falls into the realm of ritual as it submits the soul to a psychological transformation that both transfixes and transports the viewer. Lionel Corbett writes, "When ritual does perform its proper function, because of the numinosity of the archetype that is activated during ritual performance, the location where the ritual takes place is felt to be sacred space, and the time during which it is performed becomes sacred time". [123] Although the poetics of drama occur in plain sight, they alter psychological consciousness recreating sacralization of time and performance, as well as making *holy* of a place.

By its very nature, storytelling is ritualistic. It conveys the energies of the unconscious to both the storytellers themselves and the audience at large. Dramatic storytellers consciously construct the theater in order to be a safe container though which to convey their stories. Contrived as these containers may be, they are nevertheless effective at facilitating a psychological journey to wholly different cosmos. Disney plays with the traditions of dramatic storytelling, utilizing medias of stage, film and television as it does so. Their stories are the sacred texts that Disney uses to disperse the teachings of its tradition to its audience as physicalized by the parks. Understood this way, Disneyland is both temple and theater: a physical container for ritual consciously built through its ability to engage patrons in spectacle.

Eliade expands this idea through his concept of *macro-religious* time. This theory suggests that heightened states of religiosity occur around festival rituals. Eliade suggests that performance storytelling has its roots in religious and social ritual and that the stage participates in imitation ritual. He writes, "In *imitating* the exemplary acts of a god or of a mythic hero, or simply recounting their adventures, the man of an archaic society detaches himself from profane time and magically reenters the Great Time, the sacred time". [124]Stage drama is one such container for *macro-religious* time. The conscious creation of stage's imitation of life recalls the primordial act of creation. When it comes to stage drama, the audience believes because emotions are stirred, transporting those viewing

---

122 Ronald Grimes, *Rite Out of Place: Ritual, Media and the Arts*, 11.

123 *Psyche and the Sacred: Spirituality beyond Religion*, 57.

124 *Myths, Dreams, Mysteries: The Encounter Between Contemporary Faiths and Archaic Realities*, 23.

the drama to an encounter with the surreal. This experience makes us acutely aware of our own humanity. Whether it is the campfire story of a mythic hero, told by a shaman to his tribe, a fairy tale handed down at bedtime to a younger generation on a chilly, shadowy night, a play experienced by thousands in a theater witnessing the depth of Oedipus's pain, or a movie captivating gaggles of giggling girls through the three-dimensional animated movements of Rapunzel's glorious golden hair – all storytelling media contains common components: connection and transformation. Truly gifted dramatic storytelling is conveyed through the ability to connect the individual soul of the storyteller with the collective soul of the audience for the purpose of making transformative ritual. Arguably, no culture's storytelling prowess has had more of a profound effect on American mythmaking than the theater of the Greeks.

Western storytellers use Greek theater as a template because of the Greek concept of *catharsis*. The term refers to the kind of emotional purging that occurs when the theatrical patron accompanies actors on their narrative journey and is able, through identification with the characters, to release their own psychological energy. The etymological root of the term catharsis relates to the physical world. It comes from the Greek term *katamenia*, referring to a monthly shedding of menstrual blood and reproductive tissue by the female body. Aristotle is the first to use the term as a philosophical metaphor when he utilizes it as a medical metaphor for myth. Storytelling through theater is the imitation of life, as Aristotle writes, " [. . .] imitation is implanted in man from childhood . . . no less universal is the pleasure felt in things imitated [. . .] Objects which in themselves we view with pain, we delight to contemplate when reproduced with minute fidelity: such as the forms of the most ignoble animals and of dead bodies."[125] A cathartic experience transforms the patron through rituals of sensation and passion. We learn to know ourselves by ritualizing and mythologizing ourselves. Identification with story through theater creates a container for imitative catharsis in the Aristotelian sense.

Greek theater was a sacred affair, but it also straddled the realms of the sacred and the profane. One example is in the way that Greek theater uses laypersons as actors in sacred drama. Greek chorus members where chosen from the pool of theater patrons. Although they were not professional actors, they were an integral part of their religion. They helped fashion the container developed by the Greek culture. These containers need to be peopled, both by those who can construct the ritual itself, and by those who can participate. Like Greek theater, Disneyland is crafted by a series of *cast members* and *Imagineers*, some seen and some unseen. Disneyland, however, would be nothing without the patrons who, like the chorus members of ancient Greek theaters, are layperson-participants in the theatrical drama.

---

125 *Poetics*, 55.

Revealing the Animated Stage

Viewed from the air, Disneyland's landmarks are clearly visible. The park's environment is on display for all to see. It comes to life in color and texture. Subtle theatrical special effects are in use all over the park. Landscaped beds hide speakers that seem to vaporize before the patron's eyes. Again, from the aerial viewpoint, the resort boasts views of stage as well. The cast members disappear into subtly nondescript hallways, similar to the ones that lead to the backstage area of a theater. Disneyland works through this poetic ability to conceal and reveal. Its power is in its ability to hold the tension of a sacred container for play situated, as a business, in the middle of a culture that doesn't respect play's importance. The key to keeping this show lubricated is the touch of the human being, creative, though tightly regimented, to offer the show and nothing but the show.

In a brilliant maneuver, both for the sake of business and mythic ritual, Disney refers to their employees as *cast members*, rather than janitorial custodians, kitchen prep teams, dark-ride operators or dancers. The park is peopled with over 15,000 employees,[126] many of whom never put on the mantle of an iconic Disney film character, yet they are still required to act. The cast leads at Disneyland encourage their cast members to think of their work, whatever that may be, as a vital aspect of the show. Working in the park is considered acting on a stage, and cast members are expected to play their part anytime they are on that stage. For example, the custodial staff is always present somewhere on stage at any given time. Like stagehands that wear black to avoid being seen as they stealthily move sets back and forth during scene breaks, Disneyland's custodians attend to their duties swiftly and discretely. Custodians dress all in white, which effectively helps them blend into their surroundings, but also evokes a particular Disney ethos. It offers a nonverbal cue to the participant regarding the importance of cleanliness at the park.

Furthermore, a certain amount of decorum regarding dress code and behavior is required whether on stage or off. David Koenig catalogs the depth of dedication cast members are often called upon to keep up the illusion. They are required to avoid certain kinds of physical changes, gaining or losing weight, hair color changes, piercings, tattoos etc . . . in order to look the part. As Koenig notes, "It's more than a job, it's a lifestyle".[127] Cast members often attempt to find a way to make the stage their own, as many of them are not natural performers, and therefore being on stage on a daily basis can become tiresome and frustrating. They are often swept up in the excitement of working for Disney, forgetting that putting on the show requires a certain amount of predictability. The kind of daily uniformity required for production of a long-running musical, such as Andrew Lloyd Webber's *Cats*, is also a part of the

126 *Disneyland: Then, Now and Forever* by Bruce Gordon and Tim O'Day, 33.

127 *Mouse Tales: A Behind-the-Ears Look at Disneyland*, 64.

experience for cast members. It often becomes difficult, and therefore Disney has ushered in a policy of rotation in their standard operating procedure. Cast members rotate on and off stage periodically, in an attempt to keep the show as fresh as possible.

There are a few positions that offer the opportunity for any kind of improvisation. Cast members covet these roles competitively. Possibly the greatest example of this is the position of the Jungle Cruise captain. The Jungle Cruise is an attraction that dates back to opening day at Disneyland on July 17, 1955. It is themed to be reminiscent of the 1951 classic film *The African Queen*, starring iconic Hollywood actors Humphrey Bogart and Katherine Hepburn. Disney's *True Life Adventure* series was an inspiration for this attraction. The nature program that featured an episode titled *Creatures of the Wild* portrays, in Disney's narrative form, of course, the struggles African cats face in the savannah. The attraction features a canvas-covered riverboat, much like the film's *queen*, floating down the Nile River, while being steered by a daring riverboat captain who narrates the journey and protects the passengers from animals and local tribesmen. Walt originally wanted the animals featured in this attraction to be living, specimens. Though one wonders what he might have been thinking, he was able to bring in actual animals in the earliest version of the attraction.

The staff soon came to realize that depending on live animals for a show is as unpredictable as it is impractical. Many of the animals would sleep during the day, and when they were awake, they often displayed behavior that did not fit in the context of the story. The early version of the attraction meant to take a serious tone as an adventurous ride that offered visual thrills. Koenig notes "To fit the profile of a jungle explorer, the first skippers were permitted to wear goatees and earrings . . . And of course, there was a little humor, the type of puns common in the nature film series".[128] In these early days before television and Internet, the exotic was the subject of imagination for most middle-class Americans. Their only sense of life on the African, Australian, Asian, or South American continents came through magazines, movies, and film reels. Adventureland, therefore, was serious business. Although it was always meant to be a caricatured representation of an exotic *other*, a certain confidence remained among patrons that Disney was offering an image that could be trusted.

As the years went by, the attraction morphed into something slightly different. This difference came through the attraction's spiel. The spiel is the distinguishing factor of what are now known as Narrations attractions, a group which now includes Walt Disney's Enchanted Tiki Room, Storybook Land Canal Boats, and Great Moments with Mr. Lincoln. Jungle Cruise was the first of these attractions. The spiel is intended to provide a kind of stability and structure for it. It also serves its narrative purpose, providing the all-important story for the attraction. These days, the spiel is more than a script to be delivered by attraction

---

128 *More Mouse Tales: A Closer Peek Backstage at Disneyland* 52–53.

operators. It's a springboard for creativity[129] and an origin point for many a comic career. At different points in the attraction's history, the supervisors have offered small amounts of leeway with the spiel. Operators often pass jokes by the supervisor, if they are considered funny and appropriate enough for the Disney audience, they may be added to the spiel.

Jungle Cruise operators are expected to maintain remarkable amounts of focus and performance. Imagineer Jason Surrell recounts his personal experience as a Jungle Cruise skipper. In an Autumn 2010 *Disney Twenty-Three* magazine article titled "I was a Teenage Jungle Cruise Skipper", he recounts a specific trip he took around the jungle in the summer of 1989. After spending what felt like endless trips through the jungle while being shadowed by a trainer, he prepared for his first solo experience. Examining his first boatload, he recognized three faces: Danny DeVito, Rhea Perlman, and Dustin Hoffman. Surrell remembers "Try pulling focus from *that* crowd. It was going to be a challenge trying to keep my audience's attention on *me*".[130] Surrell continues to recount DeVito's admonition to "dazzle me, kid"[131] all while his elation at being able to remember and deliver his lines with wit and gusto, as well as delivering some of the ones he had written himself. The level of concentration and dedication to comedic performance is one of the most prized aspects of the Jungle Cruise attraction. It's improvisation at its finest.

The Illusion of Life

From the earliest day of the park's inception, people responded to the ability of Walt and his Imagineers to create a show so enchanting, it literally cast a magic spell. Disneyland is able to do this largely because it taps into the mythic power of the film industry, an environment so powerful in its surrealism that it seeps seamlessly into culture, making it possible to forget that there was a time when there was no such thing as a multiplex or a Fox theater, no Netflix or Amazon Prime, no VHS, DVD or BluRay, and no theme park a patron might visit to engage the ritual of venerating Hollywood's constellations. The concept of Hollywood as an icon seems to have sprung up organically, but much like other pilgrimage/temple sites there is much more calculation behind the scenes than one might originally suspect.

The roots of much of this calculation can be found in the surrealist movements of the 1920s and 30s. American anthropologist Hortense Powdermaker argues that Hollywood itself is a factory, the main product of which is dreams. She observes something quite astute about Hollywood. It's a city built on whatever

---

129 Pixar genius and Walt Disney Pictures Chief Creative Officer John Lasseter was a Disneyland Jungle Cruise operator. His humor, wit, and huge personality expressed through his amazing collection of Hawaiian shirts are a legendary part of Pixar and Walt Disney Animation's success.

130 Surrell, 14.

131 Ibid., 15.

images are considered entertaining, and that which entertains is always in a state of flux. Like a kaleidoscope, a fixed image of Hollywood's identity is virtually impossible to ascertain, because an environment developed for the sake of entertainment requires a certain amount of ontological malleability. It needs to maintain a capacity for shape shifting, because it is bound to a storytelling medium that requires it. In large part, this accounts for Hollywood's proximity and relationship to mythic ritual. This suggests Hollywood as more than its zip code, but also the icon of Hollywood, from the Hollywood sign, to Studio City in the hills, the studios in the valley, and Disneyland to the southwest.

Through its role as an icon – an artistic creation fashioned to reveal a facet of something sacred – Hollywood is inextricably linked to the film industry, a fact that one might interpret as a kind of metaphorical family dynamic. One begets the other and through mass culture we bear witness to it as though watching the struggles of Olympus. This dynamic is complicated, often bringing out the worst in humanity, but nevertheless, mythic Hollywood is a powerful force for culture making as well as myth-making. Powdermaker writes:

> THERE IS ONLY ONE HOLLYWOOD in the world. Movies are made in London, Paris, Milan and Moscow, but the life of these cities is relatively uninflu-enced by their production. Hollywood is a unique American phenomenon with a symbolism not limited to this country. It means many things to many people. For the majority it is the home of favored, godlike creatures. For others, it is a 'den of iniquity'-or it may be considered a hotbed of Communism or the seat of conserva-tive reaction; a center for creative genius, or a place where mediocrity flourishes and able men sell their creative souls for gold; an important industry with worldwide significance, or an environment of trivialities characterized by aimlessness; a mecca where everyone is happy, or a place where cynical disillusionment prevails. Rarely is it just a community where movies are made. For most movie-goers, particularly in this country, the symbolism seems to be that of a never-never world inhabited by glamorous creatures, living hedonistically and enjoying their private swimming pools and big estates, attending magnificent parties, or being entertained in famous night clubs. The other symbols belong to relatively small groups of people.[132]

Hollywood's cult of celebrity clearly embodies this. The gods walk among us in this surreal city, as Hillman suggests in his short documentary *Surfing L. A.* By musing that Hollywood itself has distinct relationship to the mythic imagina-tion, he suggests that there is something metaphysical about the way culture develops there. Images from classical mythology suggest both Olympus and the Underworld.

The gods peer down on humanity from their Hills, interacting or not as they will. Hades, the lord of the death, is present through geological instability, a constantly evolving psychological instability, and an identity created and shaped by illusion. Stories of death, and transformation are endlessly present in Los Angeles, even prompting several *Haunted Hollywood* tours. Some of these, such

---

132 *Hollywood The Dream Factory*, 16.

as the tragic Manson family murders and the dismemberment of the Black Dahlia are a fusion between myth and fact. These literalize the mythic energy present in Los Angeles. Others, such as John Carpenter's horror classic *Halloween*, filmed in nearby Pasadena and the popular *Film Noir* genre are fiction. Whether fact or fiction, these stories reflect the reality that the Earth under Hollywood is in a constant state of instability, mythically and literally, as Zeus and his fire reside in the mountains, Hades is just below the unstable fault lines, and Poseidon's realm lies across Pacific Coast Highway.

This constant instability shapes the city's identity as a kind of a film set, or backlot. It's designed to be stricken and rebuilt time and again like those housed by the studios on either side of the San Gabriel Mountains. As Alain Silver and James Ursini note in their pictorial exploration of the city of Los Angeles's presence as a character in the genre of Film Noir, "'The dream of Hollywood' is in many ways just another slightly more profane version of the American dream, that Puritan ideal of a 'city on the hill' – although, in this case, it is mostly in the flatlands".[133] The city itself is its own kind of liminal space, its own unique type of temple. Temples involve mirroring, an often impenetrable veil that both makes the gods present while simultaneously retaining their stature in the cosmos. The mythic nature of the film industry has prompted many a Hollywood critic to bemoan what performer Johnnie Davis first crooned in the 1937 film *Hollywood Hotel*, "That phony, super Coney, Hollywood".[134] And much like temples across time, the city of Los Angeles itself invites both visitors and locals alike deeper into new levels of initiation into its surrealist story.

Surrealism developed out of the Dadaist movement, which in turn developed out of Paris in the early 1920s. It hit its peak in the United States after World War I, a response to the insanity of the war and its ensuing modernist rhetoric. In part, it is an artistic attempt to integrate the trauma of the modernist period, but also, as suggests, a provocation against bourgeois ideas of exceptionalism, notions that the surrealists thought to be the result of a depraved and overindulged culture.[135] Surrealism is characterized by the juxtaposition of non sequitur images, working through absurdity. This ethos of the absurd guided the development of the young city of Los Angeles. Although this artistic movement has its roots planted firmly in 19th-century German romanticism and the artist community of early 20th-century Paris, the impact of surrealism found its way into the development of the studio system as the film industry began to develop in the mid 1920s and 1930s.

Surrealism is strongly resonant with Jungian analytical psychology, because it

133 *L. A. Noir: The City As Character*, 18.

134 The composition team of Richard Whiting (music) and Johnny Mercer (lyrics) wrote *Hooray for Hollywood* for the 1937 film, *Hollywood Hotel*, and since then it has become an anthem for the city, as it celebrates the surrealist facade of the industry that built the city.

135 Michael Richardson, *Surrealism and Cinema*, 15.

emphasizes the importance of unconscious motivating factors on the cultural soul. Hence, the Surrealists develop a deep interest in popular culture. It is important to remember, however, that they do not valorize popular culture, nor do they attempt to break down distinctions between the two. Instead, they seek to express the way they see it working in tandem with their own artistic pursuits, almost as a parallel universe, a dream world, or Alice's looking glass might relate to waking consciousness. Many early filmmakers were fascinated by this art form and combined aspects of surrealism with irony. Michael Richardson writes:

> Even if, in its heyday, Hollywood was called 'the dream factory' the dreams it manufactured [. . .] were overwhelmingly ones upon which the Surrealists were more likely to choke than to be nourished [. . .] Hollywood sought to regulate dreams in ways that annulled any Surrealist attitudes of spontaneity and moral rigour [. . .] Nevertheless, the Hollywood system still left a place for the imagination.[136]

Film is capable of committing the surrealist's dream-like qualities tocelluloid. Alfred Hitchcock, in particular, is well known for being a proponent of both surrealist vision and Freudian psychology. He directed *Vertigo* and *Spellbound*, two films made in collaboration with Spanish surrealist, Salvador Dali, an artist often considered to be the most famous one of the period. These projects reflect the absurdity of surrealism mixed with the genre's interest in the darkest, most picturesque, and pathological inner landscapes.

Surrealism's lasting impact on film is its ability to take catharsis one-step further than theater into the realm of complete mythic identification. Whereas theater works like an alchemical potion in the cauldron of a stage, the mind of the theatrical patron still retains the ability to recognize the drama as just that – a drama acted by players on a stage. By virtue of the naturalism it attempts to achieve, however, film dissolves barriers between fantasy and reality, waking and dreaming. David Thomson writes "…in the movies, those on the screen do not know we are watching. We are like voyeurs, spies or peeping toms. We do not exist in the old way."[137] By dissolving these barriers and making this illusion of life real, film fuses the media of visual art and cathartic stage drama. It makes myths more real than real, while simultaneously removing the actual human interaction of the stage. Film creates the same kind of communal ritual environment as theater does. It's created through costumes, imaginal worlds, and play, and it's traditionally experienced in the contained environment of the theater, in the dark with other patrons. By removing direct interaction between the players and the audience, however, it becomes a different kind of ritual experience, something more surrealist and dream-like, and thus participation in it becomes simultaneously less communal and more symbolically potent.

---

136 Ibid., 61.

137 *The Whole Equation: A History of Hollywood*, 49.

Film combines visual art with dramatic narrative. Images are projected on the screen in such a way that hold the audience's attention in a more focused way than the vitality of stage can convey. Each moment is a snapshot, and thus there are tactics that work in film that simply doesn't work on stage and vice versa. Like traditional temple cults, film can offer an experience of thresholding, because it juxtaposes life with art in a psychologically unsettling way. However real the film may seem, the soul senses alienation from the persons doing the acting. When, as in the case of contemporary culture, technology allows motion picture to be accessed on mobile devices and personal computers, the experience becomes even further alienated from the cathartic group experience of traditional storytelling or drama. Motion picture takes Aristotle's concepts of myth and the imitation of life to a higher peak of imagination, as the patron must juggle the complete illusion they identify with the images themselves with the isolation normal to this kind of experience.[138]

Because participating in film alienates the viewer from life while also presenting such a believable illusion of it, it is able to create the fantasy of a shared cinematic experience between all of humanity. As it shapes culture that shared experience itself becomes mythic. Built entirely out of the trappings of film culture, Disneyland participates in this tradition. Disney historian Jeff Kurtii writes that the "*Disneyland* Resort is one of the most-photographed locations on earth for a reason: pictures of the resort are not only charming and beautiful; they tell evocative stories, call to mind memories, and create a genuine longing to visit the actual place – and enjoy the real experience".[139] It is able to do this because it expands the cinematic experience outward; immersing the patron even further into a hyperreal environment, physicalizing the surreal by immersing the patron into a film set brimming with Disney characters. Like film, it is ritual, as it is both transformative and transcendent, and it is temple, as it creates a liminal atmosphere for the purpose of containing the story.

Animating the Backlot

Imagine: If, while standing in line at a club, a restaurant, or even a clothing store one were to notice a small mouse scurrying across the floor, one might jump out of the way, scream about health concerns or, at the very least, tell someone who works in the vicinity about the presence of rodents. Now imagine being in line at the Matterhorn in Fantasyland at Disneyland. Imagine standing, listening to the sound of the screams of the roller coaster, waiting with anticipation for your turn. You look down, and you see a tail disappear beneath the garden beds of the park outside of the queue. The crowd around you squeals with delight and shouts, "Look! It's Mickey!" True story – it happened to me.[140] The presence

---

138 *Storytelling and Theater: Contemporary Storytellers and their art*", Michael Wilson refers to German playwright Bertolt Brecht when he writes ". . . naturalism reflects reality, narrative refracts it …" 121.

139 *Disneyland Through the Decades: A Photographic Celebration*, 8.

of a giant mouse wandering around the park signing autographs and giving hugs and kisses to children and adults alike desensitizes the community to the oddities of the surreal environment of a theme park, not to mention the norms of the mundane environment outside of it.

Former chief executive officer of The Walt Disney Company, Michael Eisner, once said: "Transforming movies into attractions is the basis of Disneyland, from Davy Crockett to the early animated films. Disneyland is the three-dimensional realization of two-dimensional celluloid product."[141] In a 2010 documentary titled *Waking Sleeping Beauty*,[142] Walt's nephew, Roy E. Disney said, "The heart of this thing was, is, and always will be, the movie business". Walt recognized that film has become a mythic force for storytelling in cultures across the world. Through the medium of motion picture, myth-makers are able to transmit image, sound and story to the entire global community simultaneously and without variation. However, Disney also recognized and was fascinated by the links between the global consistency of film, and its surreal effects on the viewer.[143] Walt set a theatrical standard and ethos at Disney that extends beyond the studio to everything they do, in order to expand the surrealistic effects of Disney movies. Any trip to Disneyland makes one thing clear: Disneyland is a Hollywood backlot, where cinematic dreams are built and rebuilt, acted and reenacted, at will. The surrealistic aspects of Disney film most effectively link up with the imitative practices of the backlot through the use of the storyboard, one of the most important and potent Disney contributions to film making.

Storyboarding means drafting several images that represent the most integral scenes of the story being told. In fact, though storyboarding is now a common practice in the film industry, it has its roots at the Disney Studio. Christopher Finch credits Webb Smith with creating the storyboard, [144] a series of drawings in comic book format that is then pinned to a board in sequence. This format is used to work through the flow of the story, effortlessly cutting and pasting pieces of the story during the pitch and brainstorming aspects of the project.

---

140 This occurred during a personal trip to Disneyland in May 2006.

141 *Disneyland: Secrets, Stories and Magic*, DVD.

142 This documentary, directed by animator Don Hahn, explores the "Disney Renaissance" animation films that began in the mid 1980s with *The Great Mouse Detective*. Roy E. Disney was instrumental in bringing Michael Eisner, Frank Wells, and Jeffrey Katzenberg into the Disney organization. The period of the mid-1980s was financially tenuous for the Walt Disney Company, as stocks dipped low enough to attract the attention of corporate raiders, and the live action films of Touchstone Pictures and later Hollywood Pictures almost completely overtook the animation department. It explores the period when Disney's animated films were, despite the presence of some of the best talent and materials in the business, not great. It chronicles the triumphant return of Disney animation to the art form, culminating in the release of *Beauty and the Beast*, which is, in my opinion, one of the greatest motion pictures ever made. There is not another animated feature that rivals the artistic achievement of this film as far as the quality of its animation style, music, and power to stir emotion.

143 Walt was fascinated by Dali's work, and the two of them developed a project titled *Destino*, a short that was eventually abandoned in 1947, only to find a renaissance with its completion and limited theatrical release in 2003. https://www.youtube.com/watch?v=1GFkN4deuZU

144 *The Art of Walt Disney*, 27–28.

Storyboarding suggests different camera angles and storytelling choices. It explores the emotional content of plots and character arcs. Disney animators utilize the storyboard to present their story to a larger film crew, often to their bosses, by acting out the story on the board. For this reason, animators are often referred to as actors with pencils. Lead animators are required to be able to tell their stories and speak to the needs of their characters.

They are required to develop the characters to which they are assigned in a similar fashion as actors in a film or a play. Disney Legend, Glen Keane, who animated such classic characters as Ariel, the Beast, and Tarzan, discusses how Ariel came to him during the process of drawing her. He writes, "The Princess I draw is alive and breathing. She tells me what she wants to do. My pencil does its best to keep up." [145] Like other traditions of icon making that suggest the saints live in the materials the artist uses to make the icon, Keane uncovers Ariel as he draws her. He recounts the way she spoke to him, engaged with him. He notes that dialoging with her allowed him to tell her story. As the artists at Disney engage with the characters through the creative process of brainstorming and storyboarding, they also translate that same sensibility in building the park. They allow the story to come alive around them as they board it out, creating concept art for new characters and lands that they share with park patrons at events like the D23 Expo and on their Facebook pages.

The enterprise of animation is key to Disney's entire myth, the root of their ethos, and the basis of everything they do. Drawing cartoons - creating the illusion that characters rendered with pencil, ink, and paint have a life off the page - is the cornerstone of the entire enterprise. Indeed, the word *animation* draws its etymological roots from the Latin *anima*. To animate is to imbue with spirit, with life and breath; it suggests the liveliness of nature.[146] Legendary "nine old men" members, Ollie Johnston and Frank Thomas write that, "For some presumptuous reason, man feels the need to create something of his own that appears to be living, that has inner strength, a vitality, a separate identity – something that speaks out with authority – a creation that gives the illusion of life".[147] This illusion of life in animation offers a heightened condition of life. The audience is conditioned by its experience with film as an imitation of life to enter the space of animation as an illusion of life. The space this illusion creates is a place where soul creates temple.

Disney's temple is a painted land. If it is to be made sacred, this land requires the touch of masterful, poetic artists that are also able to deliver meticulously detailed work. The process of animation has a hyper obsessive and compulsive quality to its work. It is ritual-like in the way the action is repeated with only slight differences each time. In this way, it functions like the Disneyland trip

145 *The Art of the Disney Princess*, 2.

146 *Oxford English Dictionary* online.

147 *The Illusion of Life: Disney Animation*, 13.

itself. Those who are held captivated by the Disney stories are held compulsively in the world they create. The park works every time, like a charm. No matter how well one is aware of the park's details, one is always transported to a magic illusion of the acted-out storyboard, a tool that found its way into the development of Disneyland. Walt himself often referred to Disneyland as *the show*. According to Finch: "The bottom line was that visiting Disneyland would be like spending a day *inside* a cluster of Hollywood films, each one spilling magically into the next".[148] Artists and Imagineers used their concept of storyboarding to set out to make their early mock-ups of Disneyland. They painted sets, created models, and costumed those models as if they were outfitting a backlot. Once these early miniatures were tested and shown to be effective, the sets themselves were built. Imagine this intoxicating juxtaposition: the obsessively detailed imitation of life on one hand and the presence of painted fantasy on the other.

Disneyland's animated backlot is most clearly evident through its threshold opening, Main Street, U.S.A. This is Walt's personal projection of America now, and although that now is, at present, over 100 years in the past, it nevertheless speaks to American myth through iconic statements of larger myth-themes, such as the emotions which arise from an interaction with ideology and the global future of a Tomorrowland where peace, efficiency, freedom and the role of leisure time are all vital aspects of society. By design, Main Street U.S.A. is the first themed space the patron encounters when entering the berm. As soon as one steps foot out of the tunnel of the berm, one is transported to what Marling calls an environment of reassurance. Everything - from the colors, the shapes of the building, the music playing in the bushes, to the perfectly groomed cast members milling about - contributes to the detailed illusion of a stylized version of life in 1901 Marceline, Missouri.

From the fire station to the ice-cream parlor, from the decorations in the windows to the names of the Disney legends/merchants on the windows, Main Street, U.S.A. is detailed with the same level of consistent stylization and attention to detail required in the animation studio. It's is a surreal dream. Anyone who visits the park must know that life was never actually this idyllic. Towns were never this perfectly cheerful, not with people living through a life that Thomas Hobbes once called, "nasty, brutish and short".[149] Real life in 1901 was even more perilous than today, before the prevalence of vaccines and antibiotics took away fear of death from the common cold and flu. But Disney has reproduced an idealized version of it with such nostalgic accuracy that patrons buy the illusion. It works the same way memory does – mythologizing events, remembering details to make the myth seem even more real, and often tweaking aspects of the memory the soul finds unappealing. Like the sisterly

---

148 *The Art of Walt Disney,* 397–398.

149 *Leviathan* (ch. 13, para. 9).

relationship between Greek goddesses Mnemosyne (memory) and Lethe (forgetting), who inspire the poet and encourage the dead to forget the land of the living, Disney's imitation of life is present in both its dogged attention to detail and through the way it glosses over or re-mythologizes what might be unpleasant.

Another example of surrealist inspiration at Disneyland is present in the art of Mary Blair a woman who, as one of Walt Disney's favorite concept artists left an indelible mark on Disney history and mythology. Mary Blair was born Mary Robinson in McAlester, Oklahoma, in 1911. Her path to Disney legend status is itself rather mythic. A naturally gifted artist, she was honored with a scholarship to the Chouinard Art Institute.[150] After completing her courses at Chouinard, Mary began to seek employment in the precarious environment of the depression-era art world. She married Lee Everett Blair in 1934. For a time, the couple worked for Disney together. She was one of the select few, and the only female artist, to be hand-chosen by Walt for the 1941 *Good Neighbor* excursion to South America, setting her on the path to becoming one of The Walt Disney Company's most underappreciated artistic geniuses. On that trip, Walt took particular notice of her talents. The exposure to South American folk art left a lasting impression on her style that influenced a specific segment of Disney's look forever. Her influence is present in her depiction of the caricaturized human form, a perfect match with Disney as caricature is central to the language of Disney animation Her characters tend to have short, chubby torsos and small eyes.

However fascinated Walt Disney was by surrealism, its raw, pathological nature did not fit the ethos of the Disney Studio. In order to be able to engage in this kind of surrealist juxtaposition of images, the studio needed to find an artist who was able to translate the kind of imaginative space surrealism explores without spiraling out of control into the darker aspects of the unconscious. He trusted Blair with the concept art for the animated features that are the crux of what has often been called Disney's Golden Age: *Peter Pan, Cinderella,* and *Alice in Wonderland*. Her artistic voice was colored by a fascination with the contemporary craftsman style of the mid-century era she helped shape. The final look of these films was true to Blair's original vision, both in color and in spirit, and consequently, the look of the Disneyland attractions followed suit. Blair herself has reached mythic stature in the Disney community, often known by fans as *Our Lady of Flair*. For many she is an image of tranquility in the early days of the studio, a quiet genius that was able to meet Walt's challenges with the soulful eye of a poet and the joy of a child. Her graceful demeanor balances Walt's lively exuberance. She is one of the few women with whom Walt worked closely, both at the studio and the parks. Her gentle love of whimsy captivated his artistic adoration.

In 1964, Walt chose Blair to develop concept art for an upcoming exhibit at the

---

150 This eventually became CalArts under Disney's tutelage.

New York World's Fair. Her brilliance is evident in a televised broadcast of Disneyland's 10th anniversary special when Walt and Blair present early plans for her iconic attraction It's a Small World, an attraction that is arguably the most quintessentially Disney concept art created. The look of her art does belong to the elusive land of dreams, but not the kind of dreamlike state that is present at an amusement park house of mirrors. While riotous with color, her images never feel oppressive with it. They are childlike in tone, while being surrealist in their masterful complexity. The lines of her images indicate the kind of circuitous environment so often present in surrealist art, but safely confined within the world of the bedtime story.

Her work captures the essence of surrealism while simultaneously depicting Disneyland as a reassuring place. Ultimately, Blair's style is a bit of a paradox in Disney's myth. As much as she's loved, she was often treated with artistic ambivalence. Walt cherished her style. He nurtured and encouraged her as an artist, but he stops short of fully embracing her wild and whimsical style. For whatever reason, perhaps, and I'm speculating here, because he feared animated films needed to have a naturalistic style to be taken seriously, or perhaps because she was a woman, and he was unaccustomed to working with women, he always holds her work back just a little bit.

Walt encouraged as much naturalism as possible in his finished animation projects. He often uses Blair to create concept art for the characters and not for the backgrounds or vice versa. In the case with *Cinderella*, for example, the look of her concept drawings was eventually largely set aside in favor of a more naturalistic style for the characters, but he keeps the style of her background art as though placing real life characters in a painted world. It's as though he feared pushing the boundaries of surrealism too far. The backgrounds could be surreal, but the characters needed naturalism. Even from the safety of Blair's innocent style, surrealism remains slightly too subversive for Disney. The paradox of Blair's work with Disney is that although he always holds her work back a bit, he also seems deeply aware that there is something in her work that *is* the Disney style. He may hold her animated projects on a leash, he also hands her what is arguably the most important and strongly worded statement of Disney's entire mythos – It's A Small World.

The Living Room's Lens on Life

Since its inception in the early 1950s, television has become America's national pastime. Much to the surprise of many early critics, it does not replace other pastimes, such as baseball and film; it contributes to them. Nor does it eclipse other such sacred rituals as worship, family pilgrimage, and even communion with the natural world. Rather, it becomes the filter through which many Americans experience these rituals and ritual-like life moments. Television is both instructor and student to American mythic culture in a way that encapsulates the ethos of the information age. In the earliest days of the television fad,

77

indeed almost the instant television catches on; it becomes a vehicle for myth and a ritualistic medium for the poetics of culture. More than any other cultural medium, television embraces the sensitive space between fantasy and reality. The same networks dedicated to journalism's *just the facts* ethos also offer fine drama and comedy. NASA's Moon landing, traumas of Vietnam, and the abject horrors of 9/11 share cable space with *The Brady Bunch* and *Grey's Anatomy*. This reflects the Surrealism inherent in American media of entertainment at its most complex and confusing. The juxtaposition of images, between dogged realism and fantastical entertainment, requires a postmodern ability to hold these kinds of tensions in psychological balance. J. Fred MacDonald quotes Richard Hubbell's 1942 insight about television and American culture,

> For all its insufficiencies, national television performed for most Americans 'a combination movie theater, museum, education, news reporter, playhouse, daily picture magazine, political forum and discussion center, propaganda, and counter-propaganda dispenser, art gallery, vaudeville show, opera, ballet theater, plus a few other things rolled into one.[151]

Through the medium of television, we see ourselves reflected both as we are and as we (perhaps) would like to see ourselves, a very Disneyfied sentiment to be sure. All parts of the cultural soul, from the beautiful to the pathological, are on display in the world of television.

Television breaches the lines of containment drawn so carefully on the stage. It delves more deeply into the naturalism of film because it's the height of popularization. Reality television, television productions that feature everyday people, has been a medium staple since the earliest days of television. Game shows like *Truth and Consequences* and *Password* are an early example of this. Through the pairing of luminaries with "average Joes", game shows capitalized on the ability of television to crawl into the daily life of Americans and make television shows relevant to Americans as more than spectatorship and/or art appreciation. This is not to suggest that the actors on reality shows are images to which the audience can relate. They are still stylized, and they are often even more inauthentic than images on the stage or film screen. Nevertheless, they still offer a sense of the *civilianization* of stardom not often present in iconic Hollywood. These shows intimate rumblings of what have been called four-dimensional immersive experiences of entertainment. Television takes the entertainment of voyeurism to a different level, as it makes the subjects accessible to the audience. Through reality television, the people sitting in front of the television set become the stars. This emphasis on the common person as star is directly responsible for the theme park-ing of American entertainment. At Disneyland everyone becomes the star of his or her personal hyperreal reality show.

Today's reality shows are a staple of television, prompting dramedies[152] like

---

151 *One Nation Under Television*, 69.

Un-Real that poke fun at the idea of the shows as reality, Internet sites like YouTube and Vine, and Apps like SnapChat and Facebook Live, furthering television's early attempts to fuse together entertainment with art in daily life. Perhaps the most fascinating aspect of the mingling together of these two realms is advertising's use of television as a media that shapes cultural identity. Disney masters the art of selling identity through television. Disney's ability to fuse the mundane with the magical through advertising is the most potent aspect of the way they build culture through television. Commercials for the Disney parks utilize the television's magical qualities to equate Disneyland the place with Disneyland the merchandise.

The individualization of the temple is television's most significant contribution to the ideological temples of entertainment from which Disneyland arises. If there is a lack of identification with place, that may can have more to do with a loss of ownership, of identity, than with any kind of deficiency in its presence. In order to make a temple, a story, and a ritual matter, these things must feel like they belong to the persons participating in them. One takes a pilgrimage to a temple not simply to consume or to be a spectator to it, but also to become an interactive part of it. Television revives this tradition for Americans, many of which became spiritually complacent in their sacred interactions by the time television became more than simply a fad or the latest technological gadget.

Although much of what is presented on the small screen is offered for the sake of consumption with little (if any) consideration for the persons watching it, television still maintains an ability to present itself as a magical portal offering entry points to a whole new kind of sacred environment. This environment, especially via the genre of reality television, is interactive as well as mythic. Reality television makes the gods feel accessible. Pathological though they may be, their draw is undeniable, and clearly explains much of the success Donald J. Trump had in the 2016 Presidential election. Television has the opportunity to usher the viewer into temple through a magic box, a magic mirror located in one's own personal space. Psychologically speaking, that kind of interaction, however contrived, is both potent and volatile. It revives the psychic energy typically generated through stage drama, but it does so in the interactive, often unpredictable way.

Television Builds the Park

The development of new and technologically progressive media meant to springboard his products constantly fascinated Walt. In the early 1950s, he plunged his company wholeheartedly into television. It captured his imagination as completely as animation and film. His long-cherished dream of creating a park where fans could interact with the myths of his studio seemed out of reach until he moved into the realm of television. Disney was struck by the intimacy

152 A term that combines drama and comedy.

of television. Through it, he was able to fuse his love of education and entertainment with his charismatic personality and unaffected charm. At the project's inception, Walt was reticent to be the face of this new forum for his products, but when he committed to it, it soon became clear that he was the perfect choice to host the show.[153] Suddenly, it seemed possible to reach into the homes of his fans and encourage them to try his products.

As Walt began to build the park in 1954, he expanded his presence on the television. He stuck a deal with ABC. They would host the show on their network in exchange for $25 million in shares.[154] When it aired on October 27, 1954, viewers were treated to a variety show, segmented into four parts, like the four major lands of the original park: Frontierland, Fantasyland, Adventureland, and Tomorrowland. These segments present Disneyland as more than just an amusement park in Anaheim. *Disneyland*'s audience is transported into the mythic space of Disney's "lands" through the series, a themed space made real by the park in Anaheim. Each week the viewer enjoyed a story that drew them into the park. Each segment is a couch for the different aspects of Disney's mythology.

Walt used the structure of his *Disneyland* television show to make the park an icon, while simultaneously transporting viewers there. But, the *Disneyland* television show did much more than that. It created an icon, an *axis mundi*, a holy mountain, and a temple. Walt knew that the success of his park hinged on memory. Visitors might venture to the park out of curiosity, but they return because of the memories they created while they were there. Disney knew that he had to find a way to use television to create the kind of memories one makes on a family trip and, if he wanted to have a profitable first year, he needed to do this before opening day. Television was the perfect medium to bring this project into being.

The Disneyland Television Show had the unique ability to relate Disney's storytelling canon to an airtight association between the stories and characters that the audience had grown to love and the place – Disneyland – where they would be found in the physical realm. Without television, although the results may have eventually proved the same, it would not have happened in time to turn a profit, and therefore save the fledgling and deeply in debt Walter Elias Disney (WED). Critics might bemoan his use of television, calling the move manipulative advertising. The simple truth, though, is Disney had poured all of the studio's resources and much of his own personal wealth into the Disneyland product. As he had in the late 1930s, when he was told that he couldn't make a full-length cartoon people would actually watch, he had gone all in with the project. He couldn't afford to see it fail, because to do so would bring his entire

---

153 *Walt Disney: The Man Behind the Myth* 2001.

154 According to Watts, Disney and ABC had stuck a deal that garnered ABC thirty percent of stock in Disneyland in return for the vital influx of capital they offered.

family's work down around him. But his ambition was for more than financial security. He was driven by an impulse to create a park that would mean something to humanity.

The Disneyland Television Show weaves a single narrative for the park, combining Disney's iconic characters with their adaptations of historic people and places, exotic adventure, and the optimism of atomic-age science. It develops psychological associations between history, fantasy, psychology, a religious sense of the sacred, and dreams of the future. During his Disneyland progress report, which aired originally on February 9, 1955, Walt said, "We hope that through our television shows that you will join us in the building of Disneyland and that you will find here a place of knowledge and happiness". This is a vital aspect of the temple experience – worshipers need to have the personal experience.

Watts recounts an analysis of television by journalist Edith F. Hunter in 1957. It begins with a question: "Have you worshipped with your children today? No, I don't mean have you been to church with them, at eleven o' clock Sunday morning, but right at home in front of your television set, every weekday at five pm [. . .]"[155] The practice of ritualized Mickey Mouse clubs goes back to the 1930s in film houses and neighborhood meeting places all over America. By the time the *Mickey Mouse Club* arrived in 1955, the park was open and Disneyland's status as a paradisiacal world center was engrained on the psyche of the American public. The show was filmed in Fantasyland, across from the carousel and next to the Snow White Scary Adventure.[156] The *Mickey Mouse Club* was the first television variety show developed especially for children. It features a group of young people preteen to early teen who sing, dance, and play scenes meant to educate and entertain under the watchful eye of their club leader Mickey and his emissaries Jimmie Dodd and Roy Williams. The club's uniforms are famous: white turtlenecks with the club members' names on them, dark pants or skirts, and those iconic ears.

Childhood is a particularly potent time in the mythic life of humanity, because most children do not firm distinctions between concepts of time, space, fantasy, and reality. Reaching into the soul of childhood through a television set seals the viewer's role as an insider to the tradition, developing a lifelong affection for the show and the place where the show was filmed. According to Watts, "A former cast member reported that during her tour of Vietnam with a rock-and-roll band in the late 1960s, without fail a soldier in the audience would stand and request that she lead them in singing the show's theme song".[157] The experiences of childhood are the basis for Disney's carefully cultivated ritual

---

155 "Because We Like You", Children's Religion, Aug. 1957, 23. Qtd in Watts, 335.
   http://bit.ly/2bRl7kP

156 The building still stands today. In good, proper Disney fashion, it has been repurposed. It now houses the Pinocchio's Daring Adventure attraction. It is interesting to note that opening day Disneyland did not have a *Pinocchio* attraction.

157 335.

experience. This is how rituals become part of one's mythic canon. It's what makes one a true insider.

The devotion continues among the parents and grandparents of young children that visit Disneyland today. While grandparents remember growing up with the *Mickey Mouse Club* of Annette and Cubby,[158] parents now recount the way the careers of Justin Timberlake, Christina Aguilera, and Britney Spears began while singing the *Mickey Mouse Club* theme song. In many ways, watching the *Mickey Mouse Club* is like being there. It is like being initiated into the holiest part of the temple, and viewers watched children just like themselves converse with Mickey Mouse and his friends. It is the ultimate in television's ability to create vicarious living experience, and all of that begins at a central, mysterious location – inside the *Mickey Mouse Club* Theater.

Walt continued to host his show until his untimely death of lung cancer in December of 1966.[159] Through this era of social upheaval in America, his presence on the show had become iconic, and that presence continued through years of network, time slot, and title changes. His Uncle Walt persona began to transform from a connection to the actual person, whose foibles were memorable, to a brand. Many began to relegate Walt to the same sphere as the golden arch's Ronald McDonald – a fictional figurehead that represented his product. His continued presence on television as well as the prevalence of the urban legend that he is cryogenically frozen and waits to be revived at the perfect time further distances him from his natural life.

The public continued to trust Disney, but two decades after his death, the original Disneyland television show format began to show its age. As a result, ratings struggled. In 1983, CBS cancelled the *Walt Disney* television show. This occurrence corresponded with the birth of The Disney Channel, a new cable channel owned by Disney. An early *modus operandi* of the network was to continue the flow of Disney staples to the audience. In the early 1980s, cable television was a hot commodity. It was considered a luxury product, not the purveyor of mass culture typical of the cotemporary Internet era. Much like Walt did during the early years of television, Disney took a risk, knowing that the industry was likely to grow and become the same kind of cultural force for myth-making as film, radio, and basic television were. Led by Michael Eisner, Disney brought their partnership with television into the next era of technological development. This inherent trust of technology continues with Disney today, as the company continues to expand and develop into the latest and greatest new thing.

Although it no longer focuses most of its time on the early canon, and rarely

---

158 There was also a version of the Mickey Mouse Club in the 1970s, but that one didn't produce iconic characters of popular culture.

159 Walt Disney was a well-known chain smoker. Interviews with those closest to him reveal that it was this habit that let directly to his early death at the age of 65. *Walt Disney: The Man Behind the Myth* 2001.

showcases the Uncle Walt image of the early years, Disney television continues to point back to the theme park(s) as iconic center for immersion into Disney myths. The Disney Channel often intersperses spots that plug the park or show the younger characters at the park. One particular mini-show segment, *Movie Surfers*,[160] often takes place within the confines of the parks, both in Anaheim and in Florida. This show offers a kid's review of upcoming Disney releases. It acknowledges the iconic importance of television to the Disney parks.[161] Filming in the park lends an air of authenticity to the show. It is a symbolic statement: broadcasting to the faithful from deep within the confines of the temple and presenting the image of sanctioned communication from the gods, which in the end is television's most potent ability.

Disneyland as Ultimate in Transformative Narcisissm

All of this discussion of how Disney creates the park leads back to the to the ultimate question of why this temple is necessary. I've previously written that a temple pilgrimage is generally understood as a journey to a sacred center. Since the mid-20th century, American tradition has suggested that, at least in part, tourism can be considered a pilgrimage. Since ancient times, the image of pilgrimage has represented a journey undertaken for the purpose of traveling to unfamiliar territory. The central reason for travel to a distant land is to experience something outside oneself in a wholly different environment. One responds to the call to this kind of journey because one desires to gain perspective different from one's own. Since these journeys are often expected to effect a transformation due to an encounter with what Martin Buber calls the *wholly other*, one might ask whether Disneyland can truly be considered a pilgrimage.

Disneyland is a temple unlike any other, as it is created in the image of the world around it as an illusion of the world itself. Jean Baudrillard refers to this as hyperreality. He suggests that Disneyland is more real than the world around it, that hyperreality is the natural state of American reality and that as a simulation it is that which is truly real. He writes that "Disneyland: a space of the regeneration of the imaginary as waste-treatment plants are elsewhere and even here".[162] His sense is that, in this context, all experience is a simulation without a signifier, and as such, it's the simulated experience that constitutes the real experience. He further suggests that, being a culture without what he calls "a past or a founding truth",[163] America's simulation is one of true utopianism, and

160 This show began to run in 1998.

161 Hollywoodland located in Disney's California Adventure park offers an attraction known as Playhouse Disney: Live on Stage. It is a stage-show version of a popular toddler series on The Disney Channel. This show presents Mickey and his friends from the television show, while holding the illusion that this attraction is the seat of their television show.

162 *Simulacra and Simulation* 13.

163 *America*, 76.

that this creates a culture that has become a symbol without a signifier; an image without meaning.

Insofar as it relates to the experience of other, becoming fixated and transformed by a trip to Disneyland is an exercise in what I call *transformative narcissism*. The term *narcissism* has been developed by the psychological community as a way to describe a certain set of personality disorders. Narcissistic personalities are understood as persons who are self-serving, capricious, and un-self-reflexive. At first glace, one might think that a Disney apologist, such as myself, might find this concept deeply troubling. An imbalanced relationship with narcissism is dangerous, but it's also true that a deeper gaze into Disneyland's narcissism, as revealed through the story in book three of Ovid's *Metamorphoses*, reveals that there are positive messages to take from the myth as well. This myth tells of a hunter named Narcissus who, though he is renowned for his beauty, is cruel to those who love him. One day, while out on a hunting exposition, he notes his own reflection in a pool, and immediately falls in love with it. Unable to break his own spell, Narcissus cannot pull himself away from his reflection, not even to feed himself, and he eventually falls into the pool and drowns.

Some of the motifs of the myth are found in Disney's version of *Beauty and the Beast*. Jeanne-Marie LePrince de Beaumont originally penned the fairy tale. Disney's version is similar to this retelling of this fairy tale with one telling difference – Beaumont's story focuses on the beast's physicality as repulsive to Belle but Disney's version focuses on his cruelty and anger as his *beastly* qualities. In Disney's version, the tale opens with the story of how the haughty little prince becomes a beast. The prince opens the door to his castle one evening during a bitterly cold night. Outside, he spies a beggar woman, asking for shelter. When he turns her away more than once, the woman reveals herself to be an enchantress, turning him into a beast until he is able to find out what it means to truly love and be loved. As is typical of the storytelling device of fairytales, the beast carries a magical item. He has a mirror, which, as he gazes into it, allows him to see not only his own reflection, but also images of whatever he asks it to show. He lurks in his tower, surrounded by images of himself as he was, which he has torn to shreds. Of course, as the story continues, the beast literally holds Belle captive before finding true love with her.

The image the mirror denotes a similar motif as Narcissus' pool of water. It represents the captivation one feels when making an inward journey – the gaze into one's own soul. When patrons traverse the cobblestones of Main Street, U.S.A., gazing up at the windows with names of Disney Legends painted on them, wander around the *dark rides* of Fantasyland, take "hitchhiking ghosts" with them from *Haunted Mansion*, or shoot the rifles at the range in Frontierland, they are gazing on Disney's own image. And though they may be aware that these representations are idealized and do not truly represent the outside world, they are still transfixed because they accept the perspective of the storytellers as their own. The images presented clearly mirror Disney's mythic messages.

But, Disneyland also contains aspects of the exotic as well. Adventureland, is entirely based on the concept of the exotic Other, whether it is through a trip down an African river on the Jungle Cruise attraction, an introduction to the Polynesian gods at Walt Disney's Enchanted Tiki Room or a quest into the depths of an Indian temple in Indiana Jones Adventure, that which is tantalizingly non-native to California is present at Disneyland. With the development of postmodern American pancultural globalization, this kind of narcissism has become engrained in the collective imagination of the world. And with an emphasis on the development of mass culture and the unique brand of humanism that it brings, Disneyland becomes a temple that belongs not just to Hollywood, but also to all of humanity.

Disneyland suggests that to the Disneyland patron the wholly other is that which stirs the imagination. To those who love the park, stirring the imagination is Disney's unique brand of magic. It is an imaginal reality that all Disney narcissists have in common, the fascination for which, if experienced consciously, can be actualized as a positive one, and not an ever-rising pool of water. As Finch writes:

> Animators before Disney knew that all this was possible, but it was Disney, with his great sense of structure, who was the first to make it work coherently and who had the courage to invent bigger and more spectacular dreams. It was this that made him a great American original: a liberator of the imagination.[164]

Disney's mimetic storytelling takes up the challenge of creating a temple environment to the American mythic imagination. In doing this, Disney offers an animated mirror image of this imagination for the sake of becoming what Walt suggested during the opening day speech might become "a source of inspiration for all the world".[165] For the patron, Disneyland represents all of these things. It represents the American ideal that crafting one's identity and the relationship to one's own imagination does not need to be dictated by the demands of culture or social structure, and it offers, through the physicality of the park, an environment dedicated to interaction with these ideals.

---

164 *Walt Disney's America*, 294.

165 *Disneyland USA*, DVD.

Chapter 4

Disneyland as the Work of Worship

Legend has it that Walt never learned to trust blueprints. Like the old-time carpenter who measures rafters by holding every board in place, he believed in things that looked like they really worked, models he could examine from all sides, objects he could touch and turn over in his hands. – Karal Marling[166]

Archetypal Liturgy

Hillman proposes that human beings create images around them that reflect their sense of the illusive, universal archetypal energies of the soul. He calls this personification, which to him "implies a human being who creates Gods in human likeness much as an author creates characters out of his own personality. These Gods depict his own needs; they are his projections."[167] Disneyland straddles the personal and the universal, participating in Hillman's concept of personification by offering a buffet of archetypal images safely from within the confines of the park. In earlier chapters, we discussed Disneyland's personification as a ritualized temple and the ways in which it is consistent with traditional mythic and religious rituals. As part of that, we considered the hand of the maker in this process of creation. Now, let's focus on the mechanics and details of the park itself.

Disney's myths come together to create a place that is the archetypal image of a container, allowing Disneyland to be a beacon that travels out to the world at large. Once the patrons arrive, the interaction with deeply personal archetypal narratives is the thing that engages them. As a temple, Disneyland is the home

---

166 *Designing Disney's Theme Parks: The Architecture of Reassurance*, 79.

167 *Re-Visioning Psychology,* 12.

of mythic gods or archetypal images that, within this context, exhibit a life of their own. Any criticism of Disneyland as a contrived environment neglects to take into consideration the vitality of the relationship between archetypal images, the poetics of ritual, and individual patrons. The painstakingly detailed work Disneyland's makers engage in would mean nothing if the park didn't resonate on an archetypal level with the patrons. Any time the creative touch of the soul occurs; psychic energy is activated. Because the archetypal is always present in humanity's creative endeavors, an attempt to distill a place like Disneyland down to simple puppet-mastery by corporate sales and marketing is the ultimate in hubris. The power of Disneyland is only threatened if the place becomes too symbolic. If it lacks its ability to change, it loses it psychological fluidity. The park's true magic is present in the crowd as it interacts with rituals imbued with mythic resonance.

Understood from this point of view, participation with Disneyland is its own special kind of liturgy or worship. The word *liturgy* means "public service, service to the gods, public worship".[168] It refers to all the work of the people in the context of what is sacred. In its role as mythic liturgy, Disneyland comes alive with psychic energy through a cornucopia of archetypal choices. It continues making the practice sacred because patrons identify with Disney's images. Park patrons practice this liturgy through the touching of these sacred attraction relics, through the recitation of the litanies of the park, through the donning of ritual vestments, and through the collecting of (and often the making of) souvenirs as iconic representations of the kinds of archetypal images that move their soul. The liturgy of the park offers shrines for the purpose of venerating sacred images, and the merchandising of the Disneyland experience for the remembrance of and identification with Disneyland on home altars. This practice is the heart of liturgy.

Touch a Turnstile, Touch a Relic

A temple is the central location that interprets archetypal material. Broadly speaking, it offers a container for the entrance into the imagination. Disneyland is this kind of central location, bound together through agreed-upon myths where both the gods and the saints of Disney's tradition abide. The park patron engages in a personal relationship with the characters and immersion into their narrative. Disneyland lays out this experience by creating themed environments like the shrines that populate temples and churches throughout the world. The etymological root of the word "shrine" comes from the ancient Latin *scrinium*,[169] referring to a chest reserved for papers and books. This root alludes to the world of the scribe, the myth-maker or poet who creates the images, but it also conjures the image of a container necessary to house the images. A shrine's purpose is to

168 *Oxford English Dictionary* online.

169 *Oxford English Dictionary* online.

ascribe meaning to the images it contains. It is a crossroad where the archetypal becomes the human. If the temple is the holy mountain, the shrine is the summit. When a tradition is alive, the personal is at play within the shrine, offering a specific experience of a culture's interpretation of a specific story.

Small-scale shrines are typically created within a temple for the purpose of relating personally to the gods and/or saints at hand. In the Eastern Orthodox tradition, for example, the iconodule, or "one who serves the purpose/power of the image", creates and venerates the image. Their connection with image is generally expressed through shrines inside chapels or churches in both central and remote locations alike. They venerate the images in the sacred space and take the sacred out of the central location into the mundane spaces of the world. Disneyland's shrines, like other traditional forms of shrine, establish relationship between the patron and characters from within a particular mythic orientation The attractions are housed in Disney's lands, and, like the shrine of a patron saint inside a church, a stained glass window, or a personal god, Disneyland's attractions allow the patron the ability to emotionally connect with the rituals that call to them.

How does it do that? Disneyland consists of eight themed lands – lands that act as smaller chapels that come together to form the greater temple as a whole: Main Street, U.S.A., Adventureland, Frontierland, New Orleans Square, Critter Country, Fantasyland, Toontown, and Tomorrowland. Each one of these lands functions as a shrine *to* an aspect of the American mythic imagination. Each land houses a specific facet of Disney's stories. While developing the original concept of Disney's lands, Walt coined the term *weenies*, which I previously mentioned in chapter three. As iconic centers of the shrine-land to which they belong, Disneyland's weenies are distinct to their land. Within the context of each land, Disneyland develops what they call attractions to define their structure for immersion into narrative. Weenies focus attention toward attractions. In many cases, these attractions are the homes where the characters live. The weenies are the building blocks of the lands as shrine. They stake out the boundaries of each land, and they are crafted in such a way as to allow for a smooth transition from one attraction to another.

Sleeping Beauty's Castle is a weenie. It is one of the focal points of Fantasyland, often suggested to be the heart of the park itself. In fact, if you look down as you pass across the drawbridge and through the gates of the castle, you can see a brass colored nail flush with the cobblestones. This mark draws patrons through the story, as it marks, at least in their imagination, the centermost part of the park.[170] The castle, as is the case with all the other weenies, orients the patron regarding the particular mythic ethos of the place. In the case of Fantasyland, the focus is traditional fairy tale and the transcendent imagination. The castle is home to the princesses and the villains themselves. It defines the boundaries of the land, as

---

170 Although this spot is not quite the center, the image is nonetheless effective.

it reminds the patron that they are about to cross over from Walt's projection of small town America to the realm of ancient story and fairy tale. The buildings that surround it are painted a soothing color palette of pinks and peaches. These colors are meant to be an innocuous way to transition from one part of the story to another, creating definition for the shrines in a way that simultaneously speaks for individual weenies and promote the park as a whole.

By creating distinct shrines to house the different aspects of the Disney imagination, lands allow for a continued experience of re-assurance. The structure of the lands transport the patron through the park and shrink ideological icons to a manageable size, a size that feels comfortable to a culture that doesn't generally feel comfortable having its mythic images to be too big or too powerful for them to control. This personal encounter cultivates an emotional connection between the patron and the mythic energies within the shrines. Tarzan's Treehouse, for example, stands at the top of a 70-foot tall *tree* in the center of Adventureland. It offers the tallest vista point in the park. It can be seen from the corner of Frontierland and across to the center of New Orleans Square. It draws the crowd toward it, as it creates the mood of the land. Like all the other weenies, it is made of vinyl, resin, and concrete, but it creates an illusion of nature. Landscaped with ferns, it immerses the patron into Tarzan's story, effectively creating an image that spills over to the rest of the surrounding land, guiding and moving the psychic energy of the place as it suggests a kind of unified environment for other local attractions.

While Disney's lands are the shrines that house the attractions, the attractions are the container for the experience of the stories. They are the basic building blocks of the shrines as they themselves are symbolic, and as they are the home of relics. The keeping of *relics*, Anglo-Norman word,[171] is central to the traditions of western Christianity; important in this context as it is the root tradition of Walt and many of his animators. Christian relics are holy objects such as bones, hair, and pieces of cloth that tie the owner directly to a holy person, be they a saint, martyr, or even Christ Himself, as is the case with the Shroud of Turin.

Holy relics are often kept in churches, temples and shrines for the purpose of veneration and healing. The guiding concept is universal. It exists in all times, all traditions, and all religions. Archetypal images, on the other hand, are specific. They reflect the energy that collects around the archetypes. They help form an understanding of these powerful energies, for a person, a people group, a nation that would otherwise would remain in the unconscious. Disneyland attractions participate in this tradition becoming both the space that house relics and the relics themselves. In a Spring 2011 edition of *Disney Twenty-Three Magazine*, the sacred nature of Disneyland attractions was explored in an article written by Mark Lark titled "The Elephant in the Room". This article explores Richard Kraft's[172] fabled San Fernando Valley home, dubbed "Kraftland", filled with

171 *Oxford English Dictionary* online.

vintage collectibles from Disneyland. Lark's conversation with Kraft indicates that he experiences Disneyland's attractions as holy relics. He writes:

> I grew up in Bakersfield as a bored child who got an annual trip to Disneyland . . . I would live for the other 364 days by staring at the Disneyland souvenir map on my wall. My older brother was chronically ill with Crohn's disease. Our annual trip to Disneyland took place only when he was healthy. So I have this double positive association with Disneyland. We only went when my family was in good shape . . . When my brother passed away in 1993 I went back. I knew I needed to be at Disneyland. I wanted to smell the water of *Pirates of the Caribbean*, put my hand on the handrails in the queue, hear the *King Arthur Carrousel*. It so reconnected me with my brother. That's when my hardcore collecting really kicked in. Many people, me included, collect for tactile memories. You can look at photos, but actually touching a memory means a lot.[173]

Kraft's collection goes far beyond the collections of snowglobes, photos, and Mickey Ears owned by most patrons. His collection includes the organ from the original Swiss Family Robinson Treehouse, a car from Snow White's Scary Adventures and the Sea Monster from the original Submarine Voyage. Clearly, this kind of collection is not feasible for most patrons, nor is it possible without the right kind of connections with Disney itself, however, his collection does illustrate that the experience of Disneyland is akin to the tradition of relics. The psychological association with place and the mythologized meaning of objects is reflected through the patron's attachment to Disneyland. Through this article, Kraft acts as the voice of the average annual passholder, as well as the yearling whose trip to Disneyland mark a particular occasion. The ability to return to a place imbued with archetypal energy and participate with ritual in that context is an act of recreation. Such is the psychological impact of the relic, whether inside the temple or taken home to continue the ritual via satellite.

One particular example of Disneyland's attractions as relic is present in Fantasyland. Fantasyland, the literal heart of the park, is often considered the most iconic of all Disneyland locations and is the land most often associated with Walt. This section of the park was the first part of Disneyland to reflect Disney's established narrative in attraction form, a process that has since become central to Disney theming. From the point of view of the patron on Main Street, U.S.A., Fantasyland is located at the head of Disneyland. Patrons in Fantasyland can become King Arthur as they pull Excalibur from the stone under Merlin's watchful eye or journey to Wonderland with Alice. Perhaps the clearest example of the Fantasyland attractions as relic, however, is present in Peter Pan's Flight. This attraction is by far the most popular one in Fantasyland. True Disney aficionados and day-trippers alike love it, and though it was present in Fantasyland on opening day, it ranks among the least modified attractions in the Park.

172 Richard Kraft is a Hollywood music agent. His client list includes such Disney talent as Alan Menken, Richard Sherman, and Tim Burton favorite, Danny Elfman.

173 47.

On any given day, patrons line up in a long queue, less themed and more exposed to weather than most, simply for the sake of entering a flying pirate ship for a two-minute ride. Why would they do that? It does not boast amazing thrills like Matterhorn Bobsleds, or Space Mountain. Nor does it have impressive techno-logical advances in storytelling like Indiana Jones or Finding Nemo's Submarine Journey.

The answer is present in the story itself, and Disney's interpretation of it. A fantastically über-mythic Neverland and its characters, Peter Pan and the lost boys – a group of orphans who never grew up – his fairy ally Tinker Bell, a group of pirates hell-bent on killing Peter led by a hook-handed captain, and a group of *Darling* children all sprung from the imagination of Scottish playwright and novelist J. M. Barrie.[174] Peter Pan first appeared in a novel Barrie wrote for adults titled *The Little White Bird*, published shortly after Queen Victoria's death in 1902, a symbolic event that shifted mythic consciousness for both Britain and America. Two years later, Barrie oversaw production of a play that centered entirely on Peter.[175] The play became an immediate success. In 1905, *Peter Pan* opened for American audiences on Broadway. The show toured and at some point between 1909 and 1911 a road show of *Peter Pan* traveled through the American Midwest. When it reached Missouri, a schoolboy named Walt Disney broke his piggy bank to buy tickets for the show. The magic of Neverland had such an effect on Walt that when *Peter Pan* was later chosen for his elementary school play, he auditioned for and landed the role of Peter. His drive to produce his own animated version of *Peter Pan* came early in his career, and he began negotiations to buy the rights to the play as early as 1935.

Perhaps more than any other story in Disney's mythic canon, *Walt Disney's Peter Pan* embodies Disney's guiding narrative: the primacy of the imagination and the role of adults in the realm of the child. Since his creation, Peter has been a subject of fascination for the public, eventually becoming a topic of psychologi-cal speculation, as he has often been interpreted as an archetypal image of the *Puer Aeternus*. Peter is the embodiment of the child complex, an archetypal image for those struggling with identity in a changing world. For an adult Walt, he symbolizes childlike wonder, curiosity, and bliss. Embracing these charac-teristics was deeply personal for both Barrie and Disney. Both of these men led complicated, often eccentric lives punctuated by their obsession with childhood. Barrie's unhappy marriage, the death of his beloved Sylvia Llewelyn Davies, and rumors of sexual impropriety with his adopted sons[176] and Disney's traumatic childhood, tumultuous career, and obsession with innovation left these creative geniuses hyper-aware of the soul's need for the return to the carefree state of

---

174 Film icon, and Disney pirate Johnny Depp immortalized J. M. Barrie in the 2004 film *Finding Neverland*. This film, directed by Marc Forster, is based on Alan Knee's play *The Man Who Was Peter Pan*.

175 J.M. Barrie, *Peter Pan, or the Boy Who Wouldn't Grow Up*.

176 Andrew Birkin, *J. M. Barrie and the Lost Boys*.

childhood, an return that is achieved through Disney's most enduring symbol of the freedom and tenacity of imagination – Tinker Bell, the spirit guide of Disneyland.

As a symbol of the imagination conveyed through the traditions of Walt's Scots-Irish heritage, it makes sense that the fairy is placed in this role. Fairies have an ancient history in the folklore of Ireland and Britain. According to British folklorist K. M. Briggs's book *The Fairies in Tradition and Literature*, a long history has been attributed to fairies as the harbingers of daily tasks and rituals. Fairies are often conceived of as the people of old, the immortal races that lived before humanity. They are often thought of as unseen helpers or workers. Briggs notes "Skill in various crafts is often a gift of the fairies". Fairies, such as the Leprechaun in Ireland are often thought of as the invisible craftsmen of the pastoral. Much like the gypsy "Tinkers" that roam the countryside even today, fairies are responsible for fixing broken machines, tools, and household items. Their magical abilities, however, also make them a facilitator for healing. Fairies are often credited for human abilities and the presence of the miraculous in life. As an image that participates in this folk tradition, Tinker Bell is the often unseen force behind the scenes, making magic happen. Her *pixie dust* is the catalyst for Disney magic She lightens the soul, allowing psychological heaviness to dissipate so the soul can "fly".

In her role as Disneyland's spirit guide, she helps Peter Pan defeat Captain Hook. She crosses the boundaries of fantasy and reality when she arrives on the *Disneyland* television show. Tink is never more than a shout away. Walt often calls upon her to sprinkle pixie dust on his show. She is a feminine hermetic image; always willing to share her magic with those Walt asks her to help. In contemporary Disneyland, Tinker Bell's home, Pixie Hollow is an attraction that allows the patron to join her in her natural habitat. Entry into Tink's Fantasyland means access to the deepest level of the fairy realm. This ethos finds ultimate fulfillment in Fantasyland as it seeks to encapsulate the litany engraved on the Fantasyland plaque that, although Walt approved it, was never placed in Fantasyland itself:

> Here is the world of imagination, hopes and dreams. In this timeless land of enchantment, the age of chivalry, magic and make believe are reborn – and fairy tales come true. Fantasyland is dedicated to the young and the young-at-heart – to those who believe that when you wish upon a star, your dreams do come true.

The attraction reflects this sentiment. Imagineers begin to consider the way they want the patron to experience an attraction by choosing a mythic point of origin. Since the intention of attractions is to place the patron in complete identification with the characters in the story, point of view is of central importance. If the point of view is off, the attraction struggles. Snow White's Scary Adventures, for example, is often confuses patrons because the story is told from Snow White's point of view, rather than an omniscient third person like the film. Because this point of view was fixed in the minds of the Imagineers, there was no representation of Snow White in the original attraction, leading patrons to be confused as to the character with which they should identify. Although the Imagineers eventually did include a representation of the princess in the attraction, the intention remains the same: to tell the story from an established point of view.

Peter Pan's Flight does an effective job of creating both point of view and mythic orientation. Its point of view is reflected in the reprise of the movie's song *You Can Fly*.

"When there's a smile in your heart. There's no better time to start. Think of all the joy you'll find. When you leave the world behind. And bid your cares goodbye. You can fly! You can fly! You can fly!" Why fly? Flying is freedom. In myth, the motif of flying often represents transmission between parallel worlds. The Greek tradition has Hermes with his winged sandals, which allows him to transmit the messages of the gods. Likewise, in Norse mythology, Thor's helmet bears wings, which is representative of his role as Odin's champion. Winged fairies like Tinker Bell share this motif. In the context of ritualized relics, Peter Pan's Flight effects a shift in consciousness when the patron, adult, or child, *becomes* a Peter, a Darling child, or a lost boy.

The ultimate expression of this shift occurs when the patron enters Pan's flying pirate ship and goes off to Neverland. This attraction suggests that any kind of darkness can be overcome by the power of the imagination and the innocent joys of childhood. This message makes Peter Pan's Flight a defining attraction of Fantasyland, and explains both its popularity and minimal modification. The attraction sprinkles pixie dust on the patron's ability to experience the park, applying the healing balm of the fairies to otherwise world-weary adults and enthusiastic children, initiating them all into Disney's tradition of childlike wonder. Imagineers use the entire experience of the attraction as relic. As a reflection of Disney's role in Hollywood, they are aware that identification with narrative begins as soon as the threshold is crossed. Never willing to let an opportunity slip by, Disney Imagineers set up the reality-illusion of the story as soon as the patron crosses the queue entrance. In doing so, they make the queue itself an experience of relic.

Star Tours, Disney's foray into George Lucas's *Star Wars* epic, is one of the park's clearest examples of this. *Star Tours* opened in Tomorrowland at Disneyland in 1987. It has been a guest favorite ever since. It closed in July 2010 for an extensive renovation that included the addition of 3D technology, as well as the addition of over 50 different revolving storylines. A patron would now be required to visit the attraction over 100 times in order to begin to have a chance to see the same story more than once. In doing this, Disney not only ensures the lasting freshness of the show for *Star Wars* fans, who are some of the most loyal fans of myth on earth, but also allows the attraction to expand inclusion of a broader spectrum of *Star Wars* characters. Upon entering the attraction, one enters an aircraft hanger queuing up through an area much like an airport, with timetables on electronic screens and dutiful droids busily making sure that the equipment remains operational.

Patrons file up the queue, taking in this experience of their favorite travel companions. After reaching the front of the queue, they then take in the safety spiel from the spaceport flight attendants. Of course, the flight attendant speaks to the patron from the screen, emphasizing technology as a tool for protection. All of this preparation is not simply preparation. It begins the process of immersion into the story. This kind of theming is one of the defining differences between Disneyland and other amusement parks. One is not simply a patron standing in a long queue waiting for a thrill ride. The patron *is* a Jedi waiting at a spaceport for a familiar trip. The audio-animatronic droids in the Star Tours queue recognize the patrons and respond to them, making the patrons both a vital feature of the Disneyland story as well as part of Lucas's mythology as well.

With a Smile and a Song

In the context of worship, a litany is a series of calls and repeats between the parishioners and the priesthood or clergy. From the ancient Greek meaning *supplication*, litany suggests a request for something. It generally consists of listing numerous petitions. Litany creates worship through utterance. Ancient mythic traditions have often centered around the generative aspects of the word. The opening sequence of Genesis one reflects this: "Then God said, 'Let there be light', and there was light / And God saw that it was good".[177] Language is often attributed to the power of the divine, and as such, myth shares this attribution. Whether in sacred text or the fireside tradition of oral storytelling, language conveys revelation from the divine. Hillman writes "To be in a mythos is to be inescapably linked with divine power, and moreover to be in mimesis with them.[178] The divine lives in language. Humans have intrinsic knowledge of this. One can feel the power of speech, listening and participating with it. This power manifests in the ability to destroy someone or heal them with just one word. The ability to change a person's consciousness, to create or destroy a cosmology for them, is a true power of language.

Our gods speak to us and for us. Since language is a major source of human communication, God's language, and the power of this language, is integral to how human beings develop knowledge. Hossein Ziai reminds us of this when he writes that the Koran states, "God said to it, 'Be!' and it was".[179] In the book of John, the Bible tells us: "In the beginning the Word already existed. He was with God, and he was God. He was in the beginning with God. He created

177 Genesis 1:3–4.

178 *Healing Fiction*, 11.

179 "Beyond Philosophy: Suhrawardi's Illuminationist Path to Wisdom", qtd. in Ziai, 223.

everything there is. Nothing exists that he didn't make. Life itself was in him, and this life gives light to everyone [...]. So the Word became human and lived here on earth among us.[180]

The word is the generative utterance, whether it is sacred text read aloud or the creative utterance of the Sanskrit *Om*. This creative utterance is a vital aspect of the act of ritual, and thus the recitation of sacred litanies is a vital aspect of the practice of ritual. This sacred act continues to circulate spiritual energies in motion. Sacred traditions of nearly all kinds argue that there is power in the speaking of a name. There are countless other examples of a human mythological, spiritual, and philosophical understanding of the transforming power of communication, and not only do our gods speak to us, they speak through us. This is why we participate in litany. Two aspects of litany are particularly potent in the context of Disneyland. First is the role and presence of the Imagineers, cast members, and the characters in the attractions as a kind of priesthood leading the patron through the experience. This is the work of the priesthood: to create, facilitate, and organize the ritual for the sake of the participants of the ritual. Secondly, the essential function of musical repetition in the soundtrack of the park creates an environment for the memorization and recitation of litany amongst patrons.

The Animatronic Priesthood

Walt Disney's Enchanted Tiki Room opened on June 23, 1963. It is the first attraction at Disneyland to feature a new technology known as audio-animatronics, mechanized characters that engage the audience seemingly independent of living cast members. The presence of audio-animatronics is not intended to replace or usurp the place of the human cast members in the context of the show. Audio-animatronics and human cast members work together in harmony to create the show. Many have spoken out against these stereotyped, misappropriated mid-20th-century cersions of Polynesian gods, and rightly so. But remember that other characters suggested to be Irish, German, Mexican, and French. They caricatured and are also intended to be silly. In an essay on illusion and simulation in Walt Disney's Enchanted Tiki Room, Craig Svonkin argues that an attraction that cultivates an environment, which is "inauthentic, but fantastic".[181] The environment, created in the early 60s when tiki culture was the height of sophistication, is not realistic. It is a caricature of an island reality, and if it's damagingly so that is for those of Hawaiian heritage to judge. In the context of Disney culture, these audio-animatronic birds of Walt Disney's Enchanted Tiki Room culture effectively create a dependable, re-creatable litany for the patron. Because they are mechanized and recorded, the birds of the Tiki Room recreate the show in an identical fashion every time, removing the need for

180 John 1: 1–4, 14.

181 "A Southern California Boyhood in the Simu-Southland Shadows of Walt Disney's Enchanted Tiki Room", 108.

thinking from the process of recitation. Their vocalizations are exact, down to the last lilt and note.

The patron enters the waiting area of the attraction and is treated to a preshow. The Hawaiian pantheon begins the story of Walt Disney's Enchanted Tiki Room. This is transportation to the islands through the ultimate in Disney kitsch. The gods, invoked by the sounds of the Tiki drums, introduce themselves through a scripted narrative heralded by the flow of water, wind, and rain.[182] This preshow initiates and sets the mood for the audience, transforming the atmosphere from the dry desert winds of Southern California to the trade winds of the Polynesian Islands.

The preshow goes as follows:

Drum solo:

Maui:[183] "My name is Maui. Natives call me the mighty one. I tame the playful sun, and gave my people time. Now they set their clocks by mine. For I am tropic standard time."

Koro: "Aloha! Wahine kâkou Mana.[184] I am Koro, Midnight Dancer. Today, my magic feet no move, my head sore. But last night, all Tiki gods have big time. Some luau. When drums begin to pound, my head full, big sound."

Rongo: "Ua mau ke ea o ka aina I ka pono.[185] Me Rongo, god of agriculture. My land so good to me, I got time for sport. I fly kite. Me number one kite flyer. Too bad I no have teeth. Then me, I find electricity."

Pele: "I am Pele, goddess of fire and volcanoes. Some say I torment poor Ngendei the earth balancer. For when my violent temper rises, the earth trembles on its foundation."

Ngendei: "Legends say I'm balancing the earth, but sad to say I'm just hanging on".

Pele: "I'm the one who's really sad.

For when I smile it comes out mad."

Tangaroa-Ru: "They call me Tangaroa-Ru, the east wind".

Hina: "And, I am Hina, goddess of rain".

Tangaroa-Ru: "We often travel together wind and rain through tropic lands across the seven seas".

Hina: "Come closer, so that you may see what magic there is in fantasy".

Tangaroa: "I am Tangaroa; father of all gods and goddesses. Here in this land of enchantment, I appear before you as a mighty tree. Stand back.

Oh mystic powers hear my call. From my limbs, let new life fall."[186]

---

182 For more on the written texts of Hawaiian Mythology, visit: http://sacred-texts.com/pac/hm/index.htm

183 For a audio transcript of the preshow: http://disney-pal.com/Disneyland/enchanted_tiki_room_queue_details.htm.

184 May there be love between us (humanity and the divine).

185 This is the state motto of Hawaii, which means "The life of the land is preserved in righteousness". http://www.oitc.com/Disney/disneyland/Secrets/Adventure/Tiki.html

186 For an interview with early imagineer Rolly Crump about his inspiration for the Tiki gods, visit: http://www.disneydispatch.com/content/columns/the-truth-of-the-matter-is/2011/rolly-crump-pleases-the-tiki-gods/.

Once the gods have spoken and the doors open, the narrator announces a welcome. The audience shuffles into a symmetrical theater, and after a few moments and announcements, the human cast member comes out to note that José,[187] the host, has fallen asleep again. The audience is admonished to wake him up, and as they chant, "Wake up José", he offers a "Buenos Días" to the crowd. When Walt originally envisioned this attraction, he wanted a restaurant, a place where people could experience the dinner theater environment that was a hit of the era. Eventually, the idea of food was ejected, in favor of a show where people would focus on a shorter fifteen-minute show that could be recorded, mechanized, and controlled. The litany begins with the first song, *In the Tiki, Tiki, Tiki, Tiki, Tiki Room.*[188] The show invokes the call and response nature of the animal, and in particular, the aviary world. The audience is placed in identification with nature itself, a place where "all the birds sing words and the flowers croon" as though they were sitting under a shelter they had just built in the wilds of a Polynesian island.

As soon as the audience is captivated by the repetitive nature of the first song, the show launches into the next song, *Let's all Sing Like the Birdies Sing.* A mesmerizing, brightly hued "enchanted fountain" springs up from the floor, and a "bird mobile" comes down from the ceiling with "the girls".[189] This time the audience is asked to participate. The birds begin the song:

> Let's all sing like the birdies sing.
> Tweet, tweet, tweet, tweet, tweet
> Let's all sing like the birdies sing.
> Sweet, sweet, sweet, sweet, sweet.
> Let's all warble like nightingales.
> Give your throat a treat.
> Take your time from the birds.
> Now you all know the words.
> Tweet, tweet, tweet, tweet, tweet.

Again the repetitive nature of the song soothes the audience, and makes for a familiarizing, soothing experience. Next the flowers burst into action. Orchids come down from the ceiling, singing a peaceful Hawaiian tune. Birds of paradise join the orchids as the natural world joins the aviary world in song. Music places the audience in complete identification with the natural world, and the song picks up the pace as the soundtrack turns to drumming.

Drumming is a traditional part of the process of making rituals of recitation. Drums play a vital part in trance, a dream-like state that is linked to hypnosis and is a traditional ecstatic practice in ritual. Walt Disney's Enchanted Tiki

---

187 Voiced by Disney legend Wally Boag.

188 Written by Disney's favorite Sherman brothers.

189 Female singers: Collette, Fifi, Gigi, Susette, Mimi, and Josephine. These singers reflect the typical sweet, full vibrato sound popular in the early 60s.

Room itself comes to life, illuminating drummers above the seating areas. The drummers are joined in chant by totems on the wall that also illuminate as their features move and sing. As the room is imbued with spirit, the animatronic birds and flowers join the drummers and tikis in a frenzied song combination of voice, drum, and birdcalls. Suddenly, the thunder claps and the lights go out. Michael, the Irish parrot, admonishes the audience to be careful because "all this celebrating" has angered the gods. After a song of "farewell and aloha", the exit door on the opposite side of the theater opens, and the audience is ushered out to a slightly modified version of the iconic tune *Heigh-Ho* from *Snow White and the Seven Dwarfs*.

This entire attraction is a guided ritual of repetition. With such a long history in the park, one would anticipate that there would have been script changes made over the years. But Walt Disney's Enchanted Tiki Room is one of the most beloved attractions in all of Disneyland. In fact, it bears the honor of being the only attraction in Disneyland history to have an F ticket related to, and specifically developed for the it. Until 1982, Disney sold separate tickets for their attractions. The alphabetical association of the ticket with attraction designated how exciting the show was for that attraction. Generally, the tickets only went up to E. Walt Disney's Enchanted Tiki Room was so popular it required a new kind of ticket. At least until October 1966 when plans for New Orleans Square went into effect, it had their own separate booth, its own separate tickets, and its own separate price. This indicates its popularity with guests, as well as Disney's sensibility that this attraction was a whole new kind of experience. The soundtrack of this mechanical *priesthood* is a source of comfort for many Disney patrons. Each time a visitor returns; they are treated to this attraction that recreates the tikis of yesteryear.

The mechanical birds, flowers, totems, and tikis lead the audience through Disney's own version of a sacramentalized liturgical practice. By delivering consistency, they deliver reassurance. Consistency is so vital to the success of many of these attractions that if and when Imagineering does make a change to a part of the attraction, there is an immediate outcry among those who love the park and subscribe to the experience of it as a personal mythic ritual. This is particularly potent in the contemporary moment when Twitter accounts, blogs, and websites send out messages instantaneously and have demonstrated the ability to effect change in Disney policy. The dogged clinging to the continuity of attractions proves their function as a guiding structure for the development of the audience's devotion. They literally lead the audience through Disney's stories, as the recitation imprints on the soul in a deeper way than a live show ever could.

Across the Small World and the Bayou

Walt Disney's Enchanted Tiki Room soundtrack is so great that repetitive music expressed through a cast of mechanized characters, subtly controlled by cast members soon became the recipe for other attractions destined to become Disney animation's classics. The next opportunity to use audio-animatronics came in 1964 when Walt Disney was approached to craft a series of exhibits for the New York World's Fair.[190] As previously noted, Disney handed the project to one of his favorite artists, Mary Blair. Commissioned in honor of UNICEF,[191] this attraction was intended to be a gift to the children of the world. The resulting creation is It's a Small World, an attraction that continues to draw audiences today with its nearly 300 audio-animatronics representing over 100 different nations. Walt decided that since the look of the attraction and its subsequent audio-animatronics were so spectacular, the attraction required a song that was equally spectacular. It had to be simple but infectious, a song that encapsulates the sentiment of the attraction while providing continuity for the attraction as a whole.

For a song that captures the guiding ethos of the entire Disneyland experience, Walt turned to his favorite songwriters, Richard and Robert Sherman whom he famously dubbed *The Boys*. In 1964, the Sherman brothers had just begun their careers. With the Cold War at its most tense and the Cuban Missile crisis a recent memory, the Disney Imagineers working on It's a Small World was eager to promote a message of peace and tolerance through diversity. They wanted the attraction to be a message, as well as homage, to all the children of the world. Richard Sherman admits that the song was originally written as a slow ballad. He calls it a *prayerful piece*, suggesting that it should start slowly and then move to an up-tempo as it goes to the chorus. He plays a bit of it, upping the tempo toward the end of the chorus.[192]

The tempo they chose indicates that the composers were aware of the liturgical aspect of their work. But Walt saw something different. He insisted that the entire piece be up-tempo. With its simple theme and catchy hook, "It's a Small World After All" is Disneyland's true litany. It sticks with the patron. Whether one despises it or adores it, all Disney patrons know it. From an ego-consciousness point of view, that is, from the point of view of identity and the way Disney wishes to present itself mythically, and frankly, it works. Guests internalize this message. It's a mantra for humanity in a world that often seems full of alienation and destruction. The repetition of this litany, though often complained about, serves to attend to a need for comfort and peace. It reminds us that our differences hold the key to building tolerance and appreciation for one another.

If Disney consciously crafts this kind of statement in their liturgy, it stands to reason that the mirror image of this sentiment is also required to find its way

---

190 Those attractions became known as Illinois' Great Moments With Mr. Lincoln, General Electric's Progressland, Ford's Magic Skyway, and the UNICEF/Pepsi sponsored, It's a Small World.

191 United Nations Children's Emergency Fund. http://www.unicef.org

192 *Disneyland Resort: Behind the Scenes*. These lyrics are available on Google. They are under copyright. They can be found at the url: http://www.stlyrics.com/songs/d/disney6472/itsasmallworld512140.html

into the established canon of attractions. Unlike It's a Small World, New Orleans Square is not connected to some kind of grand cultural fair outside of Disneyland. Since the early days of the studio, Walt was fascinated by the city of New Orleans. On a personal vacation to New Orleans, he bought a music box of mechanical birds that eventually inspired the idea for the audio-anima-tronic birds of Walt Disney's Enchanted Tiki Room. He found the mysterious atmosphere of New Orleans to be full of magic. When he approached his Imagineering staff with a new land in the mid 1960s,[193] it soon became clear that New Orleans would be its subject. As a city suspended between the cultures of West Africa, Spain, France, and indigenous North American peoples with religious traditions as syncretic as the religions of the Creole, New Orleans Square has always represented the space where social reversals reign. In Disney's version of New Orleans, every day is (a tame and sanitized) Mardi Gras.

The pirates express this sentiment. The Imagineers were aware that their patrons would respond to the presence of music. However, in this case, Walt chose a different move than he had with It's a Small World. He decided to hand the project to an Imagineer with no experience in song writing: Disney Legend and Imagineer Xavier (X) Atencio. Instead of a litany so simple and so childlike as in the case of It's a Small World, Atencio pens a piece that is more complex, darker, and much more pirate-like. With several verses punctuated by repetitive response lines, this piece is crafted more like a traditional litany.[194] Although few Disney patrons make their way through the pirate caves singing every word of the verses, everyone sings "Yo Ho". The pirates call to response "Drink up me hearties, Yo Ho" evokes the traditional pub pieces, often referred to as *Shanty Songs* that this is intended to emulate. It is a rousing call to all pirates present, which, in traditional Disney attraction style, includes the patron first of all. One last thing to note: Walt died during the building of New Orleans Square. Who knows how he would have tinkered with the attractions had he lived?

The Spoken Recitation

The foreboding mansion at the furthermost corner of New Orleans Square is also home to another example of Disney litany. The murky quality of New Orleans as a place gives way to the presence of the supernatural. However, this gloomy environment still seems to transmit some kind of welcoming energy as the patron ventures through the queue and into the dark waiting area. An eerie voice encourages the "foolish mortals" visiting to enter a circular parlor room. As he reminds the visitors that there is "no turning back now", the room fills and the doors close. The ghost host continues, "our tour begins here in this

---

193 Unveiled on the Disneyland 10th Anniversary Television Show.

194 These lyrics are available on Google. They are under copyright. They can be found at: http://www.stlyrics.com/songs/d/disney6472/apirateslifeformeyoho246486.html

gallery where you see paintings of some of our guests as they appeared in their corruptible, mortal state". As the narrator continues his spiel, the pictures begin to stretch. As they lengthen, the pictures show stories that are not nearly as refined as the un-stretched images. In fact, these pictures show their subjects in twisted circumstances. A woman in a ballerina skirt holds a parasol as she stands on a tightrope over an alligator. A man in a coat is shown to have no pants as he stands over a barrel of dynamite. A woman with a rose sits on a tombstone. Men stand on each other's shoulders as they sink in quicksand. The host's spiel continues as follows:

> Your cadaverous pallor betrays an aura of foreboding; almost as if you sense a disquieting metamorphosis. Is this haunted room actually stretching or is it your imagination? Hmmmm? And consider this dismaying observation. This room has no windows and no doors, which offers you this chilling challenge: TO FIND A WAY OUT! **'Evil laughter'** Of course, there's always MY way. . . **'cut lights and scream'**.

This spiel is the subject of recited litany among Disney patrons. Much like prayers recited in temples or churches, the script is recited in this enclosed, sacred space. When one visits this attraction, one never fails to hear fellow subscribers to the cult of Disney vocalizing along with the ghost host. The timing and precision of the spiel, right down to the lilt of the voice and the cackle are repeated to perfection. The audible giggles around the room serve as a kind of badge of honor among the initiated. And it seems never to get old or die.

Collecting the Sacred Souvenir

Icons are defined as sacred images. In fact, the word *icon* is the Greek term for image. The poetic rendering of image is often experienced through the context of a location dedicated to worship. Indeed, the veneration of images is often central to the experience of temple. As previously discussed, the fusion of myth to image is central to the making holy of a place. Making images is an expression of the soul's ritual impulses. It is inextricably linked to the traditions of worship. Even in the most iconoclastic traditions that abhor the image, some kind of image is fashioned to make a place holy. In such a tradition, the temple, mosque, or church itself becomes the image. Islam, in particular, has a beautiful tradition of crafting the word as image. In this context, the language becomes the holy reference for contemplation, which is the function of icon. Michael Quenot writes, "in Islamic art, geometric principles coupled with an ingenious sense of rhythm seek to evoke limitless space – infinity – a symbol of the divine presence".[195] He suggests that icons denote beauty, and that through this beauty humanity experiences the divine. Icons, therefore, are defined as sacred images that function as objects of spiritual contemplation.

---

195 *The Icon: Window on the Kingdom*, 66.

Theory about ancient icons delves deeply into traditional uses of images, the making of them and the politics of them. Icons have been, and continue to be, the source of religious controversy as they are also defined as something precious, a souvenir or a memento kept and taken away by the devoted follower when they return home from the temple. They are icono-poetic remembrances of the experience. Quenot continues:

> In secular art, the original work and its 'worth' reflects the personality of the artist. In a way, it is something like the materialization of his thoughts and his vision of the world. Public recognition then demands new creations, plus the artist's effort constantly to innovate and surpass himself; furthermore, shrewdly planned exhibitions become a very sly form of publicity ... The iconographer nurtures his art both from Tradition and from the teachings of the Church. His personality must efface itself before the personality represented on the icon.[196]

It would be easy, therefore, to disregard any sacred aspect of Disney's images. One may question the presence of kitsch and caricature in the images, suggesting that these distort the images and strip any sacred presence from them. As caricature, Disney's images are often relegated to child's play and therefore are not taken seriously. As images intended to develop a correlation between play and the sacred, Disney's images must take the traditions of iconopoesis, aesthetics, and iconography into consideration.

Typically, the lines between sacred and secular art are clear. Sacred art does not represent secular enterprises. They are two entirely different spheres. However, with the return of the word *mythic* to our cultural lexicon, the vital necessity of imagination has returned to humanity's sense of what constitutes sacred. Globalization and an environment of religious pluralism are responsible for dissolving many of the boundaries between religions. A distrust of what is known as organized religions has caused many to look outside traditional religious traditions for spiritual and psychic nourishment. In a circumstance such as this, the designation of sacred is present in any images that truly house the archetypal, numinous energy of the soul. These images become symbols of archetypal interpretations, and as such they surpass their intended, merchandizing ego consciousness, resonating with the patrons on the deepest level of the unconscious.

Disney's images are the height of secular art, but their effects on the patrons who cling to them resonate with both the heart and soul on an archetypal level. Through the psychological meaning attributed to them, Disney collectibles become more than just a physical manifestation of the consumption of a place. They represent characteristics of archetypal emotions, relationships, and institutions that the patrons value. They allow the patron to fuse Disney's mythic canon of messages with a tangible experience of a container for these myths and (perhaps more importantly) to take home these images for the sake of remem-

---

196 Ibid., 71.

brance and immersion into the sacred experience in their profane lives. Collectibles - or, as they are often called, Disneyana - identify one as an insider to the outside world in much the same way as the images that decorate other kinds of home shrines. In their home environment, they invoke the energies they represent.

Selfies, Snapshots, and Icons of Light

Many of the earliest icons were made through visual art, particularly painting. Disney often employs the artistic sensibility of sacred painters in its iconic images on canvas. Light, shadow, and gradations of color are tools used by the painter of the image to express a message. Quenot writes, "light is *the* theme of iconography".[197] Disney employs Thomas Kinkade, the late artist famously dubbed the *Painter of Light*, to create icons of the parks and the character, many of which are present for sale at Disneyland. Kinkade expresses his sense that his work is an expression of icon on his website when he writes, "My mission as an artist is to capture those special moments in life adorned with beauty and light. I work to create images that project a serene simplicity that can be appreciated and enjoyed by everyone. That's what I mean by sharing light."[198] Kinkade associates his work with the sacred, often also depicting images inspired by verses from the Bible.

Likewise, secular masters such as Andy Warhol have also committed Disney images to canvas. In fact, Andy Warhol was fascinated with the image of Mickey Mouse, and one of his most famous renderings of Mickey was a black and white titled *Myths: Mickey Mouse*. Warhol was not the only one. He wasn't even the first one, as Roy Lichtenstein was the first fine artist to paint Mickey (and Donald Duck) due to a dare from his son, who brandished a Disney comic and asked his dad if he thought he could do any better. It was the first of his incredibly iconic series of paintings based on comic books. Clearly, the images of Disney's canon has been the subject of all kinds of artistic mediums. All different kinds of paintings – oil, watercolor, and acrylic – are displayed for sale in the park. These paintings, like those commissioned by Renaissance clergy, are available for those who have the funds to put into the temple. For those who cannot afford pieces of fine art, Disneyland offers printed versions like the printed images of saints and gods available at sacred locations across the world.

Like paintings, photographs are images held sacred by Disney patrons, and like icons, analog photographs are images produced by the chemical interplay between light, film, and the camera lens. Digital images are made up of pixels, tiny unit increments of different colors that, much like the creation of an icon, come together to produce an image. Disney merchandisers recognize the importance of photographs in the creation of memory. Since the inception of the

197 Ibid., 106.

198 http://www.thomaskinkadecompany.com/general_pages.asp?id=2000503

park, photography has been inextricably linked with the Disneyland experience. Kodak was one of the earliest sponsors of Disneyland.[199]

An established business since 1888, Kodak was a natural fit with Disneyland. Their early commercials on the Disneyland Television Show suggest, perhaps not so subtly, that collecting photographic images is vital to the experience. As suggested by Bob Iger, president and chief operating officer of Disney, "We are excited to continue this long-standing relationship and look forward to many more years working closely with our friends at Kodak to encourage imaginative imaging offerings to our guests".[200] In other words, Kodak's technology is the tool that paints Disney patrons' images. It's their company that is meant to be representative of the numinous memories the patron experiences. Although their partnership ended in 2012, all forms of photography continue to be a central to Disneyland.

Picture frames are available in the park for sale, offering prefabricated, decorative avenues for the display of the sacred family memories. These frames always bear some kind of representation of Disney imagery, whether it is Mickey Mouse, the Castle, the Princesses, or perhaps the most intriguingly, a description of *The first time I visited Disneyland*. Picture frames juxtapose personal park images against images of the Disney merchandizing machine. The creation of these kind of images brings further identification with Disney characters home, as it allows the images to be present in the patron's daily life, reminding them of the time when they walked among the animated characters of Disney's pantheon.

Holy Fluffiness

Another subset of Disney's most popular icons is their stuffed dolls and stuffed toys. Dolls and toys translate Disney's environment of holy play into a post-park environment. They encourage the continuation of sacred play. Toys are often taken for granted, assumed to have no deeper meaning other than the entertainment of children, but that is not the case. Toys have always held a vital position in the development of sacred culture. In their book, on religion and toys, Nikki Bado-Fralick and Rebecca Sachs Norris note that there is often more to dolls than meets the eye.

> Today, dolls are typically defined as small three-dimensional figures resembling human beings and used as toys or playthings for children. But the earliest dolls were not exclusively or even primarily for children, and likely had numerous and multidimensional meanings, including religious or cultic ones in which they would have played a significant role in both mythology and ritual practice within their various cultures.[201]

199 *Disneyland: Secrets, Stories and Magic* DVD.

200 http://www.kodak.com/US/en/corp/infoImaging/disney.shtml

201 *Toying with God: The World of Religious Games and Dolls*, 32.

As objects of cultic worship, dolls and stuffed toys are a traditional store of archetypal energy. They are imbued with the power of the gods and are used as pedagogical tools for children. William Wells Newell writes that dolls also serve as the physical manifestation of the soul and as an aid to the child in developing acceptance of the movement of the soul to afterlife. He notes that dolls have been found in and near temples, tombs, and shrines.[202] It would be a mistake to assume that dolls and toys can be distilled down to simple play or indoctrination. Like painting, photographs, and statues, dolls are religious icons. Because they are objects of play, they are living expressions of psychic energies. As such, they have the potential to fulfill these needs of adults as well. Bado-Fralick and Norris continue quoting doll historian Max Boehn suggesting that

> [. . .] for adults the doll '[. . .] possessed an occult significance with mystical-magical associations which in an inexplicable way united the present with the past and reached deep into the world of the unseen'. Dolls around the world have been adored as figures or idols of goddesses and gods and have acted as ancestors, offerings, fetishes, amulets, talismans and scapegoats [. . .] Clearly our modern conception of dolls as merely children's playthings needs adjustment.[203]

Dolls can serve as a ritual prop that shares the soul's characteristics. The miniaturization of prodigious images allows both children and adults to engage with their own souls in a way that is significant without being overwhelming. Like the doll, the plush toy is a central product sold at Disneyland. Mickey and Minnie, Donald and Goofy, Cheshire Cat, Princesses, even the broom from *Fantasia*, all of these characters have been sold in the form of the plush toy. Squishy, squashy, and fluffy, these toys express a basic need to offer images that provide comfort to children and nostalgia to adults.

One distinction remains between collectibles and dolls meant for children to play with. Dolls like plushes, action figures, and Barbie-like dolls are made to be torn apart, brushed, slept with, and dragged through the dirt. They are icons that live life with the patrons, often being washed so many times that they lose stitching or have parts broken off. Regardless of how broken they may become, they imbue the sacred into the mundane parts of life by reminding toy owners of the special memories of Disneyland. By contrast, collectibles such as Precious Moments statues and dolls made by particular Disney artists do the opposite. They are made to stay on the shelf or in the cabinet. They are objects that remind the patron of the mythic ideal, much like Plato's ideal of forms. They exist both in the world and yet somehow transcendent of it for the sake of giving the patron an icon to gaze upon, and escape into as they remember their own personal Disney magic.

202 *Games and Songs of American Children*, 29–30.

203 Ibid., 33.

Mickey's Animal Totems

One of Walt Disney's most enduring quotes is "I only hope that we never lose sight of one thing – that it was all started by a mouse".[204] The mouse that began as a clever troublemaker has developed into an icon of freedom and the tenacity of the human spirit. Disney merchandise has always evoked the animal realism. Animal totems date back to the earliest days of humanity. Images of sacred animals adorn Neolithic caves and churches. They also represent political structures and other secular institutions. Myth and icon scholar Elizabeth Terzian suggests that, in the Eastern Orthodox tradition of Christianity, the animal world fully participates in the creation of the sacred icon. The hair of the boar, ox, nanny goat, and the squirrel are all used, as well as egg yolk, oyster shell, bone, and fish glue. She writes that, "It is a mysterious poesis that works in depth through each organ, cell and individual characteristic each animal has to offer".[205] Humanity often expresses the archetypal through the characteristics and instincts of animals. Disney's earliest iconic animated characters are all animals. The animal realm represents both the deeply physical nature of ritual and the complete shift in consciousness necessary in order to experience the sacred.

Animals are the subject of many of the Disney characters that become toys. The rabbit, mouse, the dog, the duck, and the horse constitute Disney's central and founding icons. Dogs and cats, humanity's closest animal companions, are ever present in Disney films. Even when human characters are the central characters of Disney stories, their animal companions steal the show, often becoming the more likely candidates for merchandising. Plush toys are rarely sold in human form.[206] Whether it is Mickey Mouse as the sorcerer, the Cheshire Cat as the trickster, Dumbo as the underdog, or Maximus[207] as the warrior, these stuffed totems are imbued with the archetypal energy of human experience.

The Princess Bloc and The Wicked Cackle

One of Jungian thought's central concerns is the presense of femininity in the soul of humanity and the way it finds its expression in myth. Jungians are currently in the process of expanding traditional Jungian definitions of gender so rigidly enforced by Jung's modernist sensibilities. Current Jungians often orient from a feminist perspective that understands femininity in its own right, apart from and in relation to the projections of the male psyche. In other words, gender is constantly in flux. A definition of the feminine, although ultimately illusive, is eternally present in myth and ritual. Images of femininity are central to both Disney's mythology, and the iconic representation of it. Disney offers

---

204 *The Quotable Walt Disney*, 41.

205 *The Aesthetics and Poetics of Light in Eastern Orthodox Iconography: A Mythopoetic Perspective*, 119.

206 A notable exception is the popular princess characters.

207 Maximus is the horse from *Tangled*, Disney's interpretation of the Grimm Brothers's *Rapunzel*.

both light and dark interpretations of femininity in their myths. The Disney princess is their most controversial character type. The princesses often answer the charge of sanitization, but they are also the heart of Disney mythology. And they are the subjects of most of Disney's dolls. In recent years, princesses have taken over the park. In fact, between their presence in Fantasyland and the Princess Fantasy Faire that transformed the original Carnation Gardens into a Disney fairy tale village, they have formed a *Princess Bloc* that rivals the power of Mickey and his gang. Princesses dominate Disney's fairy tales. As vehicles for sweetness in fantasy, the princess allows the Disney patrons to feel safe in the immersion into imagination as they dive into a world that explores the complications of ego.

Disney princesses represent the ability of the archetypal maiden to deliver healing to a community. They are often criticized for being too passive, too concerned with looks and romance. This is patently untrue. In each of Disney's fairy tales, princesses are directly responsible for the welfare of their community. They call on their relationship with the animal world and a connection with community to either make change or be the catalysts for change. They do so while offering love, kindness, compassion and understanding to those around them. This is why the princesses are so often represented as dolls and plush toys. They are the sweetness of Disney's myth in iconic form. The difference between dolls and plush toys is the detail with which dolls are created. Much like Barbie dolls, Disney princess dolls are detailed miniaturizations of the images from the movies and the cast members in the park. Dolls are intended to be pure representations of the park's archetypal images.

Plush interpretations of the princesses, however, represent an extreme version of the Disney caricature. They paint the princesses with much broader strokes. They are often fuzzy and slightly out of focus, never conveying sharp angles or bright colors. The fact that Disney can do this and still make them recognizable is proof that their characters have become embedded in culture. Snow White is a clear example of this. Disney's version of Snow White has virtually eclipsed any other image of her. A princess with a yellow skirt, blue bodice, high white collar and a red ribbon in her short black hair is immediately recognizable as Disney's Snow White. This costume is all that is necessary to suggest the Disney princess. Another recent phenomenon of note is the presentation of Elsa and Anna from *Frozen*. As sisters and opposite sides of a similar archetypal image, these two characters are often sold together. *Frozen* ears are reversible, Elsa on one side and Anna on the other. Their plush dolls are Elsa on one side and Anna on the other, a method that Disney has now extended out to all the princess plushes. Perhaps the sisters from *Frozen* ignited a new of interpretation of Disney's archetypal maiden, the knowledge that interpreting these character should never be myopic. In contrast to the hero, who is often depicted in solitary action, princesses come in kaleidoscopic form. They are often depicted as a group. Disney understands that the maiden is a rich, multi-faceted image, and that the kind of healing she offers, gentle tenacious loving energy is deeply needed in the world right now.

In contrast to the ever-present princesses, the darker aspects of femininity, acknowledged as the devouring goddess known by names such as Baba Yaga, Kali, Morrigan, and Snow White's evil stepmother, are less often the subject of toys and dolls, although they are as popular as ever and eternally present in Disney mythology. This is because the destructive aspect of feminine archetypes moves an experience of Disney's ritualistic play into shadow, the realm of complexity and ambiguity. The female villains of Disney myths are present on t-shirts, bags, and other wearable vestments. They are also present in the park as cast members. They are meant to be frightening, and they are rarely turning into plush toys. They do not offer reassurance, and they are not playthings. It is clear that these images are dangerous, and therefore, although their role in Disney's stories is central, they are often considered taboo be turned into plush toys. One notable exception of this is the recent Disney baby plush dolls that offer the characters in infant form. The Evil Queen, Maleficent, and Ursula are all offered in this format. Perhaps Disney suggests that these energies are fine to engage in the context of reassurance as long as they offered outside of the context of their full power.

Donning the Vestments

Vestiture is a central part of the practice of mythic/religious ritual. The simple act of adorning one's body with the images of a narrative tradition is perhaps the most personal of all the possible ways one participates in ritual. Vestments denote hierarchy, as is the case with the priestly robes of the Christian and Druidic traditions or the ritual masking of West African culture, but they can also simply signify in symbolic form the participant's philosophical agreement with a tradition. Although the mode of manufacture, look and type of vestment may vary greatly, they all denote the patron's participation in choice. Ritual vestments complete the process of identification with an archetypal image.

With the advent of such shows as the *Mickey Mouse Club* and the *Disneyland* series *Davy Crockett*'s coonskin cap became the first ritual vestment associated with the park. In donning the vestments of Disney's images, the patron chooses characters with which to identify. The vestment allows them to literally put on the character, to become the archetypal image, to align patrons with the kind of experience they wish to have in the park. It represents a complete shift in consciousness, a complete immersion into the energy that captivates them. There is certainly no shortage of this kind of behavior at Disneyland. Everywhere one looks, it is possible to see patrons vested and ready for the experience. Hats, t-shirts, glasses, costumes, jewelry, shoes, hair clips – the choices are infinite. One might argue that Disney patrons are mere consumers, consuming Disney's wares like locusts. To some extent, that is true. The spiritual desires and needs that patrons use Disney products to fill never seem to find satisfaction. There is always more to shop for and more to buy. But a closer examination yields a slightly different interpretation. An overwhelming amount of Disney patrons visit the park wearing vestments that they save for return trips. Diehard patrons wear shirts, hats that specify special occasions, color-coded family t-shirts bearing the date of the event, and many other products, some made specifically for the Disney parks and some made especially by the patrons for the events.

A clear example of this is the 50th anniversary products. July 17, 2005 signified the 50th anniversary of Disneyland. That year was heralded as the *Happiest Homecoming on Earth*. Everything in the park was decorated in gold for an event that lasted two years. Every attraction was decorated with a golden Mickey Mouse image. The castle itself was decorated with golden spires and all the vista spots (in particular Dumbo and the tea cups) had at least one golden car for the occasion. Every retail location in the resort was full to the brim with golden products. Every conceivable wearable item came in a golden version. These products sold so well that Disney continued to make them available through the summer of 2007. When the event finally ended in August of that year, the products were removed from the shelves, and the event passed into immediate legend. These golden products maintain a presence in the park. Patrons continue to wear the golden ears, particularly the Minnie Mouse headbands, and if one listens carefully, one can hear the fabled tales being told of a time when the park was decked out in gold from top to bottom.

Tradable Icons

Another kind of park collectible functions as both collectible and vestment - the pin. It would be redundant to give detailed description of the pins sold in Disneyland. Numerous reiterations of all of Disney's images populate the pin shops and kiosks of Disneyland. Although pins have been available at Disneyland for many years, the pin-collecting craze gained momentum in 1999 during Disney's millennial celebration. Since then, pin trading has become a vital aspect of the Disneyland experience. Next to the Shooting Exposition attraction in Frontierland, there is a store named Westward Ho Trading Company. For many years, this store was Frontierland's spot for all kinds of hats. Recently, however, the products in this store changed drastically. Like other deftly located spots in Disneyland, this store now focuses specifically on the sale and trading of pins. There are three different and distinct aspects of the pin-collecting process: collection, affixing the pins/putting them on, and the trading of pins.

The process of locating and collecting pins becomes, for the Disney patron, yet another experience of touching and collecting relics and icons associated with the making sacred of Disney's images. Devoted patrons scour every location for that particular image that speaks directly to them. Collecting pins is a mini-pilgrimage in itself. Collector's books, like bird-watching guides, act as treasure maps leading the patron on the hunt for the prefect image. Pins are affixed to their corresponding lanyards and worn with pride through the park. Lanyards come in many of the colors associated traditionally with Mickey Mouse and friends, particularly primary colors like red, yellow, and blue. They also come with images on them, particularly the most popular images of Mickey Mouse, Tinker Bell, the Princesses, and the Pirates. The patron dons the lanyard much like a prayer shawl or a piece of academic regalia, allowing them to profess their allegiance through a symbol. Many of those who collect pins own far more than can fit on one lanyard. The process of choosing which pins to affix to the lanyard they will wear during their visit is another aspect of donning vestment.

Pin trading is an act of fellowship between devoted Disney followers as well as with Disney ritual and cast members. In order to keep pin trading fresh, Disney often cycles out older models of pins. They also offer limited edition pins or pins with holiday and date information printed on them. Once these pins go out of print, they become even more precious to the devoted collector. Disney continues to facilitate interaction for the pin-buyer beyond the original sale through the sanctioned process of trading pins. Cast members who wear pins, with or without lanyards, are instructed to negotiate with patrons regarding the pins they wear. Although not always required to trade, they are often encouraged to take trading seriously, especially with children. Trading allows both traders the opportunity to collect a new treasure without the expense of a new one.

Identification Through Ears

In April 2011, an official Disneyland Twitter account – @Disneyland News – released a tweet recording that in the history of the Disney Parks more than 79 million Mickey Mouse ears have been sold in the Disney Parks. That makes mouse ears the most popular Disney vestments of all time. The ears are the most consistent of all the Disney vestments. This most iconic of Disney hats was inspired by the popular 1929 Mickey Mouse short, *The Karnival Kid*, and began mass production through Disney's icon-making machine – Disney television. Roy Williams, an adult Mouseketeer, created the first version of the ears, making them an integral part of the Mickey Mouse Club uniform, and effectively creating wearable manifestation of the most recognizable of all American mythic images.

Mickey Mouse ears symbolize the basic Disney myths of play and the triumph of imagination. They have also been the subjects of the most consistent rein-vention. The earliest version of the Mickey Mouse ears was simple: a black, felt base with black ears and a patch on the front bearing a red ring around a white circle with an image of Mickey Mouse and the *Mickey Mouse Club* (MMC) written on it. The first Mouseketeers wore this on every episode of the show and their hats were an immediate hit with park goers. They soon became a symbol of unity; to belong to the *Mickey Mouse Club* was to be American, to ascribe to the basic American mythic ideals of freedom and creativity. As these children grew to become adults, they continued the tradition, wearing their Mickey Mouse ears proudly during their time in the park, and bringing their children to the place where they first experienced that kind of belonging. They gave their children hats and the tradition continued.

The paradoxical, quintessenttially American ethos of unity through individualism has also always been a part of the Mickey Mouse ears. Though the original ears all looked exactly the same, they were never intended to be fully homogenized symbols. The original Mouseketeers set the standard; their caps bore their names. Role call was one of the most important moments of the show, and this tradition carries over into the park. The hat may be a symbol, but having one's name embroidered on the hat makes it one's own. Until fairly recently, this embroidery was done by hand. The cast member would place the hat in the machine and sew it back and forth as though the machine was a pen, writing until the name was complete. It was a skill that kept patrons coming back, as the patron often preferred the *handwriting* of one cast member to another. Soon enough, the hat began to morph. Minnie Mouse ears were the first to arrive, but the ears have always morphed with their era. In the late 1970s, ears with narrow brims on the front arrived, and were sported by the Mouseketeers on a reinvention of the original series.

Perhaps the most fascinating reflection of ear hat culture has appeared in the last decade and a half. The Mickey Mouse ear hat has gone from being a symbol of identification with the plucky, universal character of Mickey to being a wider symbol of Disney's myth themes. As previously discussed, to a certain extent this has always been the case. Ears are a given upon which the patron paints their personal experience of the park. It is no longer enough to put on black ears with a patch in order to identify with Mickey Mouse, although those ears are still present and popular in the park today. Disney patrons are now offered ears that identify them as pirate Mickey, princess Mickey, even Mickey of the Haunted Mansion. Mickey Mouse is tie-dyed, spray painted, made neon, flowered, and painted plaid. Mickey top hats and Minnie veils are offered for the newlywed patrons, and the ears just keep coming.

In 2008, Disney unveiled a brand new kind of Mickey Ears – the completely customizable ones. Though these no longer exist, there was a time when a patron could walk into selected stores in Disneyland to make their own unique ear hat. First one chose a base (usually at least four or five different choices), then one chose the desired type of ears (glow in the dark, traditional, firework or flower petal, just to name a few), and then one chose from a bevy of different patches and other decorations the patron desired. Lastly, the one aspect of the fully customizable hat that is left in the park today, if the type of chosen base allows, the patron can have the hat embroidered. Instead of a simple name, hand embroidered on by a cast member, a machine does the embroidery. Patrons can choose between thread color and font. They can even choose (for an extra price, of course, as all of these extras are extra) to have an event or a date listed.

Although the fully customizable ears did not take off in the way Disney hoped, the impetus behind the idea did. In the years since the appearance of fully customizable ears, many new ear hats arrived at the parks fusing popular characters with the original ear hat formula. This sets up an exciting new dynamic way of engaging with Disney's ultimate icon. Instead of the original black ear hat with Mickey's emblem on it, patrons can wear a deconstructed version of the character they with to embody on their ears. For example, if one is a Star Wars fan, one can get R2D2 ears designed with R2s controls on the front, decorated in his colors. If one wishes to put on Dumbo, there are ears in a soft grey with his eyes and trunk on the front. There are princess ears with their fairy tale motifs included – Cinderella in blue with a glass slipper on the top, Belle in yellow with a rose embroidered on the front, and even Frozen ears that are reversible evoking Anna on one side and Elsa on the other. And, there are ear headbands. Sequined, bride headbands with the veil, and even ear headbands that invoke Disney's villainous mother figures. This brings diversity, color, and life to the application of wearing Mickey ears. It broadens the practice of wearing Disney ears as it allows them to engage with the characters while still participating with the grounding icon, which, as I've suggested, is common unifying emblem at Disney Parks – Mickey's coalescing impact is omnipresent.

One further note of Interest is the *Glow With the Show* ears. These ears were originally part of the World of Color attraction at Disney California Adventure and have now moved out to be part of other shows at Disneyland itself. These *Made with Magic* ears change color in time with Disney spectacles like the parades and World of Color. The idea behind these ears is fuller immersion into the show and to connect the patrons to a deeper sense of community. Patrons who wear them travel deeper, past their position as spectator and even past literalizing the characters. The ears help create an ecstatic atmosphere, allowing the narrative to fade into the background as the patron feels the impact of the experience rather than thinking through it, a technique commonly used to make sacred ritual meaningful.

Patrons even make their own unsanctioned ear hats, decorated with images that have nothing to do with the characters at the park themselves. They are often construed of Mickey headbands decorated with shells, flowers, or other craft jewels. I've even seen ears made with ceramic Mexican pan dulce or conchas appliqués glued on the outside. These ears are intended to indicate the patron's affiliation with the myths of Disney in their outside lives beyond the park. They solidify camaraderie with the Disney tradition. Clearly, the ear tradition has moved a long way away from the simple, messy hand-sewn names of the 1950s version, also becoming much more expensive and complicated. These changes reflect changes in culture. It is no longer enough for consumers to consume products; they must make them their own. This reflects the fact that the Mickey Mouse ears now straddle the space between sign and symbol. They have truly become an archetype, as Mickey is now something upon which one paints. He has been branded to the extent that the associate with the three circles (or two and a half circles in the case of the ears) is complete. However, the ears have gone from being a simple symbol of TV and theme park fun to an icon of the Disney tradition, similar to the stature of the crucifix in Christian tradition or the Hamsa of Arabic traditions. Every Disney product - from resorts across the globe, to Disney Store products, to cruise ships - bears Mickey's image, even if that image is subtly embedded in a place the patron never notices. Ears are woven into carpets, carved into wooden bedposts, and embossed on paper.

Those who subscribe to the cult of Disney immediately identify with Mickey. This kind of identification makes Mickey, like Jung's archetypes or the given of a mathematical equation, the starting point, the universal upon which the patrons base all their experiences. Each reinvention of the Mickey ear hat speaks volumes about a different incarnation of the mythology of Mickey Mouse. In this way, the ears themselves invoke the presence of the archetypal, and at the same time, it becomes a symbol of what the Disney patron values. It becomes a sacred image, interpreted through a kaleidoscope of archetypal images. In terms of ritual, perhaps the ear hats as a vestment are yet another reminder the experiences offers of being present in the body and allowing the process of the place work on psyche, providing deeper clues to the archetypal energies moving within the patron.

Disney continues to strive to balance corporate desires with an honest attempt to make the theme park as interactive and immersive as possible. Many have criticized Disneyland for what they might understand to be its cookie-cutter experience. The antidote for this kind of cookie-cutter experience of Disneyland comes from its patrons. This experience becomes particularly potent in the participation of the people in this process. In their willingness to take on the images and stories, they take part in crafting their own mythic identity. The experiences described above are by no means an exhaustive list of possible incarnations of Disneyland liturgy, as this kind of liturgy continues to unfold on a daily basis.

Digesting Mickey

Consumption of food is central to liturgical practice. Ritual studies scholar Catherine Bell calls this type of consumption "a common ritual means for defining and affirming the full extent of the human and cosmic community".[208] From ancient rites to modern holidays, sharing a meal means community bonding, the development of identity, sensual pleasure, and both physical and spiritual sustenance. Here's an interesting juxtaposition: both religion and

---

208 *Ritual: Perspective and Dimensions*, 123.

medical science remind us that we are what we eat, though scientists are often more concerned with the way what we eat kills us, rather than elevates us. What we consume, whether in food or beverage form, becomes our source of power, but it also becomes a source of joy because it is sensually transcendent in a way that is like nothing else we experience in life. The 2011 film *Perfect Sense* explores this idea. It's a love story that begins as an unexplainable epidemic spreads across the earth. The illness affects the senses. Each phase begins with a strong emotional reaction and ends with the loss of one of the five senses. French acress Eva Green plays Susan, an epidemiologist who attempts to explain the illness. She meets Michael, a young chef, played by Scottish actor, Ewan McGregor. Despite Susan's initial concerns about their relationship, she falls in love with Michael. The two begin a passionate romance, all the while becoming ill themselves.

It's the process of becoming ill in relationship to food that I find particularly interesting in this case. As the epidemic spreads and the characters begin to lose their senses of taste and smell, one would assume that they would also lose their interest in food. In fact, Michael himself assumes that he will soon be out of work as the epidemic progresses. Who would want to go out to a restaurant if they couldn't taste the food, smell it, or see it? But they do. In a move that shocks everyone, humanity begins to adapt to the changes in their circumstances and rather than abandoning food, they find another way to enjoy the sensual nature of it. They still go out and eat to celebrate events. The quality of the food becomes more contingent on other things like texture, the focus moving toward the eventual last sense – touch. The message of this film is clear: in the end all we have is love and our ability to touch and be touched. No matter what the state humanity may be, our experience of food and our ability to share it will always be a central part of it. Disneyland participates in this tradition in several ways, two of which are especially important in the development of their unique kind of ritual-holding sacred space for feasting and offering specific kinds of ritual foods.

The Disney Attraction as Feast

The convention of a feast is arguably the most significant practice of food consumption in ritual. It serves two central ritual functions; to mark an important occasion and to strengthen the bonds of personal relationship and community. Whether it's a wedding feast, a feast in commemoration of a deity, or simple bacchanalian joy, feasts mean something mythically significant. They require the creation of sacred space to mark the occasion. Disneyland offers three distinct types of dining experiences: the street vendor, themed spaces for casual family feasting, and fine dining for special event feasting. Hold the thought about street vendors though. The foods vendors are symbolic, and as such they are not quite part of as traditional practices of feasting in that they don't offer a space to contain the feast.

The spaces Disneyland creates to convene a feast are unique because the bridge the event that is being commemorated and the Disney story. They place the patron in the middle of the story. They are themed based on the part of the park where they are located. Given the amount of choice the patron has in regards to dining, the choice of story patrons choose to engage with when they feast is as important mythically as the characters they wear on their bodies and the icons they take home. Restaurants themselves become stories or attractions. They are cherished parts of the experience to be re-engaged with each time the patron returns to the park. One will often hear patrons extolling the virtues of the particular dining attraction they love. "Oh the fried chicken at the Plaza Inn. I have to have that every time I come." Or, "I have to visit Oscar at the Carnation Café. He's been a cast member for over 50 years." Because Disney creates such complete identification between the stories and the attractions, park patrons fuse their memories with their dining, remembering past family feasts – Thanksgivings, weddings, Christmases, Halloween times, graduations, etc... and with such complete identification between those events and the stories of the attractions, the mythic aspects are as real as the physical ones.

Although the list of immersive dining attractions at Disneyland is long and varied, one particular example is so deeply identified with Disneyland that it deserves mention. The Blue Bayou Restaurant in New Orleans Square is unique to Disney dining as the only one that actually inside a ride through attraction, Pirates of the Caribbean. The restaurant part of the attraction consists of an outdoor patio, which is actually inside, set dockside next to Lafitte's Landing, the area where the pirate boats move through toward the beginning of their encounter with the pirates. The patio is bathed in perpetual twilight. Fireflies flit across the backdrop as the air is warmed to a slightly humid temperature and frogs and crickets make their noises in the background.

The sounds of patrons screaming on their way down the drop to the pirates' lair pierce the patio occasionally and patrons smile knowing the mythic Caribbean pirates are as much a part of their dining attraction as the ride along attraction next to them. The patio is lit with colorful lanterns, an homage to the color and diversity of Louisiana's bayou culture. The menu is themed with the flair of New Orleans Cajun/Creole cuisine. Scalloped potatoes, steak, roasted chicken, pork chops, salmon, jambalaya, and the perennially popular Monte Cristo sandwich are central to this menu. Guests are treated to fine china, fine napkins, and particularly attentive service. There is only one element of traditional feasting missing from this attraction, alcohol. In keeping with Disneyland's original ethos, no alcohol is served within the confines of the original park, with the exception of the exclusive (and mythic in itself) *Club 33*, Walt's club created for his business associates. Club 33 is corporate club of sorts. It's long waiting list, short membership list, and incredibly pricey membership fees keep it well out of the realm of the average Dis-no-phile Visiting it is a feather in the cap to any true lover of Disneyland. It's an experience that I myself have yet to have.[209]

Back to the Blue Bayou Restaurant: for most Disney patrons, it's considered an expensive, fine dining attraction. It is so popular that Disney suggests booking your reservations as early as possible, up to 60 days in advance. It's the kind of place where families celebrate holidays, birthdays, and couples escape for anniversaries. It's even used for wedding/honeymoon dinners on occasion. Large parties are almost never accommodated on short notice. If one is lucky enough to score a walk in seat, and indeed even if one has a reservation, there is always some kind of wait, perhaps 10 minutes, perhaps 30. But patrons do wait, because there is something about immersing into this particular story that appeals to them. Americans have a particular fascination with pirates, and in the American fantasy of pirates, feasting, freedom and rebellion remain central to their story. Americans are captivated by images of eighteenth century privateers casting off old class distinctions in the sultry exotic land of bayou country.

Fellow Disney apologist Priscilla Hobbs makes the fascinating observation that New Orleans Square is Disney's foray into America's psychological shadow. She asserts that the city of New Orleans itself is a container for much of America's projection of its own shadow. "Because Americans have perceived themselves in a cycle of perpetual crisis", she writes, "affinity for the ghosts and pirates reflects a shift in trust of the American leadership".[210] This makes the choice to feast with them, to place our personal and cultural identity in the hand of the pirates particularly important. Pirates are murderers. They flout whatever system they live under, choosing a life of larceny over rule and order. Americans are drawn to the idea of cultural reversal and pirates certainly embody that. This makes particular sense if one considers it in terms of the political atmosphere that faced Americans in their choice between Hillary Clinton and Donald Trump in the 2016 presidential election. But this is Disneyland, and at Disneyland all myth is intentionally created to soothe the child's imagination. So, why pirates? The simple answer is because pirates play. Unburdened by the rule of law, Disney's presentation of them allows for a feast that celebrates seizing the life of the imagination with gusto. It's the ultimate Disney feast. This central dining attraction encourages the patrons to cast of the shackles of culture and immerse themselves in an alternate reality where there are delicious treats and plentiful treasure.

Sitting There With a Churro in Your Hand

Every tradition has foods specific to particular ritual events. Ritual foods are made and consumed because what they represent, either literally or metaphorically they invoke a deeper meaning into the spiritual practice of the ritual devotee. Bread and wine, sweets and savories, different things that are decorated

---

209 Here's an interesting website I found about this exclusive and elusive locale. http://www.disneylandclub33.com

210 *Walt's Utopia: Disneyland and American Mythmaking*, 90.

to look like mythic characters. There are all kinds of ways to engage with ritual foods, but all of these foods are integral to the same practice. They all physicalize the story, crossing the boundary between the physical and the spiritual. In doing so, they create and re-create the symbolic act of assimilating the mythic energies into our psyches through a sensual action that the devotee can participate in physically.

Perhaps the most obvious kinds of ritual food that serves this purpose at Disneyland is the food that comes from the street vendor. These foods are almost always hand held treats. They are meant to go with the patron as they stroll through the park, their symbolic shapes and tastes making the myths even more potent. Whether it's the pickles, the corn dogs, or the turkey legs, these Disney foods become icons in themselves. They become synonymous with the energy of the place. The simple thought of them brings pleasure and wistfulness to the patron.

Patrons are devoted to specific street foods they love. This is so true that there are Internet polls devoted to asking: which food is the best. There's the Dole Whip, a pineapple soft serve ice cream offered near Walt Disney's Enchanted Tiki Room in float form, ice cream, and juice form all decorated Hawaiian style with maraschino cherries and colorful umbrellas. Dole Whip is exclusive because beyond the Dole factory in Hawaii, the Disney parks in California and Florida are the only places to get this tasty pineapple treat. The thought of a Dole Whip conjures up hot afternoons in the hot lines of Disneyland. It offers a tasty way to get out of the heat, as Walt Disney's Enchanted Tiki Room is one of the only attractions that encourages outside foods indoors. There are bags of popcorn, Walt Disney's personal favorite treat that comes in all sizes and evokes a nostalgic memory of old carnivals and days sitting on a bench people watching. And then there is the churro, donut-like sugary cinnamon-y fried homage to California's Mexican history.

One last specific kind of street food is the absolute Mickey Mouse shaped everything. Much like the ears hats, these Mickey Mouse shaped treats are legion. The image of the Mouse is on every street vendor's paper product. It's often even on the vendors carts themselves. There are Mickey pretzels, Mickey ice cream sandwiches, and Mickey donuts. The effect of this is complete. The patron literally digests Mickey into their body as they collect his image in hat form, pin form, and clothing. In the end, Mickey is the ultimate icon. All the different aspects of the liturgy point to the same thing; a famous quip by Walt that he hoped we would never forget the place began with a mouse. Mickey Mouse is the ultimate American icon. We consume, we venerate, and we engage with the Mouse. We play with, we honor, and we love the Mouse. That is the work of worship at Disneyland.

Chapter 5

Spectacular Spectacle

> Communitas *is often speculative and generates imagery and philosophical ideas.* – Victor Turner[211]
>
> . . . *by its very nature sacred time is reversible* in the sense that, properly speaking, *it is a primordial mythic time made present.* – Mircea Eliade[212]

The Crafted Communitas of Disneyland

Imagine: You stand in front of the castle in a throng of people. You can't contain your excitement, but that's OK because neither can anyone else around you. They cheer, and you jump to your feet. You watch in animated exhilaration as you wait for the fireworks to begin. You've been there for hours. Your legs ache. You feel the push of the crowd around you, but still you wait. You want to sit, but when you do others come in to stand in front of you. You become frustrated, so you stand and wait. A voice comes over the sound system reminding you that in just 30 minutes, 15 minutes, just a minute the fireworks will begin. The light dims and the crowd cheers. The anticipation is palpable. It's one of the major "shows within the show". This is the space where *liminality* meets *communitas*.

David Mamet wrote that dramatic structure is "an exercise in a naturally occurring need or disposition to structure the world as thesis/antithesis/synthesis".[213] He invokes Hegel and the rhetorical tradition of dialectics in order to suggest that drama, if it is to work, must present points of plot before it finishes with some kind of a flourish, a conflagration of themes and messages. He suggests that synthesis is inherent to drama, though also problematic, full of

211 *The Ritual Process: Structure and Anti-Structure*, 133.

212 *The Sacred and the Profane: The Nature of Religion*, 68.

213 *Three Uses of the Knife*, 67.

conflicting images, ideas, and feelings. The syncretic nature of drama is one of the central connections between it and ritual. Drama becomes mythic ritual through the energy it creates for the crowd, energy created for the dual experience of liminality and communitas.

Grounding his theories in the context of a Durkheimian[214] style analysis of ritual and culture, Victor Turner circles around a similar idea: an authentic experience of religious imagination generally requires fellowship, and this fellowship creates its own energy, its own mythic reality. Disneyland partakes in the ritual tradition suggested by Mamet, Turner, and Durkheim through its participation with the characteristics of ritualized temple culture. It allows those present in the park to come together in a genuine practice of community. One might argue that the entire experience of the theme park is an experience of ritual fellowship,[215] and indeed in many ways this is true. The entire park itself is a spectacle, as I suggested when I argued that Disneyland is a temple fashioned through the spectacle media of stage and screen. From a phenomenological point of view, engaging with spectacle peppers the patron's entire encounter with a place, beginning with the disembodied voice that announces events to the crowd over the loud speaker and continuing with theater attractions such as Great Moments With Mr. Lincoln, and Walt Disney's Enchanted Tiki Room, as well as "gone, but not forgotten" attractions such as America Sings and the Country Bear Jamboree. Disneyland is panoply of spectacle: something to be seen, heard, and touched at every corner.

The spectacular shows, what I call, *meta-spectacles,*[216] are Disneyland's most effective attempt at creating collective fellowship, Turner calls this *communitas*. These pure spectacles transcend specific story for the sake of promoting greater Disney myththemes. Such productions (such as *Fantasmic!,* fireworks, holiday spectactulars, and so on) require very little in the way of patron activity. The act of sitting still, drinking in the experience and consuming the spectacle, however, is not the same thing as passivity. In this context of meta-spectacle, the Disney patron experiences what Martin Buber describes as mystical fusion into community. This mystical fusion cements psychological bonding between park patrons who, before crossing the threshold of Disneyland's main gate, were (most likely) complete strangers. This threshold crossing is the flourish moment of the show; it synthesizes *communitas*. As Buber suggests: " [. . .] community is the being no longer side by side [. . .] but, with one another of a multitude of personas. And this multitude, though it moves toward one goal, yet experiences everywhere a turning to, a dynamic facing of, the others, a flowing from I to Thou. Community is where community happens."[217]

214 *The Elementary Forms of Religious Life.*

215 Or Durkheim's *collective effervesence/*Turner's *communitas* or Eliade's mythic return.

216 *Meta*: prefix-*trans, spectare*: to look; *Oxford English Dictionary* online.

217 *I and Thou,* 51.

Spectacles also create community. They cross boundaries between personal and communal space. They synthesize Disney's mythic narrative, bringing together the consummate aspects of the narratives and their images. Through these spectacles, the Disneyland patron experiences the kind of ecstatic ritualized fellowship that is the psychological building block of *communitas*. They unify the crowd, developing a field of energy that consumes the spectator, like the finale of some Broadway musical or the definitive moment of the transformative ritual from bread and wine to the body and blood of Christ.

Immersion into park narrative occurs when the patron experiences interaction between one's own mythic identification and Disneyland's images (characters) and stories (attractions). Once the pantheon and temple are established and the threshold of initiation is crossed,[218] fusion with the tradition is complete. Like temple pilgrims moving through the deeper levels of initiation, they live their personal stories through ritualizing the mythic stories, by becoming the characters that appeal to them and by experiencing psychological transportation into the archetypal world that is Disney's imagination. Turner suggests that these kinds of rituals:

> [. . .] offer of lowliness and sacredness, of homogeneity and comradeship. We are presented, in such rites, with a 'moment in and out of time' and in and out of secular social structure, which reveals, however fleetingly, some recognition (in symbol if not always in language) of a generalized social bond that has ceased to be and has simultaneously yet to be fragmented into a multiplicity of structural ties.[219]

One can apply Turner's concept of ritualized *communitas* to the practice of traditional sacred spectacle, such as the one that occurs nightly in the square located between the Basilica and the church of the Holy Trinity at Fatima, Portugal.[220] The tradition begins with liturgical music. A musical litany is performed, and then the chosen (multicultural) priests from Rome pray the Rosary, each in their own language. After five decades[221] of the Rosary, the crowds disperse to process. At the head of the procession, clergy members carry a statue of Our Lady of Fatima and large neon cross followed by thousands of devoted Catholics. The procession then travels the length of the great square, from the shrine itself, around to the steps of the Basilica, and back to the shrine.

---

218 The patron achieves initiation into Disneyland's ritual tradition through attraction, by living the story.

219 96.

220 The shrine at Fatima, Portugal, developed around the visions of three children, Lucia, Francisco and Jacinto who over the course six months (on the thirteenth of every month) believed they had visions of the Virgin Mary. These children believed they received mysterious messages from the "Holy Virgin" related to World War I and the conversion of Europe. Pilgrims flock to this shrine from all corners of the world. The parallels between this shrine and Disneyland are numerous and striking, from the development of pilgrimage culture to the merchandizing of the sacred to location.

221 Decade is the term for the organization of the prayers in the structure of the rosary. Three types of mysteries, Joyful, Sorrowful, and Glorious each have five subplots invoked for contemplation during the prayers. For each of the five subplots, ten *Hail Mary* prayers are said after which each subplot is anchored by one *Glory Be to the Father and to the Son and to the Holy Spirit* prayer and one *Our Father* prayer.

All the way through the processional, the clergy leads the faithful in song, the culminations of the experience of *communitas* as the people become one in song.

Disneyland has always been an environment that values and invokes these kinds of sacred rituals. Interesting parallels can be drawn between this traditional spectacle and a tradition at Disneyland that has come to be known as the *Candlelight Procession*.[222] Chris Strodder calls this tradition a ". . . parade of carolers illuminates the Magic Kingdom with the glow of a thousand candles and the music of a thousand voices".[223] As early as December of 1955, the staff at Disneyland recognized and participated in a traditional sacred ritual entered around Christmas, but couched in the Southern Californian experience of Disney's Magic Kingdom. A group of twelve carolers from the University of Southern California[224] wandered, performing for Park patrons.

This tradition of Christmas spectacle became so popular with patrons that in 1958 it moved to a central location in Town Square. In that year, singers from sixteen choirs processed down Main Street, U.S.A. to the Town Square, where they performed a concert along with a group of singers located on the balcony of Sleeping Beauty's Castle. Local dignitaries and celebrities are always a part of this tradition, providing the kind of gravitas that heads of state and church have traditionally lent to sacred ritual. The presence of such vanguards of Hollywood – from Cary Grant and John Wayne in the early years, to James Earl Jones and Craig T. Nelson in the 1980s, and Jon Voight, Jane Seymour, and Terrance Howard in the post millennial years – indicates Disney's insistence that Hollywood's performing community is the clergy of the grounding structure of their ritual.

Disneyland's Candlelight Procession is the park's first foray into this kind of ritual. Its enduring presence is an appropriate container for a combination of entertainment and the practice of sacred ritual, and both the patrons and the staff responsible for maintaining it recognize this. The presence of Christmas ritual is particularly poignant, because in the American ritual cycle, Christmas continues to punctuate the entire year. Before winter even has a chance to begin, often as early as September, stores are full of Christmas decorations and reporters speak about the economic effects of it. Hollywood studios crank out Christmas movies every year in anticipation of a season when families require entertainment and distraction. Television studios turn to Christmas-themed shows; Christmas is everywhere.

Through its power as an archetypal story, Christmas creates a state of psychological vulnerability. Like the threshold crossing at Disneyland, Christmas is a

---

222 http://davelandweb.com/candlelight/

223 *The Disneyland Encyclopedia: The Unofficial, Unauthorized, and Unprecedented History of Every Land, Attraction, Restaurant, Shop and Event in the Original Magic Kingdom*, 105.

224 The director of this group was Dr. Charles C. Hirt. He was a personal friend of Walt's. University of Southern California (also known as USC) is located adjacent to downtown Los Angeles.

liminal time, a time when anything can happen. In the Christmas comedy, *Mixed Nuts*,[225] Steve Martin's[226] character argues this in a perfectly succinct way. He says, "Christmas is a time when you look at your life through a magnifying glass, and everything you don't have feels overwhelming. Being alone is so much lonelier at *Christmas*. Everything sad is so much sadder at Christmas." In this season of vulnerability, it is particularly easy to convince the audience of the magic. It makes sense that the quintessentially Southern Californian theme park would get in on the Hollywood traditions of Christmas. The presence of traditional sacred ritual in the form of the Candlelight Procession, suggests that the kind of awe and wonder cultivated by the experience of Disneyland at Christmas creates a tension between an honest experience of the holiday and the psychological manipulation of the senses created by Disney magic.

And Now, Disneyland is Proud to Present A New Kind of Spectacle

In contrast to the deeply personal experience of attraction and identification with character cultivated by other aspects of park liturgy, Disneyland's spectacular shows return the personal to the communal, infiltrating soul through an amalgamation of Disney's images. They become what I call the pancanonial metaspectacle; a show organized and offered around specific times for the purpose of punctuating Disneyland's experience of ritual. This aspect of Disneyland spectacle is responsible for creating both an ecstatic experience of *communitas*, as well as (often) Disney's last word to their audience, their grand movement intended to inject the communal soul with mythic messages. In doing so, they distill their messages down to the most basic symbols. Although these symbols create metanarrative that becomes, in essence, Disney's version of the Public Service Announcement, they broadcast these messages at to the community through symbolic shorthand.

Disney infuses them with meaning to the audience even as they present them in shorthand. This indicates the kind of psychological power that Disney's mythic tradition holds for those initiated into it. One look at the faces of the patrons who experience these meta-spectacles suggests that they have encountered bodily transcendence of social structures and personal space. This experience, like other culminating moments of ritual, creates a psychological opening for complete transcendence into the imagination. The images of the spectacle are imbued with their meaning on such a deep level that they require no exploration through narrative. They are only required to present themselves as

---

225 Written by Nora Ephron, directed by Rob Reiner, this film was released in 1994.

226 Steve Martin himself is an important ally of Disney and Disneyland. His first job was at the *Magic Shoppe* on Main Street. He was asked to narrate a 50th anniversary short film that still runs at the Opera House on Main Street in the waiting area for *Great Moments With Mr. Lincoln*.

luminescent images of psychological, spiritual and ideological significance; through which they become *communitas*.

Parades

Parades have been a staple at Disneyland since opening day, when Walt Disney, Fess Parker, and Buddy Ebsen rode up Main Street, U.S.A. toward Frontierland. Parades at Disneyland have also often been a forum for young high-school musicians, the talent of marching bands, and occasionally for park patrons celebrating a particular milestone. The "Disney Treasures" DVD[227] explores their history in detail. This DVD explores the kinds of parades Disneyland hosts: political (1976s Pooh for President); holiday-themed (Christmas, Thanksgiving, Independence Day); and even parades that just remind the patron of their importance as Disney fans. Parades appeal to humanity's most basic need for spectacle. They allow the crowd to participate in voyeurism and exhibitionism simultaneously. They achieve this by helping the patron to become part of the show. While other forms of communal entertainment ritual often require a kind of reverential quiet, the parade actually encourages outbursts from the community. This is particularly clear in the case of the *Celebrate! A Street Party* that ran during Disney's *Celebrate You!* campaign that ran between 2009 and 2010.

In contrast to other Disney parades, *Celebrate You!* keeps the color scheme of the parade especially simple. Dancers wear a variety of costumes in the same primary shades of red, blue, and yellow. This choice of color creates continuity between performers in all sections of the parade and the patrons. The music for this parade, while punctuated by refrains of songs from the traditional Disney canon, provides a soundtrack backdrop for live performance on the floats. In keeping with its theme, this parade focuses on making the patron part of the parade. Each section of the dance is punctuated by the performer's call to the audience to "let me hear what you are celebrating". The audience then cheers when they hear their event announced (birthdays, anniversaries, weddings). The loose, impromptu atmosphere of this show creates a particularly effective atmosphere for *communitas*. Patrons at this parade leap out into the parade and dance with the performers. The infectious energy of the show, as well as the call and response style, cultivates the exact kind of unity Disney expects to constellate.

In 2011, Disneyland retired its *Celebrate You!* series of shows in favor of a new parade. "The Magic, The Memories and You" reflects this. *Mickey's Soundsational Parade*[228] that ran from 2011 until the 60th anniversary in 2015, evokes memory and nostalgia by emphasizing the primacy of Disney's canon, while combining consistency through the punctuation of each parade unit with the refrain, "It's a music celebration (come on, come on, come on) / Feel the beat what a great

---

227 *Disneyland: Secrets, Stories and Magic*, 2007, DVD.

228 The music that punctuates each parade unit is derived from Hong Kong Disneyland's *Flights of Fancy* parade. The lyrics, however, have been changed.

sensation (come on, come on, come on) / Move and Clap your hands / Get into the spirit / Let everyone hear it / So come on, come on/Soundsational!"

The parade has nine units and begins with six live drummers, echoing Mickey Mouse's traditional role as the bandleader and the popular percussion acrobatics of the Broadway hit *Stomp*. It progresses from Mickey's float, including the original *Mickey Mouse Club* theme song, to *Aladdin*, and then to *The Little Mermaid*. Next, in line is a float that honors Donald Duck and *The Three Caballeros*. After Donald, there is a float signifying the princesses, with Snow White and Sleeping Beauty on the front of the float and Belle and Cinderella on the back. This unit, while signifying Disney's tradition of European fairy tales at large, focuses on Rapunzel. Her tower is the centerpiece of the parade, and the song *At Last I See the Light* plays among the punctuation of the refrain. The next parade unit is *The Lion King*. The song *I Just Can't Wait To Be King* plays, but this float, like the princess unit also has a bit of a syncretic flavor. It combines the look of *The Lion King* with characters from *Tarzan*[229] and music from *The Jungle Book*.[230]

It is significant to note that this parade does a reverse close up in the middle section. The parade works in short increments. This reflects every aspect of it. Instead of requiring the audience to stick with the syncretic narrative as it presents it, the parade then returns to the close-up, as a unit honoring *The Princess and the Frog* makes an entrance. Although it may seem odd and alienating that Tiana has her own float, separate from the rest of the princesses, closer analysis reveals a possible mythic reason for it. As the first American princess, Tiana deserves her own unique unit. However, it seems even more likely that the *Mardi Gras* atmosphere of the film combined with its position in the canon as a newer film (though established for longer than Rapunzel) may actually be the reason. This unit celebrates Jazz music, a true American art form (not unlike the theme park). After this jazz interlude, the parade ends with two units that celebrate the musicals of Disney's first renaissance, also known as the Golden Age of Disney films: *Peter Pan* and *Mary Poppins*.

The parade is a return to a show that emphasizes the primacy of Disney's classic music and images in concert with *communitas*. This is consistent with what Durkheim calls "collective effervescence", the concept that the collective experience of the religious impulse creates a bubbling up of psychological energy. Chris Shilling and Phillip A. Mellor suggest that perhaps a better word for it might be ". . . collective *intoxication*; the process leading people to almost 'instinctively' copy the symbols, customs, affective foundations and consciousness of collectivities during the totemic rituals of effervescent assemblies".[231] This parade is an example of this kind of experience. Over a course of almost

---

229 *Tarzan*'s gorilla, Terk, was voiced by Rosie O'Donnell.

230 *I Wanna Be Like You*, written by The Sherman Brothers.

231 "Retheorising Emile Durkheim, on society and religion: embodiment, intoxication and collective life", 22.

100 years, Disney develops a canon of myths that are immediately recognizable, in symbolic form, to patrons. In order to keep those myths fresh in the minds and hearts of the littlest patrons, they develop these parades as totemic rituals, which reinforce the totemic nature of these images through an experience that fuses together the safety of the family unit with the larger community of fellow patrons.

Standing in contrast to the daytime parades, that offer an air of childlike innocence and silliness with their wild costumes and wigs, *Disneyland's Main Street Electrical Parade* is an after-dark extravaganza that still remains the most popular and longest running show in the history of the Disneyland. The first run of this parade lasted 24 years, beginning on June 17, 1972, and ending on November 25, 1996. Robert Jani, who was Disneyland's director of entertainment, developed the idea for *Disneyland's Main Street Electrical Parade*. Many of his colleagues thought that the idea was crazy. At that time, no parade had ever been attempted at night. The logistical requirements alone were considered prohibitive, and many colleagues didn't think that the parade demographic would stay in the park late enough, especially during the long days of summer.

Again, as is so common with stories related to Disneyland, that which made absolutely no sense and seemed senseless from a business point of view made perfect sense from the point of view of mythic ritual. *Disneyland's Main Street Electrical Parade* immersed the community of Disneyland patrons into an experience of altered consciousness, a collective dream. Disneyland always offers a kind of collective dream state, just as myth-makers always reflect a culture's unconscious dream material. What many skeptics underestimate about the concept of *Disneyland's Main Street Electrical Parade* is the powerful energy of the liminality of nighttime. The potency of Disneyland at night, with all its neon lights lighting up attractions, is a vital aspect of the experience. Walt himself hosted a television show called *Disney After Dark*.[232] Nevertheless, this parade marks the first time that Disneyland's designers are able to harness the nighttime energy of the place for the sake of a spectacle that they are able to manipulate and present as a production number.

Strodder contends that it is impossible to explain *Disneyland's Main Street Electrical Parade* to those who have never witnessed it. By combining the lights and sounds of the computerized virtual world with Sylvania's electrical one, this parade suggests that the truth of dreams is expressed through humanity's efforts at technology. This is a key mythic theme of the Disneyland experience. The parade expresses it through the presentation of units that reflect the liminality of the dream state. He notes, "With no marching bands or synchronized performers it was far from a traditional **parade**. The recorded narration enthusiastically described it as a 'spectacular festival pageant of nighttime magic and imagination in thousands of sparkling lights and electro-syntho-magnetic mu-

232 *Wonderful World of Color* series: original airdate April 15, 1962.

sical sounds. 'Close, but in truth, still not enough.'"[233] The parade consists of eight major units, all of which reflect some kind of connection to nighttime or dreaming.

The first parade unit features the Blue Fairy of *Walt Disney's Pinocchio*. This fairy enters Pinocchio's consciousness under the cover of night, in his dreams, providing him with the magic necessary to make his dreams of becoming a real boy come true. The apparatus that makes up the float of this unit is crafted into an image of the fairy's blue dress. The performer playing the fairy sits atop this float inside it waving a wand of fairy dust over the crowd. The next unit of the parade is the *Alice in Wonderland* float. Alice sits on top of the mushroom, the symbol of Wonderland's altered state of consciousness, with the caterpillar sitting on the front of the float next to her. The third unit begins the *Peter Pan* float with an image of London's Big Ben at night. It implies the audience's participation with the Darling children as they fly through the night sky to Neverland.

After *Peter Pan*, the circus atmosphere of *Dumbo the Flying Elephant* enters and the electrical sound of the parade's score suddenly evokes an entirely different kind of altered state of dream consciousness. The image of the circus, though not a nighttime image of the dream, presents the liminality of the more subversive aspects of culture. The unit begins with circus cages, one of which moves Dumbo along the parade route. Another float carries an immense pink elephant, which in the context of the film represents another version of altered consciousness, induced by alcohol. Of course, this is all couched in the safety of Disney's Casey Jr. Circus.

The *Snow White and the Seven Dwarfs* parade unit focuses on the diamond mine of the Seven dwarfs. The connection between Snow White's story and altered states of consciousness may not seem obvious in the way that other units of this parade do. However, much of Snow White's narrative happens when the princess retreats, in exile, to the forest. This environment that offers protection and sanctuary to the princess is made possible by the industrious diamond mining of the dwarfs. In contrast to the destructive images of Snow White's family of origin, she finds comfort in the bourgeois atmosphere of the dwarfs. A chain of mine train cars filled with shiny diamonds move through the parade route, with the hard working dwarfs and a grateful Snow White behind them all the way.

The next unit centers on the film *Pete's Dragon*, a choice that might seem surprising to contemporary audiences, but it would not be to early audiences of this parade. The Walt Disney Animation Studios released *Pete's Dragon* in 1977, and this film marks one of Disney's efforts in combining the animated world with the human world. The story centers around the unlikely friendship between a nine-year-old orphan named Pete and an animated dragon named

---

233 257.

Eliot. The parade float consists almost entirely of a large version of Eliot, with a live action performer on his back. Pete comments on what a lovely view the parade is, and how happy he is to be there. He asks Eliot to affirm his feelings about the group, and Eliot answers by snorting smoke out of his nose.

The last two units represent culminating moments for the parade. The seventh unit of the parade is a tribute to America. It presents a group of floats that ritualize the images of Americana. Floats representing fireworks, the American flag and images of the early colonists fill this unit, carried by live performers dressed in brightly colored colonial costumes covered in red, white, and blue lights. The eighth unit of this parade synthesizes Disneyland's fairytale theme of true love. The centerpiece of this unit is a float fashioned into the image of Cinderella's pumpkin coach. In a move similar to subsequent parades that synthesize the image of the princess, other live action couples representing Disney princesses and princes line the coach as they wave to the crowd. The iconic ballad, *A Dream is a Wish your Heart Makes* brings the message of this parade full circle. Under the cover of night, when the bright twinkling of Sylvania's version of Disney's *stars*, the patron lives a dream of Disneyland – a life of the imagination represented by Disney's mythic canon and the triumph of technology. One last note: in 2016, Disney announced its intention to return *Disneyland's Main Street Electrical* parade to Disneyland for a limited run. The announcement has been met with ecstatic outbursts of joy from Disneyland fans and horror from Walt Disney World fans where the parade currently resides. Clearly this parade maintains it mythic heft.

Exclamation Point / Disney's Point: Fantasmic!

The parades of Disneyland's parades, and by extension the rest of the theme parks, are so numerous and have such a chameleonic nature that tracking and cataloguing them is the task of a lifetime. They generally follow a certain formula and, in the format of traditional spectacle, they encourage participation through semi-passive consumption of images and sounds. The formula of a parade, however, generally consists of different units that may share a similar mytheme, but not necessarily a cohesive narrative. In 1992, Disneyland released a brand new nighttime spectacle at Disneyland. This show, set on the banks of the Rivers of America, marks a new kind of pancanonical nighttime metaspectacle. This show, called *Fantasmic!*,[234] has become formulaic for the Disney Parks since its release. The show itself is amazing, a triumph of light and sound projected onto water. But, perhaps even more significantly, the show is a milestone in the mythic development of Disneyland. In *Fantasmic!*, characters from across Dis-

---

234 Information on Fantasmic! comes from personal experience. The history of the attraction comes from *The Disneyland Encyclopedia* (159–160).

ney's vast canon are placed along each other in the development of an entirely new narrative.

Previous to *Fantasmic!*, Disney shows and parades generally consisted of the characters from different parts of Disney's canon placed next to each other in a production number. All aspects of sensory spectacle accompany them as they encourage participation in the stories through memory rather than the development of new narrative. In other words, when one participates in a traditional Disneyland parade, the characters process through the park on floats intended specifically to connect one's current Disneyland experience with the animated films/shorts from which the characters in the parade derive. The ritual power of this kind of attraction lies in its ability to evoke memory in the patron. It affects transformation to the past: whether the patron's nostalgia for the excitement that they may have felt the first time they saw that animated film, or sentimentality that surrounds the memory of a past visit to Disneyland, or for the little ones for whom it is an early experience of Disneyland, it comes from the excitement of meeting those cherished characters in the flesh.

In contrast to this, the transformative power of *Fantasmic!* comes from its ability to take these characters and create an entirely new story with them. This is the kind of project that only works after a canon of stories has been established for many years and has become a part of the mythic consciousness of a culture the way Disney's stories have. *Fantasmic!* begins with an invocation to the mythic imagination, much like the call to the muses or the gods in Greek poetry. A voice narrates the opening of the production, indicating that "our host, Mickey Mouse" will be the protagonist of the show.[235] Once again, the nighttime spectacular invokes the power of the dream state, suggesting that anything is possible in the dream and, therefore dangerous forces in the dream must not overrun one. Mickey enters and immediately falls asleep. At first, the images that populate his dreams are innocuous enough. In his dream, he becomes the *Sorcerer's Apprentice*, one of Mickey Mouse's innumerable manifestations, and perhaps the one that most fully reflects his role as the shamanic alter ego of Walt Disney. Mickey Mouse commands the water, he casts images onto the screen, and the audience enjoys the innocence of these images, all of which are immediately recognizable to the audience as animation sequences from *Fantasia*. He invokes Tinker Bell, who helps him turn the magical pixie dust of his imagination into elemental fire before the eyes of the patron.

Next, taking the patrons deeper in the landscape of Mickey Mouse's imagination, a float appears on across the river consisting of an immense image of Kaa,

---

235 "Welcome to *Fantasmic!* Tonight our friend, and host, Mickey Mouse uses his vivid imagination to create magical imagery for all to enjoy. Nothing is more powerful than the imagination for, in a moment, you can experience a beautiful fantasy or an exciting adventure. But beware; nothing is more powerful than the imagination, for it can also expand your greatest fears into an overwhelming nightmare. Are the powers of Mickey's incredible imagination strong enough and bright enough to withstand the evil forces that invade Mickey's dream? You are about to find out. For we now invite you to join Mickey and experience *Fantasmic!*: a journey beyond your wildest imagination."

the snake from *The Jungle Book*. Monkeys dance delightfully across the water as the units of the show that represent the different stories commanded by this sorcerer captivate the patron. The Sailing Ship Columbia, a historical attraction intended to immerse the patron into the history of eighteenth century shipping lines during the day, becomes Peter Pan's pirate ship, featuring Peter, Wendy, and the Lost Boys. The audience continues to enjoy this trip through Mickey Mouse's imagination, as Mickey Mouse himself enjoys it. The pirate ship moves down the river, away from the audience and back into the recesses of Mickey Mouse's dream. Next, the comforting balm of true love appears as a group of three floats carrying Belle and the Beast, Ariel and Eric and Snow White and Prince Charming meander gracefully down the river. The characters dance together on their floats, to the tunes of the love ballads from each film. In contrast to the high-spirited adventure on the pirate ship, this unit of the show invites the audience to smile and simply enjoy the sights and sounds of the heart.

Suddenly, seemingly from out of nowhere, a dark, disturbing cackle echoes through the audience. It is Maleficent, the dragon villain from *Sleeping Beauty*. She appears in dragon form, both on screen and in three-dimensional form on the river, and it is clear that her intention is to thwart Mickey Mouse's dreams. Maleficent often appears in shows as the central image of the incalculable negative aspects of the Jungian shadow. Her presence summons a shudder, mainly because she embodies the incalculable and negative aspects of shadow. Snow White's stepmother and Ursula join Maleficent, as these dark, consumptive images of the unconscious threaten to hijack Mickey Mouse's dream and his place as an image of consciousness driving the show. All manner of villainous images manifest, as Mickey Mouse changes from his incarnation as the *Sorcerer's Apprentice* to the *Brave Little Tailor*, Disney's version of a *David and Goliath* tale. Mickey Mouse shakes his head at the dragon, which begins to breathe fire, turning the Rivers of America into a version of the River Styx, the gateway to the underworld. Mickey Mouse lets out an exclamation, "You make me feel so horrible. But this is MY dream!" And with that, he defeats them all. After defeating them all, Mark Twain's Riverboat, the Dixie Queen appears on the river. Performers from some of the most popular Disney features make this trip down the river, waving multicolored ribbons, which may be read as a symbol of the boons of an encounter with the imagination. Mickey Mouse appears, and exclaims, "Some imagination, huh?" And, with that, the show is complete.

This show may be read as Disney's interpretation of its own canon. In *Fantasmic!*, Disney wields their mythic tradition and attempts to make the audience aware, through the use of spectacle, that there is a greater mythic theme in the occurrences at Disneyland. The park is not simply the place where the characters live. It is the place where patrons gather to participate in Disney's specific way of experiencing the imagination. *Fantasmic!* suggests that certain sentient aspects of the characters' natures exist within the park. These characters are alive in the Disney tradition, and as such they are not required to present themselves through the structures of their original narrative. This show beckons the audience to initiate further into the mysteries of Disneyland, taking the show deeper than an animation museum or amusement park that many suggest it is. It presents that because these characters live, they might not be safely contained, even by Mickey Mouse, and as such, it suggests that the audience who continues to dream with Mickey Mouse follow his example by becoming more conscious of the dragons that emerge and grip their own imagination.

Disney's central themes, the transformative nature of love and the power of the imagination, are conveyed through *Fantasmic!* It is the experience of the spectacle; however, that punctuates its ability to convey its message to the audience. Since the earliest years of this show, the crowds that have gathered to witness this spectacle have themselves become a liminal vehicle for the show. Until recently, when Disney began to offer Fast Passes intended to organize the crowds by giving them designated places to stand, passionate Disney devotees often arrived hours before the show, sometimes as early as five o' clock in the afternoon for a nine o' clock pm show. In the tradition of pilgrimage, park patrons are willing to endure all manner of physical discomfort and financial burden in order to experience this spectacle. This sea of humanity forms an immovable wall across the front of New Orleans Square, often stretching all the way to Frontierland. The sight of the crowd itself is overwhelming, as the trek from Critter Country back to Main Street, U.S.A. can take two or three times the average time and is only possible through the efforts of cast members whose job it is to navigate the crowd for patrons on the move. The experience of this kind of crowd dissolves boundaries between individuals, leaving the patron to experience a kind of sensual, ecstatic alchemical experience that bonds individual park patrons into one body of cheering Disney fans.

On with the Show: World of Color

And the tradition of pancanonical metaspectacle continues in both Disney Parks today. While *Fantasmic!* continues to run, the Disneyland Resort finds itself in the midst of constant renewal of these traditions with an ever continuing effort to find newer ways to present the show. In particular, Disney Imagineers continue to re-vision their fireworks show as an offering in tandem with *Fantasmic!* as well as create new shows like the *World of Color* show which opened in June 2010 as a part of the expansion of Disney California Adventure. These attractions continue to develop the technique of show as symbolic amalgamation.

Although it clearly evokes its *Fantasmic!* heritage, the *World of Color* show is also loosely inspired by a combination light, water, and sound show that runs at the Bellagio Hotel in Las Vegas, Nevada. The staff at the park continues to learn from their experiences of crowd control, and as such, the experience of the *World of Color* show is quite different from the ones at Disneyland Park. In contrast to the congested area around the Rivers of America and Sleeping Beauty's Castle during *Fantasmic!*, and Disneyland's nightly fireworks show, Paradise Pier features a self-contained viewing area for the show. Each day, patrons flock to the main gate of Disney's California Adventure as soon as the gates open in order to queue for passes that will allow them into special viewing areas for the show. These passes are included as part of the patron's entrance ticket, and they are collected by cast members immediately upon arrival for the show. Fast passes have created a less chaotic, and, some might suggest, a less authentic experience at the new shows. Furthermore, this show participates in the tradition of the distillation of Disney's mythic images into iconic form. Instead of giving the audience a brand new narrative vehicle for Disney's characters, *World of Color* turns the images into symbols. It seems to be expected that the audience at this show is well aware of the stories invoked through the show. While this is true of all of Disneyland's spectacles, this new show takes the experience to a new level of initiation.

The show bookends this experience with Disney's images as collected ideology. The show begins with an invocation to vintage Walt Disney television with the theme song to Disney's *Wonderful World of Color*. The show then presents animation segments in proximity to each other, like the parades, as well as under the cover of night, like *Disneyland's Main Street Electrical Parade* and *Fantasmic!*. Yet, in contrast to these shows, *World of Color* organizes the show into larger mythemes, like true love, the importance of family, the fierce independence of the pirates, and nostalgia. However, the show bookends by returning to a synthesis of ideological images rather than an entrance into the narrative itself. The unit representing Disney's fairy-tale image of love is the clearest example of this. The song, *So Close*, from Disney's *Enchanted*, couches the entire unit, an interesting choice for this unit considering the message of this song centers on alienations that often keep lovers apart.

It does not progress through the narrative of any of the films through this unit. It does not even necessarily feature images from the feature film from which the music originates or offer the audience a general feeling of the story by presenting snippets of the story the way the other sections of the show does. Instead, it presents an amalgamation consisting entirely of images of Disney's *true love's kiss* moments from the fairy tales. These images flash quickly across the aquatic screen, evoking the tradition of the animation cell. The show ends with the kaleidoscopic images associated with Walt Disney's original *World of Color* show.

This entire group of spectacles that comprise Disneyland's shows are a flourish-style sleight of hand. They solidify the illusion of the stories being told. However, in reality, the impact of the new para-narrative spectacles exists entirely in the imagination of the patron as they draw on their own personal associations with Disney's canon, and the fact that these shows are so incredibly successful indicates that in large part, Disney is aware that the true power of their myths lies in the relationship between their ability to create the magic and the patron's ability to draw their own associations to it. This sound-byte experience proves Disney's ability to adapt to changes in culture and the audience's entertainment needs. It reflects the effect of the virtual world on our culture, as Disney attempts to interpret what the role of narrative will be in the postmillennial world.

Chapter 6

Renewing the Magic

Question: How many Imagineers does it take to change a light bulb?
Answer: Does it have to be a lightbulb? – Kevin Rafferty[236]

To all who believe in the power of dreams, welcome. Disney's California Adventure opens its golden gates to you. Here we pay tribute to the dreamers of the past: the native people, explorers, immigrants, aviators, entrepreneurs and entertainers who built the Golden State. And we salute a new generation of dreamers who are creating the wonders of tomorrow, from the silver screen to the computer screen, from the fertile farmlands to the far reaches of space. Disney's California Adventure celebrates the richness and the diversity of California . . . its land, its people, its spirit and, above all, the dreams that it continues to inspire. – Michael Eisner[237]

Re-animating Tradition

Rejuvenation is an integral part of any living mythic ritual. It indicates re-animation, demonstrating the life and vitality of the soul in relationship with tradition. Ritual is not effective without it. Minus the presence of the re-inventive, mythic imagination, ritual becomes a curio, an archaic piece of archeological material better suited for display in a museum than a house of worship. Although repetition itself is an act of liturgical participation, to truly engage with tradition and be transformed by it requires the soul's interaction with the structures of the tradition. Take, for example, the experience of the pilgrim and the soul's yearning for sacred landscape. In both theory and in practice, the impact of pilgrimage and sacred space on the soul are deeply personal. They reflect the archetypal movements of the soul, something that is,

236 Kevin Rafferty, *Walt Disney Imagineering: A Behind the Dreams Look at Making the Magic Real*, 11.

237 Michael Eisner, 2001 http://www.laughingplace.com/News-PID502110-502112.asp

in essence, the epitome of the interiority of soul. In its basest form, ritual must be personally meaningful. Driver writes "Ritual acts as if everything is alive and personal".[238] Sacred action must be a practice that moves the soul to continue to create, not simply to imitate.

A ritual tradition is a grouping of personal practices woven together to produce a corporate ritual tradition. By this definition, a corporate ritual tradition represents a body of individual souls in agreement that a particular ritual tradition is meaningful and transformative for them. The significance of a corporate body derives from the desire of the individuals; those who continue to make sacred pilgrimage, to continue to engage with it because it means something to them individually and as a whole. In other words, the process of making ritual is renewal unto itself. Hence, reinvention is the central function of sacred action. If this doesn't happen, ritual moves into the realm of meaningless habit, or tradition, without dialectical relationship to the soul. Furthermore, the renewal of ritual often occurs without notice, because it often occurs during the natural course of interaction with a living tradition.

There are infinite possibilities for renewal. Since change requires intentional reflection on both personal and collective story and action driven by the need to change, renewal is often a painful process. A group of individuals rarely get together to agree on the kind of shift necessary in a ritual system. There has been no shortage of bloodshed over changes to the systems that house mythic ritual throughout human history. This applies vast global traditions such as Christianity, Hinduism, and Islam, as well as secular sets, such as the Hellenized Roman world and the fascist face of contemporary politics. These mythic systems have been and continue to be guided by political, social, and ideological motives as well as psychological and spiritual ones.[239] Renewal often comes cloaked in revolution, and when the dust of revolution settles, the masses may not prefer the revolution to the previous order. They may long for the stability of the old order, however corrupt, and may fear the change necessary under the new order, as well as the set of dysfunctions the new order may bring. Renewal may occur amicably though, as the participants of a tradition respond to unconscious shifts in culture without conflict. Often, it simply means reinvention, the influx of great ideas that encourage initiates to think, feel, and act more profoundly. The following focuses on Disney's participation with the practice of renewal, specifically as it relates to Disneyland Anaheim's transition from the small park behind the berm in the middle of the orange groves to the Disneyland Resort into which it has currently developed.

238 174.

239 An exploration of the different religions and their renewal movements would make for a fascinating study. However, it would drag this study woefully off course. It is not the intention of this study to introduce a new complication here or to generalize or simplify mythic/religious history, but to suggest that these kinds of movements do in fact exist in all traditions, and that they have borne their share of conflict, confusion, and resistance.

The growing pains of re-invention, the rally cries of revolution – Disney is an organization that has survived all the different facets of transition. Since the Disney brothers began their California animation business in 1923,[240] their work has experienced the gambit of renewal. The simple fact that Disney has faced bankruptcy, employee strikes, questionable product quality, and instability in leadership – all without falling to debtors or corporate raiders – is a testament to the organization's commitment to re-invention. These revolutionary actions can be understood as the guiding mythic ethos of the Disney organization. It balances itself on the tightrope that is the tension between tradition and re-invention. This is particularly evident in the parks, beginning, of course, with Disneyland.

Disneyland itself is a renewal movement in entertainment. While trying desperately to secure the funds he needed for Disneyland, Walt assured skeptical bankers that unlike the seedy amusement parks going out of business all over the United States, his park would be, "a different kind of park – a theme park … ".[241] Disneyland is a synergistic concept, one that came to Walt as he sat watching his daughters experiencing the kind of environment he hoped to re-create. As previously suggested, his vision for this new park was about more than simple amusement. Walt Disney's vision was immersion into story, through his point of view. He found it difficult however, as many visionaries do, to convince possible investors that it was possible to re-Imagineer the concept of the amusement park, the fair, or the town square.

The fire of renewal flourished thanks, in large part, to Walt's own belief in his concepts of entertainment. When his wife Lillian asked him why he would want to get into the amusement park business with all the griminess and ethical dubiousness related to it, he replied that his park would be nothing like that. His original idea, a park that reflected his own values, where families could enjoy themselves together, gathered energy as it took shape in Walt's personal psyche. Like many visionaries, he was an intuitive individual, and as he worked to place his own mark on the industry of animation, he also developed his plan to re-craft the entire industry of entertainment – an industry he had, for two decades, intuited was ripe for a renewal. Re-invention is therefore at the heart of every aspect of the Disneyland experience. Disney's obsession with plussing[242] the show quickly became more than the hallmark of a controlling taskmaster. It becomes their guiding creative ethos. As a reflection of the park's dramatic origins, few parts of Disneyland are intended to be permanent. The park is a

---

240 One might even suggest that it would be possible to go back even further, to the old Laugh-O-Grams days to see the beginning of renewal in Disney's creative life. Walt Disney's move to California itself can be understood as a renewal. That would make a great study, but it falls outside of the scope of this project.

241 Finch, *The Art of Walt Disney: from Mickey Mouse to the Magic Kingdom*, 139.

242 Disney's concept of plussing the show refers to a procedure of operation that focuses on continuous re-invention. Disney's Imagineers are never content to walk away from an attraction or spectacle. Inherent in the Disney method is the drive to discover a better way to do and present the show.

stage, and in tandem, cast members and Imagineers alike strike this stage on a consistent basis. Tensions between devoted patrons who wish their *sacred almighty*[243] attractions to remain just as they have always been, and the Imagineers, who work to keep the show fresh, is evident in this process of re-invention.[244]

The 10th Anniversary Special

Walt once said, "Disneyland will never be completed. It will continue to grow as long as there is imagination left in the world."[245] In 1965, during Walt's last days, plans were implemented for a new section of the Disneyland Park. The farthest reaches of Disneyland, previously utilized for such short-lived play areas as Holidayland, were under construction, covering sections of the park with tarps and walls that teased the suspicions of many Disney patrons. However, it was Walt's presence on a television special that once again led to the imaginative sacralization of a place as yet undeveloped. A 10th anniversary special, which aired on January 3, 1965, showcased a dignified looking Walt Disney, clad in his signature suit and smile, with an elegant young woman by his side. The purpose of the special was two-fold. First, and foremost, it was an opportunity to celebrate the success of Disneyland and entertain loyal fans, while thanking them for their patronage. Second, it was a brilliant marketing ploy. It was an opportunity for Walt to continue plugging the park as he had since the early years of the *Disneyland* television show. The 10th anniversary special provided a glimpse into the coming Disneyland expansion by offering both a glimpse into the future of the park and highlighting the development of the park over the previous ten years.

So, why a 10th anniversary special? A decade changeover often marks a time for renewal. Ten is the first two-digit number. It's both the ending of an old cycle and the beginning of a new one. Mythically speaking, cycles of ten have often suggested powerful moments of completion. Moses returns from the mountain with the Ten Commandments and the people were liberated from Egypt after ten plagues. The first letter in the Greek word ten (deca) formed a triangle, and Pythagoraeans often took their oaths by the number ten. Hindu tradition still awaits the perfected 10th avatar of Vishnu who will end the destructive Kali Yuga and usher in a renewed order.[246] Symbolically, this simple number change itself constellates energy of renewed continuity. Disney has always participated in this tradition, marking each decade change as an opportunity to renew their mythic

---

243 This term refers to attractions that have become Disneyland institutions. Although the attractions considered to be sacred almighties clearly differ from patron to patron, the term refers to those attractions without which a visit to the park is incomplete.

244 Disney has long employed survey personnel at the main gate to take information regarding the patron's park experience. In doing so, they weed through the differences between the desires of the annual passholders and out-of-towners to get a sense of what their client base considers important.

245 *The Quotable Walt Disney*, 61.

246 Jean Chevalier and Alain Gheerbrant, *Dictionary of Symbols* 981–982.

canon and offer new park experiences that express the culture of each particular decade. Their participation in this tradition began the original 10th anniversary special.

As previously explored, Walt used television as an avenue for icon building; but this television show indicates Disney's self-conscious participation in the tradition of renewal. The show begins with Walt talking to a young woman named Julie Reems, Miss Disneyland Tencennial. She was chosen to be an ambassador for the park, traveling across the globe to promote Disneyland like a town crier, extolling the virtues of the place as it was, is and shall be. After a short introduction, Walt proceeds to walk Ms. Reems and the audience through the section of the studio populated by Imagineers working on new attractions for Disneyland. Some of the attractions Disney he presents in this special were originally installed at the New York World's Fair the previous year. Imagineering luminaries such as Mary Blair (It's a Small World), Harriet Burns and John Hench (Plaza Inn), Mark Davis and Rolly Crump[247] (Haunted Mansion) and Blaine Gibson and Claude Coates (Pirates of the Caribbean) describe their projects as Disney stands watch, making sure the park is being properly promoted. Each Imagineer is presented in the context of their talents as concept, model, costume, or story artists. They are self-consciously priestly, creating identification between Ms. Reems and the viewer, as though the audience is walking through a tour of the Imagineering department itself.

After Ms. Reems finishes her tour of the attractions to come, Walt reminds her that "anything is possible at Disneyland" and calls in Tinker Bell to transport the audience to Disneyland for a birthday party reminiscent of the parades discussed in chapter 5. The audience is returned to Disneyland, to the square in front of the ultimate weenie, Sleeping Beauty Castle, for a celebratory musical number with the characters that belong in Disney's mythic canon. The characters file in and form a circle around the entrance to the castle, couching the show safely within the mythic canon, and leaving an inner circle open for the forthcoming performance. A dance number commences, complete with a birthday cake that breaks into pieces, showcasing the magic of animation and the blue screen, a new technology that was particularly popular at the studio at the time. The spectacle ends with a song penned by the Sherman Brothers, featuring the lyric "ten years of growing and we've only just begun . . . ". The message is clear: Disneyland is even better than you remember it. The gang is all here. And, it's expanding. The show is fresh, and audience, you want to be here!

Next, the show moves back to the Imagineering department, as Walt stands in front of a map of Disneyland and begins to give a history of the park, beginning

---

247 In the show Roland (Rolly) Crump describes an attraction called the *Museum of the Weird*. While this attraction never came into fruition in the park, many of the ideas many of the ideas did find their way into Disneyland's *Haunted Mansion*.

with Walt himself in 1954, wearing the uniform of the mid-century Southern Californian cowboy pacing the space in the Anaheim orange groves that eventually became Disneyland. This montage moves from the 1959 expansion featuring the Monorail, Matterhorn, and the original Submarine Voyageto the Mine Train, Flying Saucers, Sailing Ship Columbia, Swiss Family Robinson Treehouse (now Tarzan), changes to the Jungle Cruise (African Belt and expanded elephants), and a behind the scenes look at the way Walt Disney's Enchanted Tiki Room works. After walking the audience through his plans for the next stage of Disneyland renovation, including New Orleans Square, he sends Ms. Reems out, like an evangelistic apostle, to spread the gospel of Disneyland in person to any who haven't yet been privy to this special.

Dancing with Heresy in Fantasyland

It is practically irrefutable that Fantasyland is the mythic heart of Disneyland. Fantasyland is certainly the part of Disneyland that holds the closest ties to Walt's heart. It represents the European fairy tales of his childhood, as he remembers them. The castle may be interpreted as the centermost image of Disney's belief in what Disneyland is about. In extreme contrast to the European implications of a castle – warfare, political power, oppression, feudal systems, and class demarcations – Disney's castle is a magical portal to the imagination. At the opening day of Disneyland, Walt read a dedication. This dedication was affirmed by Disney, but never installed in Fantasyland. It read, "Fantasyland is dedicated to the young and the young at heart and to all those who believe that when you wish upon a star your dreams will come true".[248] It is clear that, at least in Walt's mind, the image of Fantasyland carried with it the touch of the sacred, a touch of nostalgia that is meant to move the patron at the deepest soul levels. Fantasyland evokes the innocence of childhood, and any accompanying nostalgia and longing felt by the patron in interaction with it.

These childhood associations made the work of the Imagineers assigned to the renovation of Fantasyland in the early 1980s especially challenging. Imagineering veteran, Bruce Gordon recalls: "I remember Tony (Baxter) standing in the wreckage of Walt's favorite land saying 'What have we done?'"[249] Baxter goes on to call the process of renovating Fantasyland scary. Re-invention is scary, especially when it means breaking down one's ritual/liturgical tradition. Doing so may feel like heresy, but *not* doing so is the real heresy. Baxter goes on to point out that Disneyland is not a museum. It is alive with a synergetic energy that links the past to the future through the imagination. Fantasyland is an example of the guiding ethos within Walt Disney Imagineering as it applies to renewal.

248 "The Disneyland Show", July 17, 1955.

249 *Secrets, Stories and Magic*, DVD.

At Disneyland, Imagineers make a conscious effort to remember the best aspects of the past in order to re-invent the story, rather than replace the story.

The Fantasyland expansion is the clearest example of the way in which the Imagineers dance between fundamentalism and innovation. The look of contemporary Fantasyland has its roots in a Fantasyland attraction called Storybook Land Canal Boats.[250] During the work on the feature film, *Snow White and the Seven Dwarfs*, animator and Disney Legend Ken Anderson[251] was assigned an art director position on the Dwarfs' cottage. Anderson[252] translated Gustav Tenggren's uniquely European concept art into a dwarfs' cottage that remained true both to the concept, as well as to the Disney look. When Fantasyland became a reality, Anderson's designs and talents were utilized to create an attraction that displayed miniaturized versions of the houses from the classic Disney stories that make up Fantasyland. Due to financial and time constraints, the early Fantasyland had a very different look than the mythic continuity of Ken Anderson's Storybook Land Canals. It carried the look of a medieval fair, replete with canvas tents and banner flags. The façade of the land itself was not the reflection of Disney's story in image in the way it is today. The colors were brighter, reflecting mid-century amusement parks, not necessarily a fluid movement through Disney's fairy tales themselves. More of Disney's limited resources were allocated to attractions themselves, and not to the cohesive look of the park.

Viewed from above, as it is in the Disney television show, *People and Places,* the concrete bunkers that housed the attractions were a visible reminder that Fantasyland was actually a stage set, and that the façades were just that. This is not to suggest that the pre-1983 Fantasyland was in some way inferior to its descendant. The magical experience of the attractions housed in the old concrete bunkers of Fantasyland is without question. Anderson's interpretations of the classic stories represent an idealized image of classic fairy tales. This dedication to the integrity of the work of the story artists in concert with the design of Fantasyland, like breadcrumbs leading Hansel and Gretel out of the woods, is typical of the way Disney's Imagineers approach renewal. Disney has often been criticized for their (arguably) obsessive attention to a romantic image of the past and a utopian image of the future. While it is vital that no aspect of popular culture wielding the kind of mythic power held by Disney should be accepted on a wholesale level without criticism, one could argue that it is exactly the combination of Disney's ritual poetics together that are the most effective basis for renewal.

The Imagineering *modus operandi* is to create an environment that, as Baxter

---

250 Opened on June 16, 1956 and is currently still operational in Disneyland Park Anaheim. This attraction exists only at Disneyland Park Anaheim and Disneyland Paris.

251 Often known as the "Jack of all Trades".

252 As well as Disney Legend Fred Joerger.

notes, the fans consistently tell him is "almost as though it was always this way". This image – a chronologically nondescript yet charmingly European town, complete with cobblestones and "stonework" manor houses – reflects the true nature of Fantasyland because it provides the consistency that Fantasyland needs in order to become the kind of comforting environment Waltdesired for it. And, what could be more comforting, as far as Disney fairy tales go, than the look of eighteenth and 19th century Europe. The streets of Fantasyland and Main Street, U.S.A. are inlaid with cobblestones – not real stone, mind you, but manmade interlocking paver stones. The stones give the look of European cobblestones, but without the sharp, chipped edges and faded color of many of the older European villages. The stones create a safe environment on which to walk, and the colors used evoke the blue and pink of Sleeping Beauty's fairy-crafted birthday gown. There are three outdoor attractions in Fantasyland, all three of which were present on the opening day of Disneyland. These are the Mad Tea Party, Dumbo The Flying Elephant, and King Arthur's Carousel. These attractions remain much the same, with a slight shift in color and theme over the years.

The most significant change to Fantasyland comes through the dark rides. These stories belong to differing European cultures, in different periods. For example, Mr. Toad, Peter Pan, and Alice are British in origin and belong to the Victorian/Edwardian eras of the late 19th and early 20th centuries. Pinocchio and Snow White's Scary Adventures belong to the continent – Italy and Germany, respectively. The façades of the buildings return to the look of these classic Disney features in order to make the attractions, which have not been changed drastically, a much more authentic experience of Disney's fairy tales. This is done in a style that intentionally mutes the cultural differences between the stories' countries of origin, while not dismissing these differences. Subtle differences in architectural style are present in the attractions. Toad Hall has the look of a traditional English country manor with its Tudor style charm. Its closest neighbor, on the other hand - although it also has uniquely European dark wood beams, as all the dark ride façades in Fantasyland do - is subtly different, just enough so that it clearly belongs in London. And so it goes throughout the rest of Fantasyland: the buildings flow together, clearly belonging to the same tradition, but changing a shade here, and peaking a roof there, just to gently shift the flavor of the show as it goes along.

Imagineers are quick to point out that any time there is a change made to Disneyland, devoted patrons are skeptical. This makes perfect sense because, if much of Fantasyland's power lies in its ability to reinvent the nostalgia of childhood for patrons, it needs to, as Baxter says, "support older generations who grew up with this period {1950s and 1960s Westerns} of Disneyland as well as kids that know nothing about any of these stories . . . "[253] Continuity is key

---

[253] *Secrets, Stories and Magic*, DVD.

to any renewal process. Without it, the initiates within the tradition will feel as though their beloved rituals are being disrespected and destroyed. However, renewal also requires radical action: the willingness to take a bulldozer to the temple, to take the concrete buildings to the ground, to dismantle even the most treasured aspects of the ritual tradition set down by the cult leader himself, if it means that a fuller experience of the tradition is to be the end result of the take-down. This is both the most subversive and the most devout action in which ritual leaders can participate.

Mickey's 'Hood

A brand new land opened at Disneyland on January 23, 1993. New lands are a relatively rare occurrence at Disneyland, and often these new lands become side attractions at the park, rather than being central to Disneyland as an icon. Because the original Disneyland formula (Walt's four cardinal points emerging from the castle) has been elevated from simple park geography to the status of mythic icon, the Imagineers are not quick to change the original footprint of Disneyland. However, the question of Mickey's home, a physical spot that reflects Mickey's cartoon environment, continued to be a point of meditation for Imagineers. What WOULD Mickey's house look like? What would his neighborhood be like? The concept was not completely new, as Mickey always had a home environment detailed in the early short cartoons, which began in 1928. The challenge of this new land for the Imagineers was similar to the challenge faced by the Imagineers that completed the Fantasyland renovation a decade before: is it possible to take mythic material, the kind of storytelling material that has passed from storytelling into something that reflects a whole ideological, ritualized system, and turn it into something made of resin, concrete, plastic and steel that actually conveys something of its mythic soul in it? Is it possible to do justice to Mickey's neighborhood, as it existed in the imaginations of Walt Disney, Ub Iwerks, and the rest of the early studio team? Perhaps this is a basic artistic challenge of those engaged in mythic reinterpretation.

As always, the Disney Imagineers began with a story and a space. According to Chris Strodder's Disneyland Encyclopedia, Toontown's earliest working title was "Mickeyland". In the end, however, the Imagineering vision for the Mickey annex was broadened to include not just Mickey and his friends, but all characters from the cartoon world. In doing so, the storytellers at Disneyland are attempting to do something other than just creating a physical manifestation of Mickey Mouse's neighborhood. They are attempting to place themselves in the position of suggesting that Disneyland should really be home to Disney's rivals as well as to their own creations. Toontown's story has its basis in the 1988 Touchstone Pictures film *Who Framed Roger Rabbit*, directed by Robert Zemeckis.[254] This film, set in post-WWII Los Angeles, is a technological breakthrough. It is Disney's offering to the film noir tradition. The story centers on

Roger Rabbit, a beloved, if troubled, cartoon rabbit that is a top-billed star at fictional animation studio "Maroon Cartoons". Roger Rabbit fears that his voluptuous and misunderstood wife may have been unfaithful. Enter gumshoe and hopeless drunk Eddie Valiant, played by the brilliant English actor, Bob Hoskins. Eddie soon finds himself deep in the middle of a murder investigation when the information he uncovers drives Roger Rabbit to (allegedly) murder the object of his wife's (alleged) affections. Eddie soon becomes Roger's protector, eventually becoming convinced of his innocence, and the film-noir-esque plot twists ensue to their illogical, toon-y conclusions.

The idea of fusing the animated world with the real world was not a new one in animation. Walt Disney's 1920s series, the *Alice Comedies*, featured a live-action Alice in the midst of an animated wonderland. Disney himself borrowed this idea from the popular *Out of the Inkwell* series in which animated characters were placed in the material world. Furthermore, animated characters also make their way into the liminal, fantasy human environments of *Mary Poppins, Bedknobs and Broomsticks,* and *Pete's Dragon.* While the animation work in *Who Framed Roger Rabbit?* pushes this technology further, the most remarkable, and some might say presumptuous, aspect of this story is the creation of Toontown itself. In placing it just beyond the boundaries of the city of Los Angeles, it simultaneously allows animation its own place, while subtly giving reference to the film industry's traditional allocation of animation to the kid's table. The fact that Touchstone Pictures and not Walt Disney Animation Studios releases this film places Roger Rabbit's Toontown squarely within a Disneyfied atmosphere for animation as a whole, as it attempts an Eisner-era endeavor at cinematic respectability.

The Toontown of Roger Rabbit's world may be read as an alternate Hollywood, as film noir, and as the release of the darker, more self-gratifying nature of what Freud calls the id. In contrast to the fairy tale good-versus-evil take on cartoons that dominates Fantasyland, the Toontown characters seem to be unconscious of their dangerous and often-homicidal tendencies. They bend bars, laugh maniacally, and drop pianos out of windows. Most of the buildings in Towntown are smaller and 'toonier versions of such Main Street U.S.A. locales as neighborhood shops and City Hall, complete with their own Jolly Trolly public transit. Unlike the Fantasyland of fairy tale, it is very much like our own. Even so, it is a wackier version of our own. In Toontown, even the inanimate objects are animated in such a way that it sets the psyche slightly on edge. One can never be quite sure what antics the 'toons will exhibit. Although it is the home of *Disney's* 'toons, the inhabitants are still 'toons. Animated characters are, as Finch notes:

> . . . not bound by the laws of nature. They obey those laws so long as it is useful to

254 Based on a screenplay by Jeffry Price and Peter S. Seaman, which was acquired by the Disney studios in 1981.

do so – that gives them a footing in our world – but, whenever necessary, they can stretch them, bend them, and even reverse them by the exercise of sheer willpower. Whatever catastrophes befall them, they are never in real danger because they are blessed by the freedom that we all experience in dreams. For them, anything is possible; and we are not merely told that this is so, we can see it with our own eyes.[255]

Is it any wonder that they are placed outside the berm? By their very nature they are required to live outside human society.

All of this dark, twisty, Hitchcockian cartoon noir is, in the end, alloyed with Disney mythic significance. Like Fantasyland, Toontown's residents represent the freedom of the imagination from the complications of moral, ethical and social responsibilities. According to Dave Burkhart, the project manager for the Toontown project, "Because of its cartoon nature, it was actually better when a window was cut wrong. At first, it was difficult to get the workers to understand that. When they installed a door, they would ask 'do you want it to hang straight? And our response would be, 'Of course not. Crooked is more toony.'"[256] This exists in fascinating contrast to the fact that Toontown is intended for the littlest among the Disneyland patrons. This may be read as a subtle but distinct argument against Giroux's thesis that Disney is a fascist organization whose entire purpose is to brainwash entire generations into being mindless consumers.[257] Perhaps Toontown, more than any other aspect of Disneyland, infuses a subversive sense of wicked humor into babes bred and born into the Disney mythos. In Toontown, little ones are free to kick buildings, bend the bars of the local jail, talk to trolley cars ,and fantasize about turning the doldrums of daily life into silliness. They are free to go into the tunnel with Roger Rabbit, but once again, it is offered in a controlled, safe environment free of the mythic weasels and the Dip.

When Tomorrowland Becomes Yesterdayland

Walt once said, "Tomorrow is a heck of a thing to keep up with".[258] By this, he seems to suggest that tomorrow is its own archetypal image, an energy with which humanity engages, but is always just beyond our capacity for analysis. A tension is constellated at Disneyland through this emphasis on both the past and the future, and this tension can be better grasped through an analysis of the evolution of Tomorrowland. From the earliest days of the *Disneyland* television show, Tomorrowland was a favorite section among viewers. In the mid-1950s, viewers were eager for an opportunity to jettison the traumas of the past half-century in favor of optimism for the future. This was an era that, although it seemed on the surface to emphasize control and homogeny, was actually full of complications, paradoxes and contradictions. On opening day at Disneyland,

255 *Walt Disney's America*, 294.

256 *Walt Disney Imagineering: A Behind the Dreams Look at Making the Magic Real*, 144.

257 *The Mouse That Roared: Disney and the End of Innocence.*

258 *Secrets, Stories and Magic.*

145

Tomorrowland was set in the future *all the way forward to the year 1986*, and the assumption was that by then a utopian humanity would have harnessed nuclear technology for the use of travel and energy.

The earliest on-camera attraction at Tomorrowland in 1955 was a presentation on molecular science by Dr. Heinz Haber. In 1957, Walt Disney Productions released a film titled *Our Friend the Atom*, also lauding atomic power as a safe, new source of energy that was as yet untapped in its potential and as a boon for the future. To Walt, Tomorrowland was an opportunity to exhibit what he considered to be exciting new technologies, and to dream about possibilities for the future. In fact, much like opening day Frontierland, Tomorrowland focused less on carnival-esque attractions that reflect the work of the studio, and more on Walt's vision of reality.

The Tomorrowland of opening day in 1955 featured a crowd led by Disney officials who seem largely unaware of the complications of their vision of the future. Opening day announcer Bob Cummings refers to Tomorrowland as "not a stylized dream of the future, but a scientifically planned projection of future techniques by leading space experts and scientists".[259] This remark reflects the central conflict between science and mythology, ignorance of the extent to which story impacts science. This atomic story – post-Hiroshima but pre-Chernobyl – which these largely innocent Disney creators and patrons lived looked forward to a future where science would be a unifying ritual process that would erase the divisively dangerous lines traditionally created by ethnic, religious and ideological ritual.

However, as Walt said, tomorrow isn't easy to keep up with. Even in the 1960s and 1970s, Tomorrowland struggled to maintain relevance in a world that was changing faster than the Imagineers could design new attractions. In 1975, Mission to Mars replaced the attraction Flight to the Moon, which had been waning in popularity since the Apollo 11 mission of December 1969. Especially since the Apollo 13 mission in 1970, with its near misses and terrifying suspense, it became clear to Americans that daily trips to the moon were not in the near future. Tomorrowland was constantly in danger of becoming Yesterdayland. In those years before 1986, it seemed to the Imagineers like a heroic task, the likes of the curse of Sisyphus, just to keep up, despite the incredible enthusiasm generated by attractions like Monsanto's 1967 Adventures thru Inner Space and The People Mover.

The image of tomorrow, in its archetypal sense, never seemed quite at peace with the way the creators of Disneyland envisioned it. Then came 1986, yes the real one, both the year of the return of Haley's comet and Tomorrowland's original mythic year. Tomorrowland's 1986 saw the opening of Michael Jackson's Captain EO.[260] This attraction is Disney's acknowledgement and interpre-

---

259 *The Disneyland Story*, DVD.

260 September 12, 1986.

tation of their own archetypal image of tomorrow. The song, *We Are Here to Change the World* captures the guiding ritual ethos of Disneyland. It reminds the audience that the message of Tomorrowland has always been that science is meant to affect humanity's change in a positive way.

Since 1986, a large part of Tomorrowland's draw has changed from 1950s utopian optimism to a nostalgic memorializing of 1986. The opening of Star Tours, the *Star Wars* themed attraction, completed this shift. In 1986, Tomorrowland became the property of science fiction. Contemporary Tomorrowland fuses the 1950s utopian hopes for the future with the opulence of the 1980s, and produces a Tomorrowland that infuses *tomorrow* with Disney's affectionate memory of the past. All of this molten archetypal energy around this image was revealed in 1998 when, in preparation for the beginning of a new millennium, the Imagineers reinvented Tomorrowland with a new color scheme. Disney artist and historian Stacia Martin comments on this shift when she remarks that in the 1998 version, "we get a more residential Tomorrowland".[261] In the millennial Tomorrowland, the landscaping beds become a reinterpretation of the WWII era victory garden, filled with edible plant material. This echoes Disney's belief that the city of the future needs to incorporate a certain amount of utilitarianism in order to become a sustainable environment. Furthermore, changes have been made in the storytelling style and creation of Tomorrowland to further facilitate the reinvention of Disney's atomic age of tomorrow into a millennial one. All references to atomic energy have disappeared in favor of clean energy.

In 2007, the Submarine Voyage was reinvented to become the Finding Nemo Submarine Voyage. This attraction highlights the importance of protecting our underwater ecosystem, by both anthropomorphizing sea creatures and actualizing the philosophy by re-imagineering the submarine from diesel engines to "green" subs, propelled by magnetic coils. The dazzlingly colored reef is crafted entirely out of recycled glass. These are only a couple of examples of the ways that Disneyland lives its Tomorrowland philosophy. Recycling is key at Disneyland, from water to plastic bottles, to characters from re-Imagineered attractions. Disney has come to understand that responsible citizenship for humanity's tomorrow requires a reverence for the past and the willingness to live that out today. This vision of renewal has always been encapsulated in its identity as both Tomorrowland and Yesterdayland. Tomorrowland aficionados are in agreement about this. One last note: Due to the death of Michael Jackson in 2009, Captain EO returned to Disneyland in 2010 after being closed for sixteen years. Although it was replaced in 2014 by Guardians of the Galaxy, a new Marvel Studios offering, its popularity among die-hard Disney fans has not even begun to wane, as Tomorrowlanders continue to devote themselves to an innocent

---

261 *Secrets, Stories and Magic*, DVD.

image of tomorrow that, in typical Disney fashion, requires only heart and a willingness to face the villain head-on for an illuminated future to emerge.

The Disneyfication of the Golden State

Perhaps the most significant attempt to renew ritual at Disneyland occurred on February 8, 2001. This is the day that Disney's California Adventure Park[262] opened adjacent to the original Disneyland. Although a version of the Tower of Terror attraction originally opened on July 22nd, 1994 at Walt Disney World, the fact that it reflects the mythology of old Hollywood is significant. What makes this park and its version of attractions showcased elsewhere significant examples of renewal is their location in Anaheim, California, a city situated in the heart of Orange County, a symbol of Californian affluence. Disney California Adventure is, and has been since its inception, an attempt to re-mythologize and re-ritualize the image of California. The park itself bears a slight (*extremely* slight) resemblance to the state itself: long and thin with jutting edges on either side. And, it is broken up into themed environments much like the lands of the original park.[263]

These lands are Disney's homage to some of the most iconic areas of California, from the redwoods and canneries in the North to the farm land of California's valleys, to the tech hubs and vistas of the San Francisco Bay area and the movie magic of Tinseltown. Disney's California Adventure is more than Disney's homage to the state that spawned it and continues to call it home. It is the renewal of California's mythic power. It is a synthesis of the images and exports of California as those involved with the creation of the park imagine it could be, recreating it as an alternative to the smog-filled, congested mess that California often, in reality, is. In essence, Disney's California Adventure attempts to do for the entire state of California what New Orleans Square did for New Orleans. It returns California's iconic power to the imagination, renewing it through Disney's incredible ability to synthesize the images with nostalgia and excitement for the future.

The Soarin' Over California[264] attraction that ran at Disney California Adventure (DCA) from 2001 to 2016 is an example of Disney's attempt to synthesize what it means to experience California. Although this widely popular attraction was renovated in 2016 to reflect the Soarin' (Over the World) concept that exists at Disney parks in Orlando and Hong Kong, it still has its roots planted firmly in Californian aviation, so let's analyize the original attraction. It begins with a

---

262 On May 28, 2010, the name was changed simply to Disney California Adventure Park.

263 The lands are named Golden State, Hollywooland, Paradise Pier, Buena Vista Street, and "a bug's land". Within these lands are some subsections such as the Grizzly Airfield area of Golden State and the Pacifica Wharf area adjacent to Paradise Pier.

264 A version simply titled *Soarin'* opened in The Land pavilion of Epcot on May 5, 2005. It seems clear that while globalization is the theme of Walt Disney World, the Orlando park remains aware of and impacted by mythic roots that lie deep in the sandy soil of Southern California.

queue that celebrates California's contribution to the craft of aviation called *Wings of Fame*. Portraits of famous aircraft such as the P-51 Mustang and American aviation icons Amelia Earhart, Jimmy Doolittle, Jack Northup, and Howard Hughes line the walls of a queue that generally moves through this area just slowly enough for the patron to meditate on names that are either familiar or at the very least provocative. After strolling through *Wings of Fame*, patrons makes their way down a long hall reminiscent of an old air bunker toward a queue near the door of the attraction itself, which resembles an aircraft hanger. A television placed above and against the wall plays the attraction's music as it shows the names of the places in California the attraction is about to visit.[265]

After a few words of safety information from actor Patrick Warburton,[266] the queue files into one of three rows meant to simulate hang gliders. These gliders lift up in front of an IMAX screen horizontally so that the second and third rows can only see the shoes of those in front of them. The music of the attraction begins at lift off, a score intended to stir the patron emotionally as scents are pumped in to evoke the place pictured on screen – pine trees scent the air over Yosemite and Lake Tahoe, orange blossoms over Camarillo and the salt of the Pacific Ocean spray the patron while passing over Monterey and Malibu. Not a detail is spared, down to changes in temperature and humidity through the desert and over the Russian River. This virtual trip reads like a greatest hits reel, showing only the prettiest and most beloved areas of the Golden State. Again, Disney employs the technique of the synthesis of images to affect the audience. Toward the end of the attraction, after soarin' over sunset at Malibu, the perspective turns to nighttime in Los Angeles, symbolically returning the patron to the heart and origin of Disney mythology. It ends in front of Sleeping Beauty's Castle at Disneyland in the midst of the fireworks show, reminding the patron that after a stunning journey across the state, they are now back home at Disneyland, witnessing the metaspectacle and being sprinkled with Tinker Bell's pixie dust.

Previous to its renewal in 2012, the energy at Disney California Adventure, or DCA as many call it, was a bit ambiguous. It was clearly a part of the Disney organization, but didn't quite felt like a Disney experience. It was a wonderfully themed amusement park, but an amusement park, not a magic kingdom. Is it because the project began during the tumultuous millennial moment, when storytelling seemed to rank lower on the priority scale than profit at Disney? Is it because Ex-CEO, Michael Eisner, for all of his financial wizardry in protecting it from corporate raiders, isn't really a storyteller at heart the way Walt was? Is it because little details, like the presence of alcohol in the park, just don't create

---

265 *Soarin' Over California* locations: San Francisco, Monterey, Napa Valley, Lake Tahoe, Yosemite, Palm Springs, Camarillo, Anza-Borrego Desert State Park, San Diego, Malibu, Los Angeles, and Disneyland.

266 ftnalt Also known as Kronk in Disney's animated features *The Emperor's New Groove* and *The Emperor's New Groove 2: Kronk's New Groove*. He is also featured in several Disney television shows and video games. Furthermore, he has lent his voice to many other animated characters outside the Disney pantheon.

a true Disneyland – like environment? Perhaps there is an amount of truth to all of these criticisms of DCA, but when one considers the Disney parks from the point of view of ritual, temple and canon, another possibility arises. DCA simply wasn't held together by a mythic canon the way Disneyland was when it opened in 1955.

DCA was expected to be a meaningful experience to the patrons, simply because of its proximity to Disneyland and because so many devoted park patrons are Californians. A cohesive story for California, however, was not created at the park. Segues between Disneyland, the home of the characters, and their presence at DCA were weak. This created an environment that, while easy to feel affection for, was not crafted as a Disney icon from the beginning. Of course, at that point in 2010, DCA was a young park, only ten years old. When Disneyland was ten years old, Walt was just announcing the addition of New Orleans Square, It's a Small World, and the Plaza Inn. It is not a coincidence that Disney used the platform of the 2009 D23 Expo, the forums of Internet sites, Disney blogs, and the D23 Disney fan club itself to announce their 1.1 billion dollar expansion of DCA and the Disneyland Hotel. In 2015, Disney even used live stream technology to broadcast their D23 Expo announcement of the creation of the new Star Wars Land. What could be more effective today than Internet media marketing? It *is* the millennial version of the *Dateline Disneyland* television show.

Disney, You've Got a Friend in Pixar!

DCA's impact comes largely from work of Pixar Animation Studios. At first glance, making California a *Pixarland* may seem like a nonsensical choice, perhaps even antithetical to the park's mission of ritualizing the experience of California. Frankly, Disney has traditionally struggled to place its characters in the context of the DCA. Mickey and his friends are often present, but they are often portrayed as on vacation there. In the early years of this park the question persisted: What exactly is the mission of the park and who belongs there? In the early days it seemed as though the park didn't have a unifying mythic system. Hollywood Pictures housed The Muppets, and an attraction that showcased Disney's tradition of the animated feature. Likewise, Paradise Pier has seemed more like the Santa Monica Pier or the Santa Cruz Beach Boardwalk than anything actually associated with Disney. The Golden State was a pure homage to California's natural beauty with almost no reference to Disney's mythic canon.

In an exemplary article written for themeparktourist.com, Brian Krosnick examines this phenomenon. He, and I'm paraphrasing here, suggests that the central problem with the early years of DCA is the park didn't inject enough sacred energy into the creation of the place. This is likely the result of allowing Disney executives too much creative control in the development of the new park. The result is a park full of sarcastic gags, uninspired attractions, caricatures that lack the Disney touch, and Los Angeles realities that appeal to Hollywood insiders and industry types, but not to pilgrims who visit Anaheim longing for the kind of uplifting, environment for play that they are used to engage. Krosnick notes that the best example of DCA's problems in the early years is an attraction called Superstar Limo. This ride through attraction takes the patron through the streets of Los Angeles as it encounters celebrities, over the top caricatures of city landmarks, and self-effacing jokes. It seems to be an attempt to make it clear that Hollywood is nonsense; that tinseltown is all stage lighting and makeup.[267] This is one example of a larger problem that existed across the entire park in its first ten years. Underthemed carnival rides, corny gags, name-dropping, and cheap production – these values attempt to lift the veil of industry magic, but what if the audience likes the veil? What if the veil is central to effective Disney ritual?

Rather than causing the audience to giggle along and turn to the Imagineers with a knowing smile that gets the joke, this version undersells the mystical qualities of California as a mythic place. Theming California this way produces an awkward tension, because it reveals too much about L.A. culture in general and Disney culture in particular. The truth is that DCA's strength lives in its potential to do the same kind of ritual as Disneyland in a wholly different way. If Disneyland is the imaginative playground of Walt's childhood, DCA has the potential to be the imaginative playground of Walt's early adulthood. It always caters to a more adult crowd. It's the kind of place where locals can go for a drink, conferences break for the night, and industry types can laugh off the nonsense of their work. The problem is though that these people don't comprise the largest demographic of Anaheim's visitors. It turns out that daytrippers and annual passholders are the largest demographic at Disneyland, and these people come to Disneyland to partake in Disney's myth, not to poke fun at it, see through Hollywood's nonsense, or *pop the bubble*, so to speak. In an attempt to call out the shadow of Hollywood surrealism, DCA's early format makes a mistake that had it been anyone other than Disney probably would have proved fatal it alienates its core demographic. Throughout the first decade of the 21st century, park managers found that there are simply not enough patrons who come from the other crowd – the non-Disney devotee crowd – to actually make a financial success of DCA. They recognized that they needed to reinvigorate it with Disney magic, and, what is more postmillennially Disney than Pixar? In fact, the only area of DCA that actually seemed to unify the story was the section dedicated to children under the age of five, It's a Bugs Land.

Enter Pixar, Stage Left: the fledgling studio largely responsible for answering the question, "how do we begin to fix DCA?" Pixar's success is instrumental to both DCA's re-visioning and Disney animation's current mythic revival. Undoubtedly, Disney's classic characters do belong in DCA, but it's the ethos of

267 http://www.themeparktourist.com/features/20151212/31106/california-mis-adventure-how-disneylands
-second-gate-crashed-burned-and-was

Pixar Animation Studio and the resulting characters that are born there that generates a renewal of Disney's mythic method. Perhaps those responsible for steering DCA's imagineering recognize that Pixar itself creates an atmosphere that prizes the kind of renewal, reinvention, and innovation that has always been synonymous with Disney. The artists at Pixar are pioneers of a new form of animation, pushing the technology further than anyone thought possible. Furthermore, those associated with Pixar continue to have (arguably) a deeper love for Disney's mythic ethos than many of those who have been involved with Disney itself.

The story of Pixar's success is captivating, a true underdog story in the tradition of the early years at The Disney Brothers Studio. Pixar began in 1979 in Emeryville, California as a computer graphics division of George Lucas's Lucasfilm called Graphics Group. This group consisted of what Lucas called a "rebel alliance"[268]a group of scientists who were convinced that there was a way to merge art with physics. From its earliest days, many visionaries within this group believed in the application of computer graphics in animation. This group of pioneers shared a deep love for animation and, in particular, the art of Disney animation. Three names quickly come to the forefront of the Pixar story: Edwin Catmull,[269] John Lasseter,[270] and the late, great Steve Jobs.[271] Much like Walt Disney and Ub Iwerks half a century before, these names are now legend. They fuse passion, science, skill, and business savvy, a magical combination necessary for reinvention. Catmull was the first of these three men to work with the Graphics Group. His scientific mind lit the group's Promethean fire, but it's Lasseter that brought the connection to Disney. In fact, because he and Walt exhibit such similarities as both storytellers and creative leaders, it makes sense to turn to a short excursus about him.

John Lasseter is an alumnus of the Disney-owned California Institute for the Arts (Cal-Arts) in Valencia, California. He grew up in Whittier, California in an environment that was steeped in Disney's mythology. From the moment he realized that it was possible to make cartoons for a living, there was no question that making them was to be a defining passion of his life. Furthermore, there was never a question about the animation studio that was closest to his heart. He recalls his time at Cal Arts as some of the most inspiring moments of his life, professionally and personally. During this period of matriculation, many of Walt's legendary *nine old men*[272] came out of retirement to teach this new crop of young animators. They endowed the students with Disney's version of heart.

---

268 *The Pixar* Story, DVD.

269 Catmull President of both Walt Disney Animation and Pixar Animation Studios.

270 Lasseter presently holds titles of Chief Creative Officer at Pixar and Walt Disney Animation Studios as well as Principle Creative Advisor of Walt Disney Imagineering.

271 Jobs died on October 5, 2011. He held a seat on the board of The Walt Disney Company as their largest stockholder.

272 Particularly Ward Kimball, Ollie Johnston and Frank Thomas.

This emphasis on emotion in the mythic fabric of animation impacted Lasseter deeply, convincing him even more that his future lay with Disney. After graduation, he took a position as an animator at the Walt Disney Animation Studio. He worked at the Disney studio in the early 1980s, with many of the most talented animators of the era known as the second Disney renaissance – Glen Keane, Mark Henn, John Musker, and Ron Clements to name a few. He also shared the animation studio for a short period with another visionary filmmaker, and a classmate of his from Cal Arts, Tim Burton. Such a group of talents together at once can only be read as a pressure cooker of creativity.

However, some of the ideas that began to develop around the edges of the animation industry in the early 1980s made studio executives at Disney uneasy. Much like Walt before him, Lasseter was a part of that shake up. This is particularly true of those interested in the application of computers in animation. In 1983, after working on a project that combined traditional, hand-drawn animation with computer graphics, Lasseter's contract ended without renewal. Disillusioned, he attended a computer graphics conference at the Queen Mary in Long Beach, California. Catmull, a presenter at the conference, convinced Lasseter to move north of San Francisco to join a computer animation venture at LucasFilm. The group had been searching for an animator for quite some time. Convinced that they were on the track to success, the unseasoned group branched out into more complex and daring modes of artistic expression.

Pixar's road to success, however, was not to be an easy or untroubled one. For Pixar to be the renewing force it was capable of being, it required an established patron with pockets as deep as Howard Hughes and a vision as focused as Walt Disney. They found this in Apple Inc. tycoon Steve Jobs. He acquired this Graphics Group after LucasFilm released them in 1986. Per the terms of the deal, Jobs invested ten million dollars of Apple's capital. This influx nurtured Pixar as it began to take shape. In the late 1980s, Pixar developed the Computer Animation Production System or CAPS for Disney. It was the earliest digital ink and paint system. And, although the earliest CAPS projects were limited ones without the kind of financial gain that signifies success in Hollywood, both the Disney and Pixar were encouraged by the advances of this system.

In 1995, after a decade of success and struggle, Pixar Animation Studios released their first feature in concert with the Walt Disney Animation Studio: *Toy Story*, a fully computer animated feature about tolerance, insecurity, friendship, and loyalty in a toy box. The film was an immediate blockbuster success, and caused some at Disney to begin to respect Pixar's mythic voice, as well as the company's ability to drive its own destiny. With Disney backing, Pixar followed *Toy Story* with a string of phenomenal hits: *A Bug's Life* (1998), *Toy Story 2* (1999), *Monster's Inc.* (2001), *Finding Nemo* (2003), and *The Incredibles* (2004). All of these films were released by, and became synonymous with, Disney animation, and all of these films relit the fire of passion for animation in their audiences. As actor

Tom Hanks, who played Woody in *Toy Story*, said, "I feel like I'm in *Dumbo*. I feel like I'm in *Pinocchio*."[273] This statement can be read as Hanks' acquiescence of his participation in the beginnings of another renewal of animation for Disney, that he is part of the same kind of innovative work that created the defining icons of Disney mythology.

Although the Walt Disney Animation Studio has experienced many peaking moments of the renewal of their own mythic canon – perhaps most notably achieved in 1991 with the release and subsequent Best Picture Oscar nomination of *Beauty and the Beast* – the success of Pixar marks the first time in the studio's history that a separate production company developed a whole new technology outside of Disney's control. And, as guided as they were by the vintage Disney mythic ethos, Pixar returns to re-mythologize the Disney Studio itself. The staff at Pixar are so in love with animation in general, and Disney animation in particular, that they could not help but infect the resistant Eisner-era studio with their passion.

The capital they brought in didn't hurt, either. Pixar's success further marks the first time in Disney history that an outside group created their own mythic voice, utilizing Disney's formula, and succeeded in taking the studio simply by the force of that mythic voice. As a force for the renewal of the classic Disney artistic ethos, a charismatic leader needed to come forth, and in large part, that leader was Lasseter. Story artist Joe Grant says that Walt and he have something in common. They both have intuition. "He seemed to know everything before hand. I see the same thing in Lasseter. He is pretty much an image of Walt."[274] Led by Lasseter, Pixar re-injects the Disney studio with the archetypal *Puer*, shamanic Walt Disney-type energy necessary for the work to bear Disney's quality of playfully mythic storytelling.

Sadly, the success of *Toy Story* validated the Pixar's approach and divided the animation community at large. Many proponents of traditionally hand-drawn animation, at Disney in particular, found computer animation to be threatening to positions that already felt jeopardized. The presence of computer animation, combined with some stories that were not terribly strong,[275] caused a bloodletting of animators at the studio that was tragic for Disney's animation culture, and difficult for Pixar to watch. Disney's version of computer animation was nowhere near as exciting as Pixar's, largely due to a lack of attention to storytelling at Disney. One might suggest that the excitement surrounding computer animation was simply outshining the development of character. Many at Disney saw computer animation as a dangerous fad, responsible for the destruction of animation as an art form in favor of box office capital. However, the audience, as well as many within the studios, were fascinated by this technology, and

---

273 *The Pixar Story* DVD.

274 *The Pixar Story*, DVD.

275 *Home on the Range* (2003) and *Chicken Little* (2006) in particular.

compelled by Pixar's ability to tell a story. The relationship between Disney and Pixar has was always a tenuous one, but in 2006,[276] Pixar struck a deal that cemented their position with Disney and ensured their studio a continued role in Disney's mythic tradition. Disney officially acquired Pixar Animation Studios, calling for the studio's further participation in the storytelling of Disney theme parks.

After two decades in business for themselves, Pixar brought their outlandish outside the corporation thinking to Disney's corporate structure. Catmull said, "This is the true culmination of the building of Pixar, this amazing company, into something that will continue on and continue to make waves in the future".[277] This influence continues to make a mythic impact on DCA. The characters are present, signing autographs and engaging in spectacle through the parades, and although DCA has belonged to Pixar's spirit since they opened in 2001, this acquisition finalized it. Pixar continues to have an ever-expanding hold on the Anaheim park experience. From the earliest days of the *Toy Story* movies, Pixar was always present in Anaheim. Merchandizing and characters were present at Disneyland in the 1990s. Even though Disneyland opened a Buzz Lightyear Astro Blasters attraction in 2005,[278] the Pixar characters have never quite fit there. With the opening of DCA in 2001, however, these characters were reallocated for good.

In 2005, a traditional dark ride named Monsters, Inc.: Mike and Sulley to the Rescue opened at DCA, and in 2008, the midway games at DCA's Paradise Pier were replaced by an attraction called Toy Story Midway Mania. This attraction features a dark-ride environment, but with a new interactive twist. It's what the Imagineers call 4D, which means that not only does the rider see the attraction in 3D, but they experience a touch experience of the attraction as well. It's a fully sensory experience, breaking what is often knows as the fourth wall. If air brushes past their shoulder, or water squirts in their face, the rider actually feels this. The attraction's story is eponymously evident. The rider moves along on a track, stopping every few seconds to play a traditional midway game, that is, shooting hoops, bullets, water or darts at plates, balloons and other midway staples. The rider moves along, encouraged by the entire cast of Toy Story with tricks to score more points. This attraction is extremely successful, and the line is rarely short.

In 2009, Disney announced that they would construct an entirely new land as part of their DCA expansion. Cars Land, an homage to the popular Pixar *Cars* film franchise, features a small town – off the famed Interstate Highway Route 66 – called Radiator Springs. The story centers on a racecar named Lightning

---

276 At this point, the resignation of past CEO, Michael Eisner, in 2005, was still fresh in the minds of everyone at both studios.

277 *The Pixar Story*, DVD.

278 March 17, 2005.

McQueen, voiced by American actor Owen Wilson. In the story, Radiator Springs has become a ghost town, a casualty of the super-efficient freeway. It is an image of the bygone era of the mid-century American road trip. Route 66 has often been considered a portal to Southern California from the Midwest, traveling through Kansas and Oklahoma through the Southwest, and eventually to Santa Monica. In director John Ford's film version of *The Grapes of Wrath*, John Steinbeck's characters traverse this highway as they make their pilgrimage to Southern California. This highway became so iconic that Bobby Troup wrote a song about it, which was recorded by the Nat King Cole Trio in 1946. It's lyric, "get your kicks on Route 66" endures today as a symbol of the heyday of American automobiles.

Cars Land is nestled in between Paradise Pier and Hollywoodland, providing a route between Hollywood and Santa Monica to the San Francisco/Santa Cruz and agricultural areas of the park. It features an attraction called Radiator Springs Racers, a high-speed car attraction utilizing technology previously developed at Walt Disney World to bring to life the experience of a road trip across the desert to Los Angeles. In Radiator Springs Racers, visitors ride in cars with bodies similar to Lightning McQueen's. The attraction begins with a slow trip through the desert. There are rock formations in the arid landscape with a similar look as the red rocks of the Arizona/California border scenery that was once the famous Route 66. There's a majestic waterfall and music swelling through the car speakers as the slow cruise comes to an end. The car pops around the corner into a dark ride area where characters from the movie *Cars* jump out at every turn. Then the attraction moves into a holding room where your car is either painted or given new tires in preparation for a race. It then races around the track in an exhilarating high speed competition that is a fitting end to this myth about road trips.

Cars Land also attempted the re-invention of a vintage Tomorrowland classic, The Flying Saucers.[279] This attraction offered the patron the opportunity to ride hovercraft saucers across an air-pressurized platform. It was a fan favorite that never quite worked, because Imagineering did not have the technology at that time to make it a smooth, consistent and enjoyable attraction for all. This new attempt, Luigi's Roamin' Tires, failed again for almost the same exact reason, and is now replaced by an attraction called Luigi's Rollickin' Roadsters, a more traditional car spin style attraction themed to honor the Italian immigrants of California. Cars Land also consists of several shops and restaurants, as well as an attraction that square dance attraction with fan favorite, (Tow) Mater. Through this addition of Cars Land, Imagineering is attempting to bring together Disney's original concept for Disneyland, a place where adults and children can both find fun, while also playing with Southern California's myths that connect Hollywood to freedom through the automobile, as well as devel-

[279] 6 August 1961 – 5 September 1966.

156

oping an environment that attempts to balance the princess-heavy environment of Disneyland.

A Whole New (La La) Land: Renewing Walt's Los Angeles

The work of bringing Pixar to the front of consciousness at DCA, though wonderfully effective in its own right, still does not complete its journey toward renewal. For many years before the expansion of DCA that was completed in 2012 I wondered: where is Walt in all these Disney projects? If Disney was the first shaman of his tradition, to deny him presence in later projects because he has been separated from his followers by death seems not only foolish, but also downright cruel. With the influx of Pixar's mythic energy, DCA does receive renewal through an entirely new generation of bards of the Disney tradition. But where is the cult leader, the pied piper, the original visionary that captivates audiences with his fearlessness and his affection for nostalgia? Where is Uncle Walt? He's there now! In an article they wrote for the summer 2009 issue of *Disney Twenty-Three* magazine, organizers Steve Clark and Jeffrey Epstein argue for the inclusion of Walt Disney at DCA.

> Charming Victorian Architecture, the clip-clop of the horse drawn streetcar, ornate gas lamps, and the sweet smell dancing in the air outside the candy shop are likely familiar to most readers of *Disney twenty-three*. While strolling down Disneyland's Main Street, USA, it's a warm embrace of nostalgia that greets us. Bur for most, that nostalgia is rooted in the experience of another. It's the embodiment of fond childhood memories Walt Disney had for the five short years his family live in Marceline, Missouri just after the turn of the century.[280]

Much of Walt's life story has moved past historical fact into myth and legend. A great deal of his power as an icon is encapsulated by just that. Walt's closest family and friends, as well as those with interest in his organization, are fiercely protective of his image, and they should be. Just as the image of Walt in action is likely to bring a tear to the eye of many a baby-boomer, it's also likely to bring a nostalgic charge to later generations who were raised on the early years of The Disney Channel. In the last decade before her death in 2013, Walt's daughter, Diane Disney-Miller, was extremely vocal about her sense that her father's memory must be preserved and honored within Disney.

In early 2010, she partnered with her son, Walter Elias Disney Miller, to launch a new physical space for the project that they have called The Walt Disney Family Museum. Disney-Miller speaks about this project in a special feature on the DVD of her documentary, *Walt Disney: The Man Behind the Myth*. She feels that in recent years her father's image has become so mythologized that the public has lost the sense that he was an actual human being who lived his work passionately and loved his family. She made it her mission to return the life in her father's work to cultural consciousness. Her passion for this topic has found its way back to Anaheim, which has allowed for a re-infusion of Disneyland with

---

[280] "California Dreamin': Imagineering the Future of Disney's California Adventure", 30.

images and attractions related to Walt Disney. Clark and Epstein quote Bob Weis, President of the Imagineering Division:

> We said, 'Well, if Main Street is about Walt's childhood and about his dreams, then Disney's California Adventure should be about the Walt who came to California and started the legacy of what would become The Walt Disney Company of today' . . . 'A big part of what people said about Disney's California Adventure was that they wanted more about Walt – and more of a connection to the Disney legacy'.[281]

In traditional Disney Park renewal style, this expansion was completed piece-meal. The work at Paradise Pier, which began with a wholesale renovation of Paradise Pier's story that features Victorian architecture and the imagery of the early Mickey and Friends shorts, was completed in 2010, ending with the introduction of Ariel's UnderSea Adventure.

When it was completed in 2012, the DCA expansion entered the phase that deals with Disney's Los Angeles experience. The letter sculptures that spelled out the word *California* were removed from the front entrance, in favor of an entrance that evokes both the architectural norms of Los Angeles's downtown Mission style and the art deco style of the iconic Union Station.[282] The reference to San Francisco's Golden Gate Bridge was removed, and the bridge was renamed Hyperion Bridge in honor of the home of the earliest Disney Brothers Studio. Furthermore, the sculpture in Sunshine Plaza was removed to make way for a replica of the Carthay Circle Theater. The new DCA Main Street, L.A., is called Buena Vista Street, a tribute to the Walt Disney Animation Studio in Burbank, Buena Vista Pictures, and the Buena Vista music label. Los Angeles' vintage public transit, The Red Car, stops on this new Buena Vista Street, picking up passengers on the way to Hollywood, just as one would have done in the bygone Hollywood Golden Age of Disney's life. The Red Car makes three stops, including one at the main entrance: at Carthay Circle Theater near the Pump House, and on Sunset Boulevard near the Tower of Terror (soon to be Guardians of the Galaxy). In doing all this, the Imagineers invoke an image of Los Angeles as it never (quite) was, never will be, but as, they suggest, Disney's imagination dreamed it could be.[283] Utilizing images from Los Angeles's most archetypically fruitful period, the 1920s and 1930s, they may just be transforming an image of Hollywood, at least in the mind of the patron, back into the highway of dreams that Walt understood it to be. That is the power of mythic ritual: the ability to transport an audience, to take something familiar to them, smooth over the edges, and make the mythic seem more real than reality itself.[284]

---

281 Ibid., 30.

282 Los Angeles County Metropolitan Transportation Authority.

283 Visit this Disney blog for D23 Expo video on the *Buena Vista Street* renovation: http://www.insidethemagic. net/2011/09/a-peek-at-disneyland-resorts-carthay-circle-theatre-the-new-california-adventure-icon-rest aurant-and-rumored-club-33-style-experience/

284 With all due respect to Baudrillard's theories of *simulacra* and *simulacrum*, I still maintain that a certain amount of this is healthy and necessary for immersion into the imagination in a playful way.

Two central aspect of Buena Vista Street require special mention: the inclusion of Oswald The Lucky Rabbit and the theming of the Carthay Circle Theater Restaurant. Oswald is Disney's earliest icon. In 1927, after spending much of the 1920s working on a project called *The Alice Comedies*, The Walt Disney Studio released a brand new cartoon character, a furry, troublemaking rabbit called Oswald. Drawn by Walt's friend and animator Ub Iwerks, this character looks pretty much like the original Mickey Mouse with one notable exception; his long floppy ears. The studio sold the character to Universal, and the rights to a cartoon distributor in New York named Charles Mintz. All was well until Walt went on a trip to negotiate his contract with Minz in the spring of 1928. The deal Walt received from Minz was unacceptable to him, and he decided to let the character go. On the way home, according to Disney legend, Walt and Lillian developed the idea for Mickey, and when they returned home, Ub brought him to life. The loss of Oswald was a particularly painful subject to Walt over the years, but with his characteristic Midwestern attitude, he moved on to other things. In February 2006, coincidentally around the same time of the Pixar deal, Bob Iger negotiated a deal with NBC returning rights to Oswald back to Disney. Because of this, Oswald now appears as a character on Buena Vista Street, as a live character, in store form, and in merchandise. Disney fans love to wear Oswald's characteristic ears and take pictures with him near the front gate. His classic troublemaking tendencies and silent film star status cement him as a symbol of the freewheeling, pre-Mickey pre-depression years at The Walt Disney Studio.

The other Buena Vista Street expansion that deserves special mention is the Carthay Circle Theater Restaurant. Located at 6316 San Vicente Boulevard in Hollywood, this theater hosted the premier of Disney's first animated feature, *Snow White and the Seven Dwarfs*. It has become an icon of Hollywood's Golden Age. Walking into the restaurant, one enters a lounge reminiscent of 1930s Hollywood watering holes. There are black and white photographs on the walls, pictures of Walt and Lillian Disney with friends and colleagues going back to the mid/late 1930s. Occasionally there are animation cells and other art pieces on loan from The Walt Disney Family Museum. Reservations are required for this restaurant; sometimes even the lounge is so crowded that ushers form a line outside to maintain an air of quiet elegance inside. When a patron goes there to eat, the first thing to do is go to the desk to check in. The hosts check patrons in by filling in paper cards. Cast members never break character, as there is never a computer in sight. They must be there, but they are kept somewhere out of sight.

After check in, patrons relax in the longue and might order a cocktail or at least some water or a house made soda. They are particularly well known for their whiskey drinks, the Manhattan, or the Scotch Mist, Walt's personal favorite drink. When a host who comes around calling up the patron by name, they make their way up the stairs or the elevator to the towers of the theater. The walls along the way are covered with images from Walt's Laugh-O-Gram years and the earliest years of the Disney Brothers' Studio and The Walt Disney Studio. Inside the restaurant there are pictures of Oscar winners, such as Julie Andrews and the Sherman Brothers. Private rooms line the outside of the restaurant. It's an elegant dining experience. The same chef creates the menu at Carthay Circle Theater Restaurant as at Club 33 and Napa Rose, the exquisite restaurant inside Disney's Grand Californian Hotel. Carthay also has its own Sommelier, offering a broad collection of California wines and even a group of Disney *family* wines that includes wines from Fess Parker, Silverado (Dianne Disney Miller's winery), and ones from the winery of John Lasseter's wife, Nancy. All in all, it's an experience that rivals any fine dining restaurant across California. The lounge has a bar table where locals and regulars often congregate and to talk about the seasonal menu and soak up the mythic energy of Walt's golden Hollywood.

As news about the expansion swept across the digital world in 2010, Internet buzz on Disney blogs has speculated as to whether or not a new "Partners" statue would be part of Buena Vista Street. The 2011 D23 Expo released that indeed a new "Partners" statue has been commissioned for DCA. The original "Partners" statue in Anaheim was sculpted in 1993 by animator/Imagineer and Disney legend Blaine Gibson. The statue stands on a circular concrete base that forms a seat utilized often for picture taking. The statue is cast in bronze and it depicts Walt at middle age, the age he was at the opening of Disneyland in 1955, side by side and hand in hand with Mickey Mouse. Both Walt and the Mouse face out towards Main Street, U.S.A. Mickey Mouse stands with his free hand on his hip, his posture evoking the kind of "gosh, it's great to see ya" attitude one associates with an established Mickey Mouse. Walt, clad in his trademark suit, smiles and waves to the patrons on Main Street, U.S.A. as though to reiterate the welcome of his dedication. The plaque entitled, "Partners" on the front of the statue reads, "I think most of all what I want Disneyland to be is a happy place . . . Where parents and children can have fun, together. - Walt Disney." This statue presents him as shaman, beckoning the public onward to all kinds of adventures.

The new "Partners" statue, unveiled in 2012 and aptly called "Storytellers", at DCA depicts a completely different image of Walt. Rather than an established image of him as "Uncle Walt", this statue depicts a young, twenty-something Walt Disney, fresh off the train from Kansas City, waiting for a ride and looking for adventure in Los Angeles. It depicts a lean, jaunty man in 1920s era garb, complete with his signature fedora hat and a trunk. The side of his trunk reads, "Walt Disney: Cartoonist". Mickey Mouse stands on the side of his trunk with a suitcase in hand and the "ta da!" body language more typical of the Mouse in his early years, before he began to bear the weight of his role as a pop culture icon. The statue is cast in Pewter grey, in contrast to the bronze of the Disneyland statue and, perhaps even more fascinatingly, it stands on the ground rather than on a pedestal. In doing so, the sculpture's creators seem to evoke a different aspect of Disney's shamanic power. They seem to suggest that if Walt, a poor, farm boy from Missouri, who came from obscure parentage, who possessed limited talent as an artist, and who went bankrupt several times can come to California to dream and rewrite his adventure, then so can you, oh dear park patron. Look, they seem to suggest, he isn't even taller than you.

Disneyland in the Digital Age

Video games are becoming increasingly immersive psychologically as computer-gaming systems become more advanced and writers become more interested in developing entire cosmologies for their gaming systems. In 2010, role-playing game designer Warren Spector created a new game, released by Junction Point Studios for Nintendo's Wii gaming system, called *Epic Mickey*. In 2012, another game, this one focused more on Oswald the Lucky Rabbit appeared called *Epic Mickey 2: The Power of Two*, providing a powerful reunion between these two central generative icons of the Disney tradition. It's important to note at this point that the collaboration between Junction Point Studios, Spector, and Disney ended when Disney pulled the plug on Junction Point Studios in 2013. Nevertheless, the mythic power of this project still deserves consideration in the context of Disneyland and renewal, as Spector argues that to many, Mickey Mouse's importance as an iconic presence in popular culture has begun to wane.

According to *gameinformer* magazine's *Epic Mickey* issue, Spector had reservations when originally approached by Disney about whether or not he would design a game about Mickey Mouse. In agreeing to design *Epic Mickey*, Spector intends to reclaim Mickey Mouse's image for what he feels is an entirely new mythic epoch. He says: "'you've done an incredibly good job of making Mickey lame and irrelevant to anybody over the age of eight over the last 30 years. I don't do games for kids.'"[285] His sense is that the Mickey Mouse of Walt Disney and Ub Iwerks has become too saccharine to truly wield an impact in the current cultural milieu.

Although one might argue the finer points of this assertion, one especially compelling aspect of it is the renewal of the image of Mickey Mouse as the savior of the mythic Wasteland. The narrative of *Epic Mickey* centers around a sorcerer named Yen Sid (Disney backwards) and his meddlesome mouse named Mickey. The game opens with the story of Yen Sid's creation of a magical kingdom. He paints his world with loving abandon, creating a beautiful pink castle and many different lands. Yen Sid leaves his world, which frankly, looks a bit like a model, behind. The ever-curious Mickey Mouse ventures out to look at Yen Sid's creation. In his role as the bumbling apprentice, he attempts to wield paint and thinner like the sorcerer. Tragically, he spills paint all over Yen Sid's creation, and then attempts to thin it. This creates a vacuum called "the blot", Mickey Mouse panics, attempting to contain it, but the creation is lost – a wasteland.

---

285 60.

Mickey Mouse returns to his room, and a montage indicates the passage of time, from *Steamboat Willie* through the contemporary moment. As Mickey sleeps, the blot reaches through the mirror into his bedroom, drags him through, and down into the Wasteland.

The land of *Epic Mickey* is literally called Wasteland. It is a mirror image of the actual Disneyland, as seen through the eyes of Oswald The Lucky Rabbit. In Spector's cosmos, Oswald is the neglected older sibling, wallowing in bitterness toward the mouse that he believes got the lion's share of the attention from creator Disney (remember, this is a mirror image). Furthermore, Oswald resents the damage Mickey Mouse has caused to the park he inhabits and hopes the creator will notice. In the *Disney Epic Mickey Collector's Edition Guide* Spector notes that his "direct inspiration was Sleeping Beauty's Castle at Disneyland in Anaheim" (v). He calls it iconic, noting that he found inspiration in the other parks, but that Anaheim was his primary basis for inspiration. Spector's Wasteland consists of two separate gaming modes, one that is presented as a third-dimensional post-apocalyptic Disneyland as a Wasteland, complete with a "Partners" statue with Walt Disney and Oswald holding hands in the square of "Mean Street" and the Danny Elfman-sque kind of music generally heard in Tim Burton films interspersed with two-dimensional levels that can be likened to the *Donkey Kong* and *Pong* games of the early Atari and Nintendo gaming platforms.

These two-dimensional levels are an opportunity to collect "E-Tickets", and they pay homage to the old Mickey Mouse shorts, such as *Plane Crazy* and *Clock Cleaners*. In Wasteland, Mickey Mouse has the ability to choose to be kind to these fellow animated characters or to choose not to help them as he moves through Wasteland. Spector's Mickey Mouse is a bit edgier and darker. Somehow, he seems to be at home in the Wasteland, and does not always act in a manner that is trustworthy or friendly. In portraying Mickey Mouse this way, Spector returns Mickey Mouse to his depression-era roots, a time when Mickey Mouse didn't mind grinning at nemeses as he threw them off a cliff or dropped bricks on their heads. It seems clear that in presenting Mickey Mouse in this way, Spector reinterprets the image of Mickey from the depression-era. In 2010, in the middle of the "great recession", Mickey Mouse appears yet again, in the clothing of our contemporary post- apocalyptic moment, renewing both the Wasteland of our imaginations and the Wasteland that is the park itself.

The companion piece to the first game, *Epic Mickey 2: The Power of One* reunites Oswald and Mickey against the Mad Doctor who seeks to tear down the renewed park and restore Wasteland. The Mad Doctor, *Epic Mickey's* central villain, believes he can convince Oswald to help him, but he underestimates his relationship with Mickey as ultimately the two join forces to defeat him for good. This suggests that Spector is aware of the dynamic relationship between what Jungians calls shadow and ego – Oswald as shadow and Mickey as ego –

unconscious soul and conscious soul. We presume Oswald will be the baddie and Mickey the goodie, but this is not always the case. In presenting these two in vigorous relationship with each other, Disney offers a central psychological truth that has been part of myth from time immemorial; soul is complex, the forces of it are always interacting with each other, and answers are not always what you'd expect.

This form of gaming is becoming ever more interactive, and since the advent of *Epic Mickey*, there has been a video game of note that may suggest a new direction for the next generation of patron's participation with the Disneyland temple. This game was released on November 15, 2011 for the XBOX 360's Kinect. This game is known as *Kinect Disneyland Adventures*. Like Nintendo's Wii system, the XBOX 360 utilizes motion sensor technology. Unlike the Wii, however, the XBOX 360's Kinect does not utilize controllers. This gaming system utilizes the entire body as the controller. This new game offers gamers the ability to create avatars of them and play the game as though they were actually walking through the park and experiencing the attractions.

Furthermore, a gamer can now buy virtual reality goggles that provide a panoramic view, making the game even more lifelike. The impact of video games can only grow, as virtual experience seems to continue to eclipse physical experience. In fact, the current Pokémon Go phenomenon could not even exist without these games. One might suggest that, in the context of ritual studies, games like *Epic Mickey* and *Kinect Disneyland Adventures* are effective in two fundamental ways. First these games return the experience of the park to the living room, utilizing the merchandizing and mythic power of the park as a place to both sell games and, like the *Disneyland* and the *Mickey Mouse Club* shows of the past, turn the television into a magic window into the park. Secondly, they provide the ability to enter into the emotive experience of the temple from within the context of the home. One might even suggest that this kind of technology would render Disneyland, as a place, passé, an argument that might be confirmed if one sees Disney's choice to curtail some of the video game projects that many expected to be so successful like *Epic Mickey* and the expansive world of Disney Infinity, which Disney had banked on being so successful that they launched icons of the gaming characters.

I disagree. The ebb and flow of archetypal energy in the digital age continues to prove this. Many new digital offerings continue to arrive in connection to the park. In the twenty-teens, these renewals come in the form of smart phone apps, social media pages, and blogs: MouseWait, Facebook/Twitter/Pinterest/Tumbler, and *Tours Departing Daily* to name a few. MouseWait is a smart phone app that creates both community among Disney fans and an interactive practice of visiting the park. With MouseWait, the Disneyland patron can check wait time for attractions, view menus for restaurants, connect with community in the Disneyland Lounge, and access information on their apple watch. This app is fully interactive. It allows patrons to change wait times to reflect what they see personally in the park. Users can accrue points through this activity as well as through answering trivia questions. It is also connected with an app called Virtual Plaid that invokes the image of the Disneyland guides, Miss Julie Reems being one of the earliest of those, conducting the visitor around the park for a private tour.

Social media sites are also part of this digital regeneration of Disneyland. Pages such as *The Circle of Villains*, *Vintage Disneyland*, *DisneyBounders Unite*, *Disneyland Annual Passholders*, *Dateline Disneyland*, *MousePlanet*, and *Disneyland Alumni Club* are a few examples of the communities available on Facebook and Twitter. Pinterest is full of pages that offer step-by-step suggestions on creating crafts, foods, and clothes for Disney fans to recreate the park at home. One of the most intriguing practices of this is DisneyBounding,[286] the practice of creating an outfit that evokes a character and wearing it to the parks. Adult wearing of costumes at Disneyland is specifically forbidden except during the exclusive evening events of Mickey's Not So Scary Halloween Party that runs from September through the end of October every year. Generally, Disney fans are respectful of this rule, but they cannot seem to let their desire to identify with the characters end there.[287] They wear outfits that look like the characters but are not specifically costumes. One might DisneyBound Minne by wearing a red skirt with white polkadots and a red t-shirt. Or they might wear green pants and a purple tank top to invoke the energy of their favorite character Ariel. This practice bleeds out into the digital world where Disney fans can discuss tips for making outfits better and can offer supportive solidarity to each other.

And then there is *Tours Departing Daily*,[288] a blog created as a labor of love created by digital photographer geniuses Matthew and Michaela, husband and wife high definition photographers from San Diego, California. The tagline of this page is "A blog about finding joy and inspiration at Disneyland". The style of photography they employ on their page is called high dynamic range photography. This style attempts to bridge the gap between what we see when we experience something in the natural world and the way it is rendered in photographic form. It is essentially a mythic form of photography because its creation is a mythopoetic process between technology and the artist in an ever more imaginative way than usual. This form of photography does not simply attempt to convey images in an artistic but natural format. Its aim is to convey what the soul sees. In the similar way as magical realism does for literature and romanticism does for visual art, HDR captures the image in a cross between the mystical space of imaginative, hyperreal color and natural imagery. For instance, when these artists capture an image of the castle at Disneyland at sunset, the

---

286 http://www.popsugar.com/love/What-Disneybounding-35830598#photo-35830598

287 https://www.instagram.com/thedisneybound/?hl=en

288 http://toursdepartingdaily.com

colors are more vividly blue, pink, grey and green than a standard photograph could present them. And indeed they are likely more vivid than our eyes can see, and yet somehow they capture a truer image of what the visitor experiences at that moment near the castle.

This form of photography gets at the heart of the tradition of icon-making, releasing something mythic from the imagination that was always there but perhaps must remain somehow intangible to the natural world. These are only a few examples of the way digital community renews Disneyland, returns it to our home screens, and makes the park realer and truer to the patron. I suspect, and we must leave it to future revelation to prove this, that games and digital portals will serve to initiate children and adults deeper into Disney's myths, and these games will fulfill a ritual need for those who cannot visit Disneyland due to a myriad number of factors, such as distance or finance. Although it might seem as though these games will take the place of the park, I think that what will inevitably happen is that the games will become an introduction to the park and, much like the *Pirates of the Caribbean* film franchise has done, a dialectic may develop between the parks and the games, as the park itself begins to fuse with the gaming world's interpretation of Disney's mythic ritual.

Such a tantalizing idea is suggested by novelist Ridley Pearson in his *Kingdom Keepers* series, which follows a group of teens turned holograms at night by Walt Disney World's technology. These teens enter the park at night as Holograms, literally keeping the kingdom safe from the *Overtakers* or Disney's villains. This imaginative series may have begun in the Magic Kingdom, but the series ends at Disneyland in Anaheim, proving once again that the parks in Anaheim are the ultimate theme park experience in the Disney cosmos, and that anything is possible in the land where dreams come true.

This land, the child's imagination, seems to be shrinking from consciousness. Children often rush to grow up, indulging in behavior that many may feel unprepared for even as adults. In this rush to *grow up*, many children eagerly reject the wonders of childhood. The ability to engage in innocence may be in danger of being lost as part of this process, and once it is lost, it may be nearly impossible to reawaken. I am convinced, however, that a fusion of imagination with enjoyment is vital for the soul to find balance and to thrive. The joys of Disneyland – the churros, the sunshine, the characters and the thrills – come together to create an environment of ritualized levity that is so vital to both the personal and corporate soul.

For me, the fundamental significance of this kind of ritual is the permission that it gives us – once we have left the mythically immersive experiences of childhood behind – to live our dreams. Where else are we allowed, as adults, to cross back into childhood and to believe, as Dumbo does, that a magic feather will make us fly? Furthermore, where else can we jump on Dumbo's back and fly with him? Where else can we feel safe enough to lower our psychological walls and give over to the imagination? Other theme parks may offer thrills, but they do not probe deeply into the realms of the soul, contributing a soothing balm and pampering the child inside. We neglect the needs of this child at our own peril. Walt knew this. He knew that we all need the opportunity to play, and he knew that through this kind of play humanity is able to forge true community. This is why Disneyland exists. This is why it will continue to thrive.

This brings us full circle to the question of what Disneyland offers the visitor. As Americans, we often underestimate the importance of place. Disneyland shows us our myth in terms of sacred space. As British comedian, Eddie Izzard once said to an American audience, "You know, I'm from Europe, where the history comes from."[289] The vitality of Disneyland's mythic ritual comes, in large part, from the power of California as a place. The collaborative staff at Disney often endeavors to extend Disneyland's influence by homogenizing all their parks. They have begun to sell merchandise online and in Disney Stores that can be found at Disneyland. Furthermore, they often sell merchandise at Disneyland that belongs to Walt Disney World. They also share attractions back and forth between the different parks, testing attractions, shows, and parades at one park before migrating them to another. A certain amount of branding is necessary for the sake of creating familiarity in Disney's market. However, too much emphasis on Disney global is dangerous. Presenting Disneyland as a piece of merchandise that belongs to Disney global - that is, suggesting that all Disney park experiences are the same, that all the parks are one, simply defined Disney experience - sells Disneyland short. A consequence of this practice leads to unfair comparisons between parks, particularly with Walt Disney World.

Each Disney park is distinct, and each Disney experience is distinct to the place that calls it home. For Disneyland, renewal means truly honoring the it as an esoterically Californian one. It means owning Disney's California-ness. No, Disneyland Resort is not, nor will it ever be Walt Disney World, and that is an important aspect of the place. Walt called it "a place for California to be at home, to brings its guests, to determine its faith in the future".[290] Disneyland reflects the kind of creative, often laid back, always-enterprising environment that the giants of Californian industry have so typically preferred. When Disneyland mirrors the need in the Californian soul for the balance between Disney's Hollywood heritage, Southern California landscape and mythic portals into the exotic and adventurous, renewal is fulfilled. However, like any process of individuation, process doesn't suggest the possibility of completion. As Walt said, "Disneyland will never be completed. It will continue to grow as long as there is imagination left in the world."[291] One might as well insert the word ritual for imagination, and clearly, collectively we have.

289 *Dressed to Kill*, DVD.

290 Marling, 62.

291 *The Quotable Walt Disney*, 61.

To the Diamond Celebration and Beyond: Disneyland at 60

As I complete this analysis in the summer of 2016, Disneyland is in process of completing a massive Diamond celebration of its 60th year. In contrast to the 50th anniversary celebration in 2005–2006, 2015–2016 seems a little muted, not badly done, but slightly muted. The 50th anniversary tagline *The Happiest Homecoming on Earth* gold celebration brought new shows and merchandise that were incredibly impressive. Something about the golden ears and the castle bathed in an excess of gold brought home how truly amazing it is that Disneyland continues to thrive all these years later. In part, it's not a surprise that this event is muted. Disney has a lot going on right now. Between the opening of its new Shang-Hai park and an expansion of the Disney Vacation Club, the company's resources are fully engaged. The 60th anniversary Diamond Celebration had a lot to live up to, while doing so in a way that did not cause unnecessary stress on finances, and in large part it has been lovely. The diamonds on the castle, while moderately impressive during the day, become a glorious spectacle at night. What stands out most about this celebration is the way that Disney subtly, but firmly sticks to its mythemes of nostalgia and progress, deftly weaving together fan desires for offering of the past with a vision for the future that focuses on innovation. I'd like to conclude this work with a walk through the park offering a look at some of the concepts I explored in chapters 4–6 through the lens of the Diamond Celebration.

Shining, Shimmering Merchandise

This tradition of celebrating anniversaries is originally associated with marriage. Although the origin of the tradition is mythic and unclear, what is known is that it traces at least to medieval times in Europe, particularly in Germanic tribes where a husband would crown his wife with a silver wreath on the occasion of their twenty-fifth wedding anniversary. In 1922, Emily Post published a book called Etiquitte. In it she lays out cultural traditions for celebrating anniversaries. She equates the diamond as the appropriate gift for the 60th. As one might expect, Disney embraces the diamond.

The most exciting 60th anniversary merchandise is the diamond decorated everything. There are diamond encrusted picture frames, pins, t-shirts, Christmas ornaments, Mickey ears, and, for those who wish to spend a bit extra on their souvenirs, Swarovski crystal encrusted ear headbands, tiaras, and noise cancelling headphones. There are Disneyland Diamond Days, an event guests can enter to win actual Disney diamonds and diamond crusted merchandise. This evokes the meaning of the diamond as a symbol and is clearly meant to associate the archetypal image of the diamond with wearable and collectable materials.

Diamonds have an ancient mythic significance. Its luminescence and hardness make it a symbol of perfection, constancy, and clarity. In Indian tradition, alchemists associate it with the philosopher's stone, its hardness and ability to cut are particularly important in Tantric Buddhism, and in varying Western European cultures it is a symbol of sovereignty, divine love, courage, and has the power to free the spirit from fear.[292] This suggests that Disneyland is forever. In fact, Disneyland Forever is one of the mottos of the celebration. Encrusting the souvenirs with diamonds offers them as an unmovable symbol of commitment to love, courage, and the devotion to the imagination that, as is the case with any of the souvenirs, the patron can then take home and keep near them in remembrance of their connection with the place.

Blasts from the Past, Into the Future

Another importance aspect of Disneyland's Diamond Celebration is the spectacle: *Paint the Night Parade, Disneyland Forever,* and *World of Color – Celebrate!* These spectacular shows are the epitome of Disneyland's balance between nostalgia for the old Disneyland and the innovation of new work. *Paint the Night* parade originally began at the Hong Kong Park in September of 2014. In some

---

292 Penguin Dictionary of Symbols, 290–291.

ways, *Paint the Night* is the perfect mythic successor to the *Disneyland's Main Street Electrical Parade*. It has eight units and utilizes over 1.5 million LED lights, suggesting a new emphasis on energy conservation. It blends together Disney's images from the past, Peter Pan, Tinker Bell, and Mickey and friends with the new characters of Pixar's *Toy Story* and *Cars* and Disney's *Frozen*. This parade is truly what Walt called a plussed show. The enhanced LED technology makes the parade a breathtaking thing to witness and the appearance of Mickey Paintbrushes, Minnie Bows, and Glow With the Show ears all offer more interaction for the patron.

Disneyland Forever fireworks also offer an exciting bridge between the past and the future. Disneyland's fireworks have been a multimedia, multi-sensory attraction for many years, but this new show adds an added layer to it. In the past, the bulk of the spectacle around fireworks show has been focused at or just behind the castle. Any fireworks, music, and pyrotechnics were featured there, safely away from the patrons. The one exception to that rule is Christmas. During the Christmas show, snow machines release a winter surprise on unsuspecting patrons, pulling them into the show by engaging more of their senses than ever before. *Disneyland Forever* takes that one step further by expanding the spectacle out into the audience, projecting images and a light show on the buildings and even the cobblestones of Main Street, U.S.A., the Matterhorn, It's a Small World, and the Rivers of America. This shifts the audience's focus from in front of them to all around them, drawing them deeper into a state of awe while engaging the entire park.

The *Disneyland Forever* fireworks show also features two brand new songs by Disney legend Richard Sherman: *Live the Magic* and *Kiss Me Goodnight*. It is impossible to overstate the importance of having Richard Sherman write these songs. One half of the prolific Disney song writing team the Sherman Brothers, Richard penned many of the musical pieces that are now the *sacred almighties* of Disneyland, such as It's a Small World and In the Tiki Room. The show is anchored on either side with Sherman's songs. The first one is an admonishment to live like Walt did, believing in magic. As the song begins, a voice over narrates saying that "just imagine, if you were standing here sixty years ago, you'd be standing in the middle of an orange grove. One visionary man, stood right where you are now. But instead of orange trees, he envisioned a magic kingdom. This man's name was Walt Disney, and his dream would be called Disneyland." Then Walt's voice comes over the sound system, vocalizing the famous quote "Disneyland will never be completed as long as there is imagination left in the world".[293] The song speaks of belief, love, memory and transcendence through fantasy, the crux of the Disney method as it admonishes the visitor to "step into the magic". The second of Sherman's songs a sweet reminder that goodnight

293 https://www.youtube.com/watch?v=bVBToWIdWZM

kisses[294] open the door to dreams and that expressions of love and that are the take away message of Disney's myth.

If *Disneyland Forever* invokes the memory of Walt through his quotes and the songs of Richard Sherman, *World of Color – Celebrate!* goes even further in its nostalgic remembrance of Walt's early Disneyland. This show, narrated by Neal Patrick Harris begins by invoking the name of Disney's television show, *The Wonderful World of Walt Disney*. As the narrator is announced, another of Walt's most famous quotes is projected on the water: Laughter is timeless. Imagination has no age. Dreams are forever." Mickey Mouse joins Neal Patrick Harris in hosting the show. Mickey transforms from his animated character into his image and back again, and Harris describes Walt's dreams of creating Disneyland and Walt's image appears across several screens. The audience is admonished to "Celebrate a world filled with magic/Just wish upon a star that shines so bright/Enter a world of make believe/Watch as dreams come true/Tonight!"[295] Images of Walt in the early years at Disneyland appear across the screen and in the Mickey head on the Mickey's Fun Wheel attraction in the background. Then it turns into an old animation reel, as Mickey reminds the audience that he arrived in 1928. Images of Mickey shorts appear as the theme song to the Mickey Mouse Club plays. Then Mickey appears as the Sorcerer's Apprentice. Harris notes that Walt was not satisfied with his shorts, as a Snow White montage moves across the screen. The rest of the show is an homage to the entirely of Disney/Pixar's animation canon. It offers images from the earliest shorts through Disney hits like *The Lion King* and latest films such as *Tangled*, *The Princess and the Frog*, and *Finding Nemo*.

The show also offers a blended Technicolor version of the opening day at Disneyland, and the other iconic attractions previously discussed in chapter four. Then it plays a song that admonishes the audience to stay "forever young" as home movie type images flash across the screen. The motto of the Diamond Celebration remains consistent as Harris argues that although some things have changed, "Disneyland has remained a constant in our lives". Harris then asks Walt if he had it to do over again, would he, and a clip of Walt appears saying that "No, I don't think I would". Walt and Mickey appear in outlines of golden light, walking hand in hand into the distance as though they were entering heaven together and the audience is reminded that, as Walt Disney famously said, "All our dreams can come true if we have the courage to pursue them". In doing this, it effectively remakes the pancanonical metaspectacle experience as it also ties in and honors Disneyland's origin myth. One last significant aspect of this attraction is the inclusion of the musical hit from *Frozen*, "Let it go", wedding together this show with the Frozen Sing a Long that replaced the Muppets and Aladdin attractions in HollywoodLand. Clearly this attraction

---

294 https://www.youtube.com/watch?v=wZP4n3TQMWk

295 https://www.youtube.com/watch?v=WK38wHBNOJM

leverages the power of this Disney current revival while reminding the audience of its original source.

Renewing Opulence

Beyond Club 33, Disneyland has not traditionally been known for opulence. There are exceptions, of course: Everything at Disney's Grand Californian Hotel, especially the Napa Rose restaurant, Disney's Dream Suite located above the Pirates of the Caribbean, Club 1901, DCA's answer to Club 33, and the sought after themed suites on the upper floors of the Disneyland Hotel all have a reputation for opulence. With the coming of the Diamond Celebration, Disney has taken the opportunity to raise the bar on the opulence it offers to the daytripper and the casual annual passholder. The diamond decorations on the castle are beautiful, but the diamond façade on front of Carthay Circle Theater is incredible. These decorations inhabit what Disney can offer.

New experiences such as themed high tea at the Disneyland Hotel, a limited engagement breakfast in the autumn of 2015 at the Jungle Cruise that offered exclusive gift perks and an extremely high price tag, package deals, dinners, and desserts for *World of Color – Celebrate!* and *Fantastmic!*, and diamond truffles filled with whiskey and other liquors in a commemorative box at Carthay Circle Theater Restaurant and Steakhouse 55 restaurant at the Disneyland Hotel. Disney is becoming aware that their patrons desire opulence beyond the normal Corn Dogs, hamburgers, and popcorn that it offered in the past.

A Long Time Ago in A Disneyland Far Far Away

Disney has, of course, had a long relationship with LucasFilm, and on October 30 2012, Bob Iger announced that Disney had acquired LucasFilm for a staggering $4.05 billion in cash and stock options. At the D23 Expo 2015, Iger made an announcement that turned a long hoped for rumor into reality. He announced that Disneyland and Walt Disney World would be getting brand new lands: Star Wars Land. On April 14, 2016, Disneyland officially broke ground on Star Wars Land. It will open in 2019. It is also likely that it will open any time between late 2018 and early 2020. It is also likely that attractions will be rolled out, much like the renovation at DCA.

Although not much is known for certain about Star Wars Land, I couldn't end this book without discussing what Disney had done in preparation for it, what will likely be seen there, and what I believe is happening, mythically. Star Wars Land will take up some of the former Frontierland's real estate. It will occupy the space where the Petting Zoo and the back part of the Rivers of America originally existed. In fact, the River is being rerouted and made shorter so that part of this space can go to Star Wars Land. In preparation for this, all of Disneyland's animals were removed to locations off property, which includes all the horses that travel up and down Main Street, U.S.A. We don't know which

Star Wars world we will step into, if it will be from one of the films or from one that is yet to come. What we do know is that it will feature some kind of thrill attraction, and its own weenie. There are even rumors about it having its own public transit in it, much like Main Street, U.S.A. and The Red Car in DCA.

Mythically, this choice of location is intriguing. Star Wars Land will be located at the head of Disneyland, next to Toontown. Placed adjacent to Frontierland, and theoretically on the opposite side of Tomorrowland, it seems as though Disney is literally positioning it between "a long time ago" and "a galaxy far, far away". With Fantasyland below them and Toontown under their arm, Star Wars Land will bring a new level of myth to Disneyland as, for the first time, Disney creates a land that steps outside their own mythic canon. Doing this, Disney makes the assertion that Disney storytelling is a method that is more than a brand. They are suggesting that Disney is a mythic orientation. And this opens the door for more acquisitions: LucasFilm, Marvel, Indiana Jones. Who knows what will be next for Disney?

Bibliography

A Bug's Life. Dir. John Lasseter and Andrew Stanton. Pixar Animation Studios, 1998.

African Queen, The. Dir. John Huston. Romulus Films, 1951.

Alghieri, Dante. *The Divine Comedy*. Trans. Allen Mandelbaum. Everyman's Library, New York: Alfred A. Knopf, 1995.

Andersen, Hans Christian. *Fairy Tales*. New York: Penguin Books, 2004.

Aristotle. *Poetics*. Trans. S. H. Butcher. New York: Hill and Wang, 1961.

Atencio, Xavier and George Bruns. "Yo Ho, Yo Ho, a Pirate's Life for Me". Walt Disney, 1967.

Barrie, Sir J. M. *Peter Pan*. New York: Penguin Books, 1987.

– –. *The Little White Bird*. Montana: Kessinger Publishing, 2010.

Baudrillard, Jean. Simulacra *and Simulation*. Ann Arbor: U of Michigan Press, 2006.

– –. *America*. New York: Verso, 1999.

Beauty and the Beast. Dir. Gary Trousdale and Kirk Wise. Walt Disney Feature Animation, 1991.

Bell, Catherine. *Ritual: Perspectives and Dimensions*. New York: Oxford UP, 1997. *Bible, The New Oxford Annotated*. New York: Oxford UP, 2004. New Revised Standard Version.

Birkin Andrew. *J. M. Barrie and the Lost Boys*. New Haven: Yale UP, 2003.

Blystone, Lee Ann. *Disneyland: Dreams, Traditions and Transitions*. Disney's Kingdom Editions, 1995.

Brave Little Toaster. Dir. Jerry Rees. The Walt Disney Company, 1987.

Briggs, K.M. *The Fairies in Tradition and Literature*. London: Routledge, 1967.

Brode, Douglas. *From Walt to Woodstock: How Disney Created the Counterculture*. Austin: U of Texas P, 2004.

– –. *MultiCulturalism and the Mouse: Race and Sex in Disney Entertainment*. Austin: U of Texas P, 2005.

Buber, Martin. *I and Thou*. New York: Simon and Schuster, 1996.

Campbell, Joseph. *Pathways to Bliss: Mythology and Personal Transformation*. Novato: New World Library, 2004.

– –. *The Hero With a Thousand Faces*. Princeton: Princeton UP, 1968.

– –. *Thou Art That: Transforming Religious Metaphor*. Novato: New World Library, 2001.

Carroll, Lewis. *Alice's Adventures in* Wonderland. New York: Penguin Books, 1998.

Cars. Dir. John Lasseter and Joe Ranft. Pixar Animation Studios, 2006.Chevalier, Jean and Alain Gheerbrant.

Penguin Dictionary of Symbols. New York: Penguin Books, 1994.

Halloween, Dir. John Carpenter. Compass International Pictures, 1978.

Churchill, Frank and Lary Morey. "Heigh-Ho". *Snow White and the Seven Dwarfs*. Walt Disney Productions, 1937.

Cinderella, Dir. Clyde Geronimi, Wilfred Jackson, Hamilton Luske. Walt Disney Productions, 1950.

Clark, Steven and Jeffrey Epstein. "California Dreamin': Imagineering the Future of Disney's California Adventure". *Disney Twenty-Three*. Summer 2009: 30–34.

Corbett, Lionel. *Psyche and the Sacred: Spirituality beyond Religion*. New Orleans: Spring Journal Books, 2007.

Dallen, J. Timothy and Daniel H. Olsen. *Tourism, Religion and Spiritual Journeys*. New York: Routledge, 2006.

Dan in Real Life. Dir. Peter Hedges. Touchstone Pictures, 2007.

Davis, Amy. *Good Girls and Wicked Witches: Women in Disney's Feature Animation*. Eastleigh: John Libbey Publishing, 2006.

Disney Epic Mickey Collector's Edition Guide. 2010.

Disneyland Resort: Behind the Scenes. Disney Editions. 2010.

Disneyland: Secrets, Stories and Magic. Dir. Bob Garner and Pete Shuermann. Walt Disney Home Entertainment, 2007.

"Disneyland Story, The". Dir. Robert Florey. *Disneyland*. 1954.

Doniger, Wendy. *Other People's Myths: The Cave of Echoes*. Chicago: U of Chicago P, 1995.

Doty, William G. *Mythography: The Study of Myths and Rituals*. Tuscaloosa: U of Alabama P, 2000.

Driver, Tom F. *The Magic of Ritual: Our Need for Liberating Rites that Transform Our Lives and Our Communities*. New York: HarperCollins, 1991.

Dumbo. Dir. Samuel Armstrong and Norman Ferguson. Walt Disney Productions, 1941.

Dundes, Alan. *Sacred Narrative: Readings in the Theory of Myth*. Berkeley, California: U of California P, 1984.

Durkheim, Émile. *The Elemetary Forms of Religious Life*. New York: Oxford UP, 2001.

Eade, John and Michael J. Sallnow. *Contesting the Sacred: The Anthropology of Christian Pilgrimage*. New York: Routledge, 2000. 270

Eddie Izzard: *Dressed to Kill*. Dir. Lawrence Jordan. Ella Communications, 1999.

Eliade, Mircea. *The Sacred and the Profane: The Nature of Religion*. Orlando: Harcourt. 1987.

– –. *The Myth of the Eternal Return*. Princeton: Princeton UP, 2005.

– –. *Myths, Dreams, and Mysteries: The Encounter Between Contemporary Faiths and Archaic Realities*. New York: Harper and Row, 1975.

Enchanted. Dir. Kevin Lima. Walt Disney Pictures, 2007.

Fantasia. Dir. Samuel Armstrong, James Algar, Bill Roberts, Paul Satterfield Ben Sharpsteen, David D. Hand, Hamilton Luske, Jim Handley, Forde Beebe, T. Hee, Norman, Ferguson, Wilfred Jackson. Walt Disney Productions, 1940.

Feild, Robert D. *The Art of Walt Disney*. London and Glasgow: Collins, 1942.

Finch, Christopher. *The Art of Walt Disney: From Mickey Mouse to the Magic Kingdoms*. New York: Abrams, 1999.

– –. *Walt Disney's America*. New York: Abbeville, 1978.

Finding Nemo. Dir. Andrew Standon and Lee Unkrich. Pixar Animation Studios, 2003.

Finding Neverland. Dir. Marc Forster. Miramax, 2004.

Fralick, Nikki Bado and Rebecca Sachs Norris. *Toying with God: The World of Religious Games and Dolls*. Waco: Baylor UP, 2010.

Frozen. Dir. Chris Buck, Jennifer Lee. Walt Disney Animation Studios, 2013.

Gabler, Neal. *Walt Disney: The Triumph of The American Imagination*. New York: Knopf, 2006.

Gadamer, Georg. *The Relevance of the Beautiful and Other Essays*. New York: Cambridge UP, 1998.

Garci Rodriguez De Montalvo. Las Sergas De Esplandian De. Scripta Humanistica: July 2001.

Gibson, Terrill L. "Cin-Imago-Dei: Jungian Psychology and Images of the Soul in Contemporary Cinema". *Spring Journal: Psyche and Cinema*. Spring, 2005.

Giroux, Henry. *The Mouse That Roared: Disney and the End of Innocence*. New York: Rowman and Littlefield Publishers, 2001.

Gnomeo and Juliet. Dir. Kelly Asbury. Touchstone Pictures, 2011.

Gordon, Bruce and Tim O'Day. *Disneyland: Then, Now, and Forever*. New York: Disney Editions, 2008.

Grapes of Wrath, The. Dir. John Ford. Twentieth Century Fox Film Corporation, 1940.

Great Mouse Detective, The. Dir. Ron Clements, Burny Mattison, David Michener, and John Musker. Walt Disney Feature Animation, 1986. ????

Grimes, Ronald. *Rite out of Place: Ritual, Media and the Arts*. Oxford: Oxford UP, 2006.

Grimm, Willhelm and Jacob. *The Complete Grimm's Fairy Tales*. New York: Pantheon Books, 1972.

Hahn, Don. *Brain Storm: Unleashing Your Creative Self*. New York: Disney Editions, 2011.

Hargreaves, Robert, Stanley J. Damerell and Tolchard Evans. "Let's All Sing Like the Birdies Sing". 1934.

Harline, Leigh and Ned Washington. "When You Wish Upon a Star". Victor Records, 1940.

Hench, John. *Designing Disney: Imagineering and the Art of the Show*. New York: Disney Editions, 2008.

Hillman, James. *Re-visioning Psychology*. New York: HarperCollins, 1992.

– -. *Healing Fiction*. Putnam: Spring Publications, 1983.

– -. *Surfing L. A.* Dir. Kevan Jenson. Visualize This, 2005.

Hobbes, Thomas. *Leviathan*. Ann Arbor: U of Michigan Press, 1817.

Homer. *The Odyssey*. Trans. Robert Fagles. New York: New American Library, 1999.

Huzinga, Johan. *Homo Ludens*. New York: Taylor and Francis, 2003.

Imagineers, The. *Walt Disney Imagineering: A Behind the Dreams Look at Making the Magic Real*. New York: Disney Editions, 1996.

– -. *Walt Disney Imagineering: A Behind the Dreams Look at Making MORE Magic Real*. New York: Disney Editions. 2010.

– -. *The Imagineering Field Guide to Disneyland*. Hoboken: Disney Editions, 2008.

Incredibles, The. Dir. Brad Bird. Pixar Animation Studios, 2004.

Johnston, Ollie and Frank Thomas. *The Illusion of Life: Disney Animation*. New York: Abbeville Press, 1990.

Joyce, William. *A Day with Wilbur Robinson*. New York: HarperCollins, 1993.

Jung, C. G. The *Structure and Dynamics of the Psyche (1916/58) CW 8*. New York: Taylor and Francis, 1973.

– -Archetypes and The Collective Unconscious CW 9. New York: Taylor and Francis, 1973.

Kirby, E. T. "The Shamanistic Origins of Popular Entertainment". *Ritual Play and Performance: Readings in the Social Sciences and Theater*. Ed. Richard Schechner and Mady Shuman. Chicago: Seabury Press, 1976.

Koenig, David. *Mouse Tales: A Behind-the-Ears Look at Disneyland*. Irvine: Bonaventure Press, 2001.

– -. *More Mouse Tales: A Closer Peek Backstage at Disneyland*. Irvine: Bonaventure Press, 2002.

Korkis, Jim. *The Vault of Walt: Unofficial, Unauthorized, Uncensored Disney Stories Never Told*. Pike Road: Ayrfour Publishing, 2010.Kurtii, Jeff. *Disneyland Through the Decades: A Photographic Celebration*. New York: Disney Editions, 2010.

– –. Walt Disney's *Imagineering Legends and the Genesis of the Disney Theme Park*. New York: Disney Editions, 2008.

Kurtii, Jeff and Bruce Gordon. *The Art of Disneyland*. New York: Disney Editions, 2006. LaBerge, Stephen. *Lucid Dreaming: A Concise Guide to Awakening in Your Dreams and in Your Life*. Los Angeles: J. P. Tarcher, 1985.Lakoff, George and Mark Johnson. *Metaphors We Live By*. Chicago: U of Chicago P, 2003.

LaBerge, Stephen. *Lucid Dreaming: A Concise Guide to Awakening in Your Dreams and in Your Life*. Boulder, CO: Sounds True, Inc. 2009.

Lakoff, George and Mark Johnson. *Metaphors to Live By*. Chicago, U of Chicago Press, 2003.

Lark, Mark. "The Elephant in the Room". *Disney Twenty-Three*. Spring 2011, 45–47.

Larsen, Stephen. *The Mythic Imagination: The Quest for Meaning Through Personal Mythology*. Rodchester: Inner Traditions, 1996.

Lewis, C.S. *The Chronicles of Narnia*. San Fransisco: HarperCollins, – -fix this!

Lorenz, Konrad. "Habit, Ritual and Magic". *Ritual Play and Performance: Readings in the Social Sciences and Theater*. Ed. Richard Schechner and Mady Shuman. Chicago: Seabury Press, 1976.

Lyden, John C. *Film as Religion: Myths, Morals, and Rituals*. New York: NYUP, 2003.

Lyon, David. *Jesus in Disneyland: Religion in Post Modern Times*. Malden: Blackwell Publishers, 2001.

Maas, Charlie. "Disneyland is Good for You". *New West*. December 1978: 13–19.

MacDonald, J. Fred. *One Nation Under Television: The Rise and Decline of Network TV*. Chicago: Nelson-Hall, 1994.

MacDonald, William L. *The Pantheon: Design, Meaning and Progeny*. Cambridge: Harvard UP, 2002.

Mamet, David. *Three Uses of the Knife: On the Nature and Purpose of Drama*. New York: Random House, 1998.

Marling, Karal Ann. *Behind the Magic: 50 Years of Disneyland*. Dearborn: The Henry Ford, 2005.

– –. *Designing Disney's Theme Parks: The Architecture of Reassurance*. New York: Flammarion, 1998.

– –. "Disneyland 1955: Just Take the Santa Ana Freeway to the American Dream". *American Art* 5, no. 1–2 (Winter–Spring 1991): 168–207.

Marion Woodman: Dancing in the Flames. Dir. Adam Greydon Reid. 2010.

Mary Poppins. Robert Stevenson. Walt Disney Productions, 1964.

Meet the Robinsons. Dir. Stephen J. Anderson. Walt Disney Animation Studio. 2007.

Mercer, Johnny and Richard A. Whiting. "Hooray for Hollywood". *Hollywood Hotel*. 1937.

Miller, David. "A Myth is as Good as a Smile". *Depth Psychology: Meditations in the Field*. Ed. Dennis Patrick Slattery, and Lionel Corbett. Carpinteria: Daimon Verlag, (2004), 175–192.

Miller, Diane Disney: *Walt Disney. His Life in Pictures*. New York: Disney Editions, 2009.

Mixed Nuts. Dir. Nora Ephron. TriStar Pictures, 1994.

Monster's Inc. Dir. Pete Doctor and David Silverman. Pixar Animation Studios, 2001.

Moore, Thomas. *Rituals of the Imagination*. Dallas: Dallas Institute Publications, 1983.

Newell, William Wells. *Games and Songs of American Children*. New York: Harper, 1883.

Nietzsche, Friedrich. *Thus Spake Zarathustra*. Trans. Alexander Tille. London: Macmillan, 1896.

Otto, Rudolf. *The Idea of the Holy*. Trans. John W. Harvey. London: Oxford UP, 1923.

Our Family Wedding. Dir. Rick Famuyiwa. Fox Searchlight, 2010.

Ovid. *Metamorphoses*. Trans. Stanley Lombardo. Indianapolis: Hackett Publishing, 2010.

Pearson, Ridley. *Kingdom Keepers*.

Perfect Sense. Dir. David Mackenzie. BBC Films, 2011.

176

Pete's Dragon. Dir. Don Chaffey. Walt Disney Productions, 1977.

Pinocchio. Dir. Norman Ferguson, T. Hee, Wilfred Jackson, Jack Kinney, Hamilton, Luske, Bill Roberts, Ben Sharpsteen. Walt Disney Produtions, 1940.

Pixar Story, The. Dir. Leslie Iwerks. Leslie Iwerks Productions, 2007.

Powdermaker, Hortense. *Hollywood: The Dream Factory*. Los Angeles: Arno Press, 2009.

Quenot, Michael. *The Icon: Window on the Kingdom*. Crestwood: St. Vladimir's Seminary Press, 1991.

Reader, Ian and Tony Walker. *Pilgrimage in Popular Culture*. New York: Macmillan, 1993.

Religulous. Dir. Larry Charles. Lionsgate, 2008.

Richardson, Michael. *Surrealism and Cinema*. Oxford: Berg Publishers, 2006.

Rouner, Leroy S. "Transcendence and the Will to Believe". *Transcendence and the Sacred. 2 vols.* South Bend: Notre Dame UP, 1994.

Rowling, J.K. *Harry Potter and the Deathly Hallows*. New York. Arthur A. Levine Books, 2009.

Scheff, Thomas. *Catharsis in Healing, Ritual and Drama*. Berkley: U of California P, 1979.

Sherman, Richard and Robert. *It's a Small World After All*. WED Enterprises, 1964.

Silver, Alain and James Ursini. *L. A. Noir: The City as Character*. Santa Monica: Santa Monica Press, 2005.

Smiley, Sam. *Playwriting: The Structure of Action*. New Haven: Yale UP, 2005.

Smith, Dave. *The Quotable Walt Disney*. New York: Disney Editions, 2001.

Smith, Evans Lansing. *The Myth of the Descent to the Underworld in Post-Modern Literature*. Lewiston: The Edwin Mellen Press, 2003.

Snow White and the Seven Dwarfs. Dir. William Cottrell, David Hand, Wilfred Jackson, Larry Morey, Perce Pearce, and Ben Sharpsteen. Walt Disney Feature Animation, 1937.

Somé, Malidoma Patrice. *Ritual: Power, Healing and Community*. New York: Penguin Group, 1997.

Spector, Warren. "Epic Mickey". *gameinformer*. 58–67, 2009.

Spellbound. Dir. Alfred Hitchcock. Selznick International Pictures, 1945.

Spengler, Oswald. *The Decline of the West*. New York: Oxford UP, 1991.

Star Wars Episode VI: The Return of the Jedi. Dir. Richard Manquand. Lucasfilm, 1983.

Strodder, Chris. *The Disneyland Encyclopedia: The Unofficial, Unauthorized and Unprecedented History of Every Land, Attraction, Restaurant, Shop, and Event in the Original Magic Kingdom*. Santa Monica: Santa Monica Press, 2008.

Surrell, Jason. *The Haunted Mansion: From the Magic Kingdom to the Movies*. New York: Disney Editions, 2009.

– –. "I was a Teenage Jungle Cruise Skipper". *Disney Twenty-Three*. Spring 2011, 13–17.

Svonkin, Craig. "A Southern California Boyhood in the Simu-Southland Shadows of Walt Disney's Enchanted Tiki Room". *Disneyland and Culture: Essays on the Parks and Their Influence*. Jefferson: MacFarland and Company, Inc., 2011.

Terzian, Elizabeth. *The Aesthetics and Poetics of Light in Eastern Orthodox Iconography: A Mythopoetic Perspective*. Diss. Pacifica Graduate Institute. 2003.

Thomas, Bob. *Walt Disney: An American Original*. Saint Louis: Turtleback Books, 1999.

Thomas, Rob. "Little Wonders". *Meet The Robinsons*. WEA International, 2007.

Thomson, David. *The Whole Equation: A History of Hollywood*. New York: Vintage Books, 2006.

Toy Story. Dir. John Lasseter. Pixar Animation Studios, 1995.

Toy Story 2. Dir. John Lasseter, Ash Brannon, and Lee Unkrich. Pixar Animation Studios, 1999.

Tuan, Yi-Fu and Steven D. Hodscher. "Disneyland: Its Place in World Culture". *Designing Disney's Theme Parks: The Architecture of Reassurance*. Ed. Karal Ann Marling. New York: Flammarion, 1998.

Turner, Victor and Edith. *The Ritual Process: Structure and Anti-Structure*. Ithaca: Cornell UP, 1969.

– –. *From Ritual to Theatre: The Human Seriousness of Play*. New York: PAJ Publications, 1982.

– –. *Ritual Play and Performance: Readings in the Social Sciences and Theater*. Ed. Richard Imageand Pilgrimage in Christian Culture

Saving Mr. Banks. Dir. John Lee Hancock. Walt Disney Pictures, 2013.

Schechner and Mady Shuman. Chicago: Seabury Press, 1976.

Schickel, Richard. The Disney Version: The Life, Times, Art, and Commerce of Walt Disney. NY: Simon and Schuster, 1997.

Velarde, Robert. *The Wisdom of Pixar: An Animated Look at Virtue*. Downers Grove: IV Press, 2010.

Vertigo. Dir. Alfred Hitchcock. Paramount Pictures, 1958.

Virgil. *Aeneid*. Trans. Robert Fagles. New York: Penguin Books, 2006,

Waking Sleeping Beauty. Dir. Don Hahn. Red Shoes, 2009.

Walt Disney: The Man Behind the Myth. Dir. Jean-Pierre Isbouts. Pantheon. Productions/Walt Disney Family Foundation, 2001.

Walt Disney's Wonderful World of Color: Our Friend the Atom. Dir. Hamilton Luske. Walt Disney Productions, 1957.

Watts, Steven. *The Magic Kingdom: Walt Disney and the American Way of Life*. New York: Houghton Mifflin, 1997.

Weber, Max. *The Protestant Work Ethic and the Spirit of Capitalism*. New York: W. W. Norton and Company, 2009.

Zaleski, Carol. *Otherworld Journeys: Accounts of Near-Death Experience in Medieval and Modern Times*. New York: Oxford UP, 1987.

Ziai, Hossein. "Beyond Philosophy: Suhrawardi's Illuminationist Path to Wisdom". *Myth and Philosophy: A Context of Truths*. La Salle: Open Court Publishing Company, 1992.

Zipes, Jack. *Happily Ever After: Fairy Tales, Children and the Culture Industry*. New York: Routledge, 1997. Print.

– –. *Fairy Tale as Myth/Myth as Fairy Tale*. Lexington: UP Kentucky, 1994.

– –. *Fairy Tales and the Art of Subversion*. New York: Routledge, 2006.

Index

183